Love and Work

If a man has a talent and
cannot use it he has failed.
If he has a talent and learns to use
half of it, he has partly failed.
If he has a talent and learns somehow
to use the whole of it
he has gloriously succeeded,
and won a satisfaction and a triumph
few men ever know.
                    —*Thomas Wolfe*

An Original Collection of 25 years of work

The ATHLETE
by ROBERT RIGER

SIMON & SCHUSTER · NEW YORK · 1980

Designed by Robert Riger
Manufactured in the United States of America
1 2 3 4 5 6 7 8 9 10
Library of Congress Cataloging in Publication Data
Riger, Robert.
The athlete.
1. Athletes—Biography. I. Title.
GV697.A1R57   796'.092'2 [B]   80–12599
ISBN 978-1-5011-4615-2

CONTENTS

Prologue

Robert Riger views the world of sport through a romantic yet analytical series of prisms known only to him.

Although his tools are the most literal of lenses and sharp-pointed pencils, to his eye the jockey becomes a knight, the figure skater a prima ballerina, and the pro football lineman a World War II GI in the hedgerows of Normandy.

This is Riger the romantic.

Riger the analyst sees things differently. He seeks out the unromantic reasons for an athlete's success —the tiny edge in technique, invisible except to the super-slow-motion camera, that enables the ski racer to win by a few hundredths of a second; the detail of a rider's hands that lift a horse over the hedge and across Becher's Brook in the Grand National Steeplechase.

As friend and colleague, I have viewed both Rigers at close hand for almost two decades. I come across him in unexpected places—shouting down to me from his frozen perch on an alpine peak; turning up underfoot, lying in the grass to get the right angle in a U.S. Open golf championship; memorializing the weariness of a traveling reporter by photographing me as I slept in seat 7A.

Homogenize the two Rigers and you have an uncommon reporter. Get to know Bob Riger as a friend, and you realize one other thing—that his pictures and opinions are always kind. If that be fault or virtue depends on your point of view. Personally, I feel that it is easier to shatter an ikon than it is to search out and portray skill and virtue.

I think that man, in sport as in life, is more ennobled by the search for truth and beauty than he is by cynicism, acerbity and the jaundiced eye.

You can have the artist who sees only the flaws, faults and warts of the world. I'll take Robert Riger and spot you two shots a side.

Jim McKay
Host, ABC's *Wide World of Sports*
March 1979

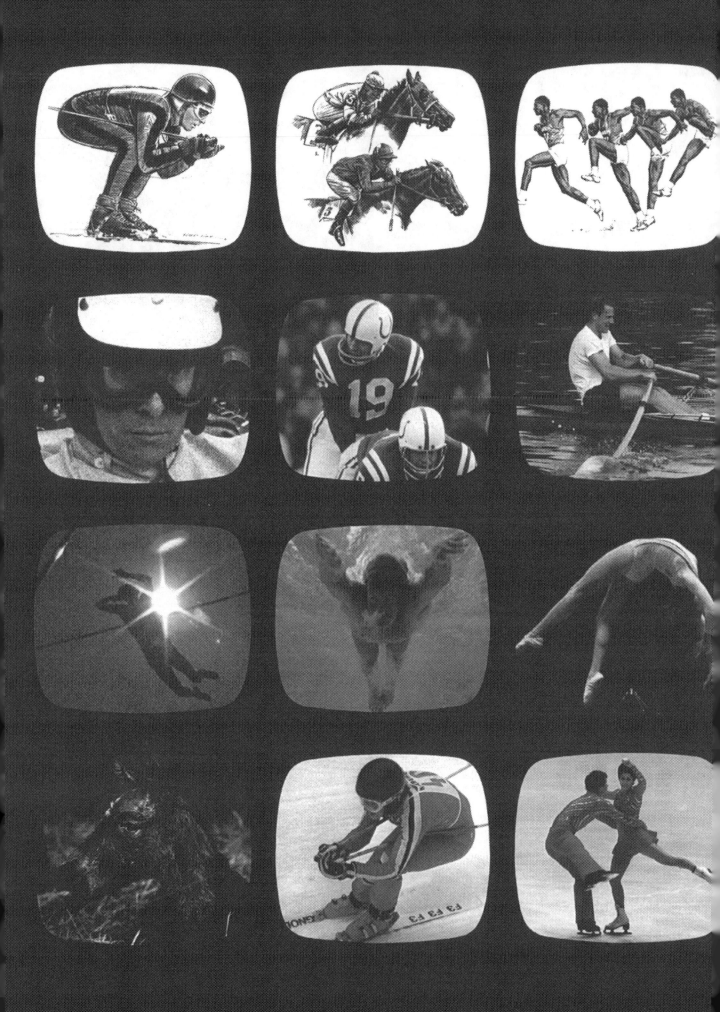

Introduction

SPORTS JOURNALISM

The pleasure of a book is enormous. The joy of authorship, especially of a book that reflects twenty-five years of one's work as this one does, is one-of-a-kind for me, and I trust for each reader. There is one neat trick that makes such a collection of pictures work, and that is to balance the book to include enough remembered pictures so that the artist is recognized, but also to include a wealth of new, never-before-published pictures of quality and interest to all so that the book is a discovery. Then the retrospective idea becomes immediate.

My career has been sports journalism. I consider myself a journalist first before any specific avocation—as a draftsman, or photographer, or television director. I was trained as an artist, developed as a photographer and cinematographer, and make my living now as a television director and writer with ABC Sports. The two questions I cannot answer are which craft do I prefer and what is my favorite sport. I never think about them as separate abilities; I only use whichever I need to report with.

Properly used they have been very effective. Each of the three forms of journalism—drawing, photography and television—is totally different, but for me in sports journalism the three are completely related as seen on the monitors at left.

The past fifteen years in television sports journalism have given me a chance to develop my artistic sensibilities as a cinematographer and shape full programs as a producer and director. The 150 programs and feature inserts that I contributed to ABC Sports programming over ten years, pieces running anywhere from two to ninety minutes, were all exciting—more exciting than the drawings or photographs because of the added elements of motion, music and voice. The most important factor about television, however, is that it offers the chance for the finest sports journalism. The sixteen seven-minute daily satellite reports I did from Sapporo, Japan, during NBC's coverage of the 1972 Winter Olympic Games were the high point in this television sports journalism. The response to my reports on ABC for the Montreal Olympics in 1976 by the millions of viewers was the most rewarding.

Roone Arledge, my executive producer at ABC Sports, and benefactor in the early sixties, saw in my work the natural journalistic transition from print to television and guided the changeover. His great talent in shaping the ABC Sports department lay in his ability to pick extremely loyal and indefatigable workers in all areas who thrived on pressure and never tired of the travel or challenge.

As this book is readied for press, ABC Sports, under Roone Arledge's name, has aired 6,890 hours of sports programming. Most all of it has been good. Hundreds of hours have been superb. (Many times it has received too much credit over excellent sports telecasts that the other two networks, NBC and CBS, have aired.) This book explores some of the phenomena of television sports journalism and reproduces in color scenes off air from my segments.

The style of this particular book represents a comparatively new form of sports journalism. Peter Schwed, my editor at Simon and Schuster, guided me through my first authorship in the 1960s with *The Pros* and *The American Diamond,* picture books that began to combine an immediate reportage in pictures with parallel text that included the captions in most cases. My intuition at the time was to influence people with lazy reading habits to read the text to find out about the pictures and not just read the captions as most readers do with picture books. In this book I have gone back to my notebooks, stories and tapes and designed it so that the text is the voice of the athlete. Harold Hayes, as editor of *Esquire,* gave me my big break as a writer in 1960, but he claimed a writer could not just print pure quotes. I disagree. It does take a certain self-effacement to step back and let the athlete speak. But this book is their portrait. The "pure quotes" pass through my ear and hand. My thoughts are footnotes to three decades of amazing sports history.

I'm basically a collector. I think that sport is art and I want to own it. I'm not really interested in who wins but how they play the game—for reasons almost as pure as those of the Baron de Coubertin. This book begins with lithograph drawings sketched from old glass negatives of the men of the *golden age* of sport. Was it? What channel was Bobby Jones' grand slam on? How many millions saw Babe Ruth hit a home run in color and then saw the replay? Who saw slow-motion and stop-action of Dempsey standing over Tunney? The golden age of sport was a lovely alloy of sweat and sentiment in newspaper prose. The 18-karat kaleidoscope of the world of sports journalism is now. I was lucky to be around at the right time and blessed with the energy to see and save some of it.

Getting Ready

My mother sent me to art school because I was talented. I didn't know what that meant in the beginning. Now, twenty-five years later, I realize talent is patience, imagination, work, competitiveness, self-confidence and love in always changing human balances. The craft itself can be quite simple.

To contend that this book represents the twenty-five years of my work would be misleading. This edition represents less than one tenth of my best effort, and to say the book is finished might suggest that I have completed my work. Rather it is little more than my apprenticeship. Last week I had an exciting assignment, next week I'll have another at some stadium in the world. Twenty-five years of work is searching, eliminating—getting ready, I believe.

The Athlete is a presentation of a series of ideas on sport that I began working on in 1950 and that can never really be fully explored. It is one man's sports journalism, an intensely personal view, and yet, I hope, a universal and significant one—a con-

vator at *Sports Illustrated* in those first years of publication, walk into the office of the managing editor, Sid James, and outline a series of sketches for the next issue and he'd say, "Fine, let's do it."

The next seven years I did ten photographic books and was able to use my still pictures, transferred to television tape, as the beginning of my television journalism. The excitement came with the expanded audience. Millions of people saw the work on television and thousands could collect the books. A book seems to be the last area of freedom for a journalist. It is the place where he can say what he wants and be hampered the least by a *group* in final production.

After the war the artist rep—selling agents for illustrators and photographers on commercial assignments—became a lucrative business, and the big guys had fancy showrooms on Fifth Avenue in New York. I had returned to Pratt Institute in the late forties and stopped in to see one with my portfolio during spring vacation. My work was detailed and

tradition I'll have more to say about. As I see the pages arranged, the book becomes a portrait, a vivid reflection of the character and skills and thoughts of the best athletes in the world.

The ability to draw, and eight years of art training, has been the strong foundation that made everything work. The fact that my drawings were published by the carload and that they were clearly "read" and that they looked like the drawings readers would like to do if they could draw made them collectible. I tried to keep them simple and honest. Those years of all-night stands and crash deadlines were exciting journalism. I would get off the ele-

imaginative. I had won the art school medal for Coleridge's "Rime of the Ancient Mariner" (above), not considered *commercial*. I remembered his French cuffs, expensive cufflinks and red suspenders, the slick interior of his office, the deep rugs and all the romantic and glamorous illustrations by the name illustrators, Coby Whitmore, Al Parker, Joe DeMers and others. This agent took one third of every check, thirty-three cents on the dollar. I wondered how much went into overhead.

I felt very uncomfortable and inadequate. I asked him after he had looked at my stale and dried-out efforts, which lacked any emotional involvement whatsoever, for advice. "How do you know what to draw when you're starting out? How do you know whether to do lovers on a couch or Eskimos fighting in a cave?" I showed him my detective story (right).

He had his hands clasped behind his head and he said, much as a doctor would, "You draw what you know best, because you'll do it best."

"The only thing I know anything about is sports," I explained.

"Then do sports." He tilted his head and stretched out his arms with open hands—as if offering me an entire subject all to myself.

I took it. Researching the "field" that week in 1948, I decided there were really only three good sports artists in the country, and they were newspaper cartoonists. I decided then that with the intensity I felt about the stadium and the athlete that sports would be my subject. I could be original. My fiction illustration (opposite page), contrived in art school, was just like the other illustrators' and in most cases not as good. I was looking for a subject where I could be the best and also not give away a third of my earnings. The fact that there was little market in 1950 for sports illustrations did not bother me. I felt the day was coming.

Growing up in New York and playing sandlot ball, I had begun following pro football in 1935 because I liked Dutch Clark—for the reasons that any kid is likely to pick a particular sports idol. I liked the way he looked and played and all I read about him. A year later I moved to Coogan's Bluff over the Polo Grounds. I began watching all the New York Giant games, at first from the rocks high above the stands, then from a bleacher seat every Sunday. I couldn't understand why everybody wasn't nuts about pro football in 1939—even in 1949. To see Tuffy Leemans crash into a ton of Chicago Bears and bounce out and keep going was a tremendous thrill. To see Mel Hein never fail, and that Owen defense try to stop Hutson and Isbell, Baugh and Battles, Luckman and Osmanski, was football at its best. I became dedicated to the pros. They were the dramatic and dynamic picture material in my mind. I saw the game as a New Yorker watching the Giants play the whole league. From the end zone I saw the pattern of play, the deception and blocking—and this perspective was football to me. I wondered how it would be if you were the quarterback to look into the eyes of the linebacker across the line. I wanted to take pictures with this emotional impact.

Having begun a career as a sports artist I was lucky indeed in 1950 when the Giants put me on the field so I could see the game as the players saw it. But I found that I could see only the quiet moments. The complex scope of football could not be drawn by looking up from a pad. The demands for accuracy

as I wished to report the game were overwhelming. After a few games of sketching, I took a camera and was amazed at the things I saw. As the years passed I gathered a great wealth of material. I had little opportunity to use it, however, until the editors of *Sports Illustrated* gave me the chance in 1954, the year the magazine was first published. On the strength of this work I had the good fortune to be retained as a free-lance artist that first month, and my initial assignment was on pro football.

The twenty or more drawings presented here are a part of the 1,400 I had reproduced between 1954 and 1976. The drawing below was the first sports drawing I tried when I was eighteen, thirty-five years ago. It was done with five different lithograph pencils and rendered in about 140 hours. It was a composite sketch from newspaper clippings and inspired by my memory of how I saw football from the end zone. It was supposed to be Army vs. Notre Dame. The cadets were the first team to wear form-fitting uniforms. Students saw it, liked it, but the first question they asked was, "What team is that supposed to be?" Pointing to a player they would ask, "Who is that?" From then on I decided to draw only specific players and specific teams. The best. I bought my first Speed Graphic and the New York Football Giants permitted me to work on the field and take my own research photographs.

Over a period of six years, I simplified the rendering down to one lithograph pencil and a watercolor or ink wash to meet the pressures of deadlines. I chose the sepia color to give the work warmth and distinction, and persuaded *Sports Illustrated* to run it on a two-color press. It was more handsome than cold black-and-white and less expensive than full color. Some of the sketches in the book took forty minutes, others took forty to sixty hours. These simple drawings of athletes became my style for sixteen years until I switched over to photography and cinematography in 1965 and began directing in television.

During the first ten years, I used eight different cameras to develop my file of football, baseball, boxing and track pictures from which I did my game reports and drawings. Football is a difficult game to photograph. Its momentum and diversity and complexity can appear confusing. You cannot photograph it well unless you know a great deal about football and the teams that are playing and their personnel. You never have a second chance in football. The fleeting moment never comes again. If you wait for it to happen it is over. You never watch a football game or you'll miss it. You have to go out every Sunday and follow every play so that when the key game assignment comes along you have the touch and are ready. All week before a game I develop a point of view for this specific game depending on the teams involved—I stage it in my mind and the players play to it. When I take a photograph I am making an illustration. It has got to be the most representative picture of that game and of all football. Like art, it must transcend the actual fact. Most sports photographs are old, awkward, accidental fragments.

I feel every artist has a concept of life, and if this concept is universal and can be understood and the artist intensifies this concept with a personal style, his art will be well liked—may even be significant. My concept is the dramatic one. My style is the documentary style. My subject is sports. It gives me an honest world to document in a dramatic way—to be contemporary, to draw the battle of the day, the hero of the hour.

After the long periods of development and the periods of career changes—which I always set in patterns of seven-year periods—you reach a chemical/creative balance which governs your productivity. Today I find that a lovely achievement in my work, a series of good photographs, a beautiful day's filming for television, makes me feel very good—but the glow lasts only one tenth of the time that the disappointment of a missed picture or imperfect scene on film will last. Consequently I need many more excellent pictures, many more days of success in television, to keep me in balance—otherwise with a five-to-one ratio I'm in a perpetual downer. I think this need for beautiful results, creations that others feel are beautiful, becomes a driving force. Some artists can't survive without a high percentage of excellence. For others one really good picture will

My philosophy as a creative artist is to *work hardest on your weakest talent*. When it becomes your strongest, stay with it and support it with a wise choice of what you do best. With intelligence and experience this will grow into a formidable overall creative strength. In the beginning, people and animals were the most difficult subjects for me to draw. Faces and careful rendering of tone and color were my strong talents, along with design and composition. I set out to master the anatomy of action in the figure and the horse, and that skill became my strength. Drawing people gave me great joy as well, which is so important. You must thrill to your work.

take them through a year. Some of the tin gods have built their reputation and careers on less than fifty negatives.

A picture, however, no matter how good it may be, is not worth a thousand words. In fact, in the context of a magazine or book it is worth very little without just the right words to complement it. I sometimes forget that readers unlike myself do not study the form and tone and line of a picture and react aesthetically alone—they react in words. The language of vision needs a voice, and it is this bridge of words that sparks the creative reaction in the reader. I began to write. My own thoughts and the words of the athlete.

The Artist

There are two kinds of artists—those who see the world as terribly real and feel that they must represent and interpret it in a very personal or abstract way that will better express this ordinary reality, and those others who see the world as an abstraction —actual in shape but with no synthesis and so no real form—and are inspired to achieve a cohesive reality. Their art is less gifted, some critics might say, because it appears less original or less inventive —you only have to look at it to see how close it is to actuality. If this is true of a photograph then the picture is meaningless and dead. But this is not true in the work of the best American artists. You have only to look at the photography of Edward S. Curtis, Alfred Stieglitz, Dorothea Lange and W. Eugene Smith—whose portraits express and preserve a vital society. Their compassion for the human spirit is evident in all their photographs. My original gods in art school days were five artists who could draw people and horses: Toulouse-Lautrec, Edgar Degas, Daumier, Frederic Remington and Winslow Homer.

Art is really an emotional trigger; whatever happens on the paper can only be related to what happens in the mind of the viewer—how it effects his spirit. If it makes him *feel*. If it makes him think. If it makes him care.

"Sports pictures," as they are called, are a national language. They are as continuous and rhythmic as the seasons and as faithfully changing and as surely recurring. They never stop. With each passing year, in each sport they give us another hero. A few of these photographs find the true character of the action and the sensitivity of the athlete. Others are only evidence.

I shaped my own sports journalism in drawings and photographs, television programs and text. I have paid a hundred dollars for a ringside seat (thirtieth row) because another network was telecasting and I could not get a press pass. I assumed, I guess, that I would take four or six fine photographs even if the fight lasted only one round. I can never enjoy a sporting event unless I photograph it or direct a telecast. I either don't go or leave early if I'm not working an event.

In this country, more than any other, the trigger response to a piece of sporting art or photography has everything to do with the subject. A significant picture of a sports subject will release a whole series of feelings, which are the sum total of what a viewer knows as legend, fact and dreams. An American who cares about sport in an all-consuming way will look at a picture of the President of the United States, his father and his favorite quarterback with different reverence, understanding and enjoyment. But he will probably know more and feel more enthusiasm for the portrait of the quarterback.

This book is a portrait of the athlete as a human being. I do not see the athlete as some extreme physical animal or gladiator or his world of competition as danger-packed exploits that need all sorts of exaggerated visual approaches to "capture the excitement."

The excitement for me is the thinking expression in the eyes of the athlete. The face of the athlete is the fortune of sport. For these men and women, their dignity and grace and balletic movement and aggressive power stem from their eyes, which reflect the total chemistry of their bodies.

The energy of the athlete seems supreme, and they are mentally fit. This well-being is essential. These pictures reflect the joy of the immediate moment, the peace of the long hours alone, the passion of the battle and the joy of competition—and it shows in their eyes. If the athlete knows fear it is only the fear of floundering. The fear of indecision. Seeing their effort to do their best for more than twenty-five years has been a rewarding experience.

It makes little difference if the athlete is alone in the corner of a practice field or in a vast stadium in the Olympic Games. The greater the crowd, the louder the roar, the higher the stakes, the more intimate for me the portrait of the athlete becomes. The moment is drawn to their thinking. Their decision. Their eyes. Everything is measured to their ability. That is why success is so immediate, so joyous. Why failure is so temporary.

The playing field is a stage for the athlete, and there is a cast of supporting actors. Trainers, coaches, officials, owners, journalists, broadcasters, and most important of all the fans. These faces are part of this book and they are important to help express the intensity of the moment.

In 1967 I directed the *Man in Sport* exhibition which included the work of my colleagues around the world and displayed the whole tapestry of sport in photographs. This edition, published for the Olympic year 1980, is one artist's view of this world of sport. I have spent as many hours alone at it as the athletes have. They know this and their respect has been an incentive. My selection of a picture follows no popular judgment—only how well it reflects the character of a certain athlete or the character of a particular sport. This character alone is essential to the emotional impact and to any enduring qualities a drawing or photograph might have.

This is a collection of portraits of gifted people in an extraordinary world: *The Athlete*. This is a book of drawings and photographs that hold the pulse beat of life, that have found a rhythm of pure action that transcends the moment, pictures that are beautifully staged; pictures that reveal the faces of athletes with expressions of thought and the inten-

The Athlete

sity that thought provokes—which is the heart of sports and all meaningful relationships. These photographs are not frozen moments in time. There is no such thing as a still picture, any more than there is such a thing as a still person.

The athlete's dedication is the same everywhere in the world. A long-distance runner from Kenya or a marathon runner from Ethiopia flies by jet air-

motor cars are flown across oceans for derbies and grand prix.

There is a holy alliance in sports that brings forth the maximum skill and strength and striving, the classic greatness and dignity in man. The paradox of sport is that in the contest and clashing, in the struggle and the race, there is almost a divine accord of beauty and grace, a poetry in the harmony of all

craft to compete in California or Japan; a ski jumper from north of the Arctic Circle jumps at Lake Placid and a Russian high-jumper is the main attraction in Madison Square Garden in New York; an Austrian farm girl wins a championship ski race in the Andes; a Brazilian soccer player commutes to Europe to play and an Australian tennis team travels the globe to retain a trophy; racehorses and

peoples together. If sport is a microcosm of life, that life is here, and these pictures hold the significance of a lifetime and are a tribute to man.

There is only one force more intimate than a picture, and that is a person's voice. The portraits that follow are the words of the athlete, private conversations over the years with some of the finest people, the most gifted athletes, one will ever know.

Part 1 THE PORTRAITS

EDDIE ARCARO

"When I ride I always want to be in a driving position, and I'll sacrifice my best form to make certain I achieve this. You have got to be in a position on a racehorse to drive at the finish. I get more power getting very low and flat on a horse during the last sixteenth of a race than if I were sitting up. That's why I carried my right iron so short to give me the great pushing action, a chance for a maximum effort at the wire—when you need it to win. It's a wonderful feeling.

"Now, the English and French don't ride that way. In fact, their style isn't close to ours. They don't push back on those irons and dig into a horse's side like we do or push on the horse's neck in a low position as we do in the States. Instead, they sort of throw the reins at a horse. I've watched Sir Gordon Richards, who won more races than I have, and by comparison he rode almost upright. But who is to say either of our styles is right or wrong.

"Of course the best ride in the world won't bring in a good horse that doesn't want to run. The same goes for a cheap horse, and they are hard to ride. A horse is cheap when you are forced to be driving at any point in the race. The good horses you never forget. They have so much will to run that there's not a whole lot of riding to a real good horse. This will to run makes you one with him. What makes horses like Citation, Assault, Devil Diver, Shut Out, Nashua and Bold Ruler good horses was one factor: they tried to run."

The sun had just lifted above the exquisite clubhouse at Longchamps in the Bois de Boulogne. It was seven-thirty in the morning in Paris and the fog was so heavy over the ancient racecourse that the windmill in the trees and the hill in the backstretch were colorless and almost invisible. The sun's circle looked eerie and the grandstand was mysteriously silent. We walked for almost half a mile to the toughest part of the course, the final turn, where the racetrack becomes flat for the first time, and in the haze we saw a few old track attendants stepping down the turf, inspecting every foot of it on this morning of the race. The setting was like a Millet painting. The Prix de L'Arc de Triomphe was ten hours away. The richest horse race in the world.

"That's my position, Eddie," I said, "right there

on that mound of earth." Arcaro and I had walked to what would be the first turn at U.S. tracks, but in Europe is the final bend, to inspect my camera angle. We wanted to be certain for a technical piece we were doing in our telecast, and Eddie slipped under the rail and walked across the track. He looked down the rail out of the turn to where the track narrows, walked the area twice and studied it carefully, then came back and agreed it would be a perfect shot.

We started the long walk back and Arcaro laughed and remembered the first time he had ridden on this track in Paris.

"I came to France with C. V. Whitney and accepted the mount on Career Boy and when I arrived they thought it would be helpful if I rode a race the day before the Arc de Triomphe to get the feel of the course. They run clockwise here, you turn to your right, and more than half the race is run up and down hill, completely different from any U.S. track. Our tracks are manicured and flat and our turns are always to the left.

"They had arranged for an interpreter for me, and when I arrived in the old paddock area I saw the biggest, wildest horse I'd ever seen. 'Who's going to ride that bronco?' I asked, laughing. 'That's your horse, Mr. Arcaro,' my interpreter answered. 'My horse! Why, he must stand seventeen hands at least,' I said, gasping. I couldn't believe it. I stood there and I watched and they could hardly hold this big animal to put the saddle on him. So I go to my interpreter and I say, 'What makes him so nervous?' So he goes to the French trainer and he asks him and the trainer says, 'He's not broken his maiden—he's never won.' 'Never won!' I said. 'How old is he?' My interpreter asked, nodded, hesitated and answered softly, 'Five.' 'Five,' I say, 'and he's never won and you picked me to ride him in a five-horse race! Why hasn't he won?' There must be something wrong with this guy, I'm thinking. How can this great big powerful animal not have won? 'Ask him why he's never won,' I say, nudging my pal. The interpreter questioned the Frenchman and then turned and said, 'He's never raced before in his life.' 'Never run!' I almost fell over. 'No, they couldn't bring him to the track. He was too nervous,' was the

explanation.

"Well, they finally got the saddle on him and gave me a leg up and the groom was hanging on for his life and when we got on the track he turned him loose. The groom went *ahhh!!* and it was like a rodeo for about an eighth of a mile. He was jumping and diving and bucking, just the greenest horse you've ever seen in your life. I couldn't settle him down, and the interpreter saw this. He had followed in a car, and when we got to the starting barrier, I saw him talking to the starter and then he came over and smiled up at me and said, 'Mr. Arcaro, I know you use a starting gate in your country,' and thinking I had never ridden under an open barrier, explained that the starter would give me a little signal with his hand before he pulled the barrier up. This would give me a head start.

"Now you know in a five-horse field going a mile and five-eighths you don't have to be in front at the gate. But anyway I sat up there and when I get this little tipoff wave I kick this big green dude and he came running all out to the tape. Just as he got there the starter pulls the tape and it goes swish right up in front of my horse's nose. He propped and wheeled, but I kept going straight ahead!

"I'm stunned and I sit up and look and the other jocks are away and all I see of this beauty of mine is his rear going back where we started from. I don't have to tell you about me sitting on that Parisian soil on a one-to-four shot. You know it's pretty em-

barrassing. So I whistle at this nervous fluke and he wheels around and comes back toward me. I figure it's a long race, I'll remount and make a respectable showing. I tried to catch him, because when he wheeled he went in the opposite direction to the end of the chute and then had to turn around. I stood in front of him waving my arms like mad, believing for all my life that a horse wouldn't run over you, when voom, he run right flat over the middle of me. *I'm dead!*, and he disappears down the track. I get up with a mouthful of dirt and they ride me back in the car to the finish line.

"I'm trying to hide when suddenly I hear the loudspeaker call the race off because of a false start. They were trying to take me off the hook! The crowd booed so long and loud that they let it stand and the next day I'm glad I didn't understand French because all the newspapers said I needed some lessons on riding and the open barrier.

"When the big race came up on Sunday I was still shaky, but a great horse, Ribot, won it by fifteen lengths so it didn't matter. I was caught in the pack back at that very turn we just looked at and they were bunched so tight I got banged off fourteen times. They just picked my horse up and carried us. I didn't hit the ground for at least ten jumps. So watch out for that turn today, ol' buddy. It's gonna be gangbusters!"

We went to get some croissants and coffee down the road near the track. It would be a long day.

James McKay, Esq., stands tall (below) with Edward Arcaro as they are fitted for the formal dress required at Epsom. The English derby was one of the five greatest horse races in the world that were part of our ABC Sports 1965 tour of thoroughbred racing. My drawing, at left, "The Hand Ride," is from the *Art of Raceriding*, and shows Arcaro at his best in the stretch.

"One thing is certain as you watch the jockeys over here," Eddie explained. "They don't appear to be working as hard in the stretch as we do in the States. Although it is correct to say that every foot of the way is important in each race, it's a fact that nine times out of ten the money is waiting for the horse and the jockey who get the best job done from the eighth pole to the wire. It is over the last two hundred yards that I preferred to forget my whip and give my horse, instead, the benefit of what we call the hand ride. What a rider does in the hand ride is to tune himself completely into the motion and rhythm of his horse. When the horse is on his hind feet, you must be in position to shove with your hands. And as he pushes off on his jump, you go with him with your hands. Naturally, you must push as hard as your power will permit you to. The harder you push, the more you feel you're urging your horse and helping him. I get more power with my head down in an all-out drive. They never ride that way over here; their irons are too long, they can't get the leverage. In hand riding, with the great push and thrust going for you, so that you feel *one* with your horse, and he's running for you, you almost never hit him, you would break the rhythm. If you urge him, and drive him in the stretch with the hand ride, he'll give you all the run he has in him."

JIM FITZSIMMONS

"We have damn few good racehorses in America today. That is the way it has been for over five years, and it will continue to be that way. In 1956 when we had Nashua, Swaps and Summer Tan were also running and there wasn't a hell of a lot of difference between those three. They were all-time great horses. Then I trained Bold Ruler. He is a great horse and he could be a great sire. But here we are in the sixties and one horse—Kelso—becomes the only big horse around for three years, and although Kelso is good he's not that good to be on top all by himself. It is apparent that the foundation for training thoroughbred horses that was chipped away in the past ten years is now in bad shape. The big racehorse is becoming a legend."

The morning work with the horses was about over and Sunny Jim Fitzsimmons sat talking over coffee in the little wooden cottage across the road from the barn at Belmont Park where the fifty racehorses he trains are quartered. It was April 1961.

The old man went over to the icebox and took out a bowl of pancake batter and made his skillet hot and picked up the bowl and nice as could be poured four cakes in a circle. The pan hissed and he watched without saying much and he took the spatula and flipped them over without any flourish. In a few minutes, after he had made a stack, he served them and we sat together on the rickety table with the flowered oilcloth. Now, you have to understand that Mr. Fitz's pancakes are famous and this was a rare treat. They were without question the most delicious pancakes ever tasted and when asked about them Sunny Jim laughed and said, "Well, I don't know if they're famous. All I know is that everyone likes them and that's the important thing. When we first started out long ago things were pretty tough. If you didn't win you didn't eat. This fella Miller and I used to barnstorm, and things were so lean we couldn't afford to throw anything away—so Miller used to take all the leftover beans and rice and all the scraps and mix them with flour and water and make a pancake batter. One day I asked him how he made them. 'Oh,' he said, 'they're mystery cakes.' The mystery was no one knew what the blazes was in 'em. Those mystery cakes of Miller's became the basic recipe for my pancakes, and I added and developed and eventually used the mix. Plenty of eggs, plenty of butter. I use cream instead of milk and I put syrup in the batter. My granddaughter Kate says that makes the difference. It's sort of a ritual.

The important thing is I never follow the instructions on the box. I guess I train horses that way too."

Sunny Jim Fitzsimmons has suffered through the years of the outlawed tracks, the lean years under the Hughes Bill when racing was all but snuffed out in New York, and the desperate early years as a trainer. He has known the great days of the twenties and thirties and then beginning in the late forties has seen thoroughbred horseracing prosper and grow and then explode into the fantastic decade of the plush racing factories, the swollen pari-mutuels, and the astronomical purses.

This quiet, friendly man, with his quick smile and gracious manner, has a legion of friends in racing, and he has in the last twelve years trained horses whose earnings totaled $7,500,000. His stakes victories are extraordinary. He has won the Kentucky Derby, Preakness, and Belmont Stakes, racing's hallowed Triple Crown, with Gallant·Fox in 1930 and with Omaha in 1935. In 1939 another Derby and Belmont with Johnstown, and a Preakness and Belmont with Nashua in 1955. His phenomenal successes at distance races fill the record books: seven Jockey Club Gold Cups, six Belmont Stakes, ten Saratoga Handicaps, five Suburbans, eight Wood Memorials as well as his three Kentucky Derbies. Diavolo, Gallant Fox, Faireno, Omaha, Isolater, Fighting Fox, Johnstown, Nashua, Bold Ruler—all great Fitz-trained horses down through the years, plus the superb fillies and mares, Vagrance, Misty Morn, High Voltage, and the rest. Eddie Arcaro paid him the highest tribute: "Getting a horse ready for a distance race Mr. Fitz is the greatest trainer who ever lived."

The eighty-eight-year-old man looks at you with his clear light-blue eyes and speaks his mind. He is critical without malice. He offers only his appraisal of thoroughbred racing in America which turns out to be a paradox too, because the days he has known can never come again and the consequences of time and place are making a mockery out of the training of a racehorse.

"Your help today around the racetrack is a major problem. The wage and hour business and the unions cut us down. You can't train in the East as you did in the past. You can't get the help today around a stable. No one seems to have the time or cares any more. I collect seventeen-fifty per day for each horse from my owners for training their horses. That's my price for feed and help and it includes my profit, which is nothing. It costs twenty dollars a day to do it right and it will go to twenty-five per day soon, I'm sure. I collect ten percent of the purse for stakes winnings. So if I don't win now, I don't eat—same as the old days. The owners pay the veterinarian's bill and the track is responsible for the upkeep of the barns.

"We need a crew of about thirty-four men and boys to run the stable, and last year our books showed we had employed eighty-six. Some stay for two weeks or less. Then they float around somewhere else.

"The boys have changed too. It used to be just as important to make jockeys as yearlings. But now you can't get the boys to stay. The green young ones come around and the first thing they want to do is race and there's no chance of that in New York so they leave. We don't make any boys. You can't get them to ride around New York. We need more weight concessions, and we don't get them, so they ride elsewhere. The Racing Commission doesn't think it's important. Jockeys are greedy, too. They're all businessmen with agents, and where they used to get a fixed fee to ride each race on the card and ten percent of the stakes purses, *now* they want ten percent of *everything*. It takes at least six months before you can let a boy race, but you can't ride him in New York against all the good jockeys with only a five-pound allowance—that's just not enough allowance to give him the chance to win. My idea is that the only way to encourage the boys to stay is to give them a ten-pound allowance until they've won twenty races. By that time the owner has gotten some good use of the boy and a return on his investment. The number of thoroughbred tracks has increased from seventy to one hundred and twenty-nine in the last twelve years, and there are many places a boy can go to win outside New York. You can sign a contract, but there's no sense in making him ride and chancing that he'll ruin your horse if he has a chip on his shoulder and wants to go elsewhere. I won't try to make boys unless I get enough concessions to make it worthwhile. The Jockeys' Guild talks about making riders, but they don't really do anything about it. Nobody does, and there is a great influx of jockeys coming in from outside the United States and they're good riders. But we're not making any here that I can see.

"The condition book today has become a big problem for the trainer. When I bring my horses to a track they are usually *all* ready to run. The difficulty is for the racing secretary to put races in the book for the horses I have. I've got to run my horses according to the conditions in the book, and if the conditions don't fit my horses, I might have fifty horses and can't run any. They have claiming races. Well, I don't have cheap horses, so that's out; nonwinners of two races, well, I have few horses that haven't won two races, so that's out; nonwinners of so much money and so forth. Well, there are so many eligibility requirements that squeeze you out. You can't run your horse if he is not eligible for the conditions in the book. There are six claiming races in New York each day, and chances are the horses are worth from three thousand dollars to fifteen thousand. Well, cheap horses are always in the majority, and so the racing secretary, in order to fill out his card, has to set up most of his races for these horses. Of course the people don't care. They bet on anything.

"If I told you the difference between how we trained in the old days and how we train today you would think it was fiction. When I first started we did it all on the track. Take a string of fifteen horses out and each boy would go off, work his horse, walk his horse, sponge his horse right there on the track. You can't stay out there today or you'll get run over. You just get on and off quick. I used to go around the sheds at old Aqueduct in the winter four miles each day with my two-year-olds and when they came out of those sheds they were fit for most anything. True horsemen are hard to find. Today everything is piecemeal—do the best you can. Just run them and hope for the best. You can't develop a super horse that way.

"Horses need a lot of work and a lot of care. They don't get it anymore, or at least not like they used to. We don't have the space—the stall space—or room for grazing. In the past a two-year-old was brought along slowly, wisely, and sometimes we did not race him until he was three. This was not unusual. If the long days of slow, steady training were there I could always go on from there with the fast work. Today there is little chance for this. You can't get stall space for any two-year-old horse some places unless you're going to run him. If he's not scheduled to race, then the track authorities prefer to give the space to horses that are. Now, what am I to do?

"Owners race their two-year-olds before they are ready, and all the time and good breeding and money spent is washed away and a lot of good horses go wrong. Training a horse takes a long time, and the track owners won't give us this time. We have to be on and off the track at a certain hour. They think you're greasing automobiles on a rack.

"You can't put anything into a horse. If you just protect what they've got and develop the qualities they've got, then you've done a good job as a trainer. A trainer is responsible for the sound, full development of their muscles, legs, and hearts. If I get a horse ready to work a stiff half mile well, rather than take any chance I'll only work him three eighths of a mile. I always want to be sure in the spring he is ready. For a mile race, I'll let him go three quarters. Of course, over the years if a three-year-old horse made a good showing in the Wood Memorial, this was the test for me for the Kentucky Derby. Then the owners would decide whether or not to ship him to Louisville.

"There are no mean horses. There are horses with different dispositions and you have to learn that some horses are lazy and others want to do too much. Others like to play a lot. The horse that wants his own way will need a good crack to bring his mind on his business. The exercise boys are very poor today, and they can ruin a horse very quickly, and you have to watch the boy as much as the horse so he will not

"There's only one thing a trainer needs to be successful, and that is the best horses. No matter how good a trainer you are if you don't get the horses you can't win. And the test of the good horseman is to develop the young horse and bring forth all his good habits and overcome his bad habits. The second requirement is after you have developed a good horse to his peak condition to keep him there. But we all must have the best horses to start with.

give the animal bad habits by doing something he shouldn't be doing. We get them schooled at the gate and ready to run, but then we take the horse to the races and hand him over to a jockey that maybe has never seen the horse before in his life. And the starter and assistant starters in the gate take over and put the finishing touches on it and it's out of the trainer's hands. If you get a good jock you try to keep him on the horse and not learn bad habits.

"My whole creed as a trainer has been based on something that I was told long, long ago. I guess about 1894, and I never forgot it. There was this man named Allhouse and he had this horse called Bartender, but most of his others were trotters. He came to me and said, 'Jim, I'd like you to train Bartender for me. Will you do it?' 'Well,' I said, 'if you think I'm good enough, I certainly would be tickled to death to do it.' I considered it quite a compliment. 'Well, Fitz,' he says, 'nobody ever made a bad horse good. But,' he says, 'there's been many a trainer that's made a good horse bad. You won't do that and that's why I want you to train for me.' Of course a trainer who didn't know his business could have the best horse in the world and he could ruin all the potential before the horse even got a chance to show it."

After a hearty meal we pushed our chairs back and relaxed and Mr. Fitz talked about the old days long ago when he was very young and Brooklyn was meadow and woodland. He spoke with such firecracker swiftness and such alertness about each name and place and incident it was hard to realize he was a man of eighty-eight years who had fallen in love with horses when he was only five.

"I guess it was a coincidence or something, but I was born in a house that my father owned in 1874 and in 1879 we had to move because they tore the house down to build Sheepshead Bay Racetrack on the very spot. In 1880 the track opened. We moved over here to Irish Town and lived here ever since. In all these years I watched horse racing change and Brooklyn change too. It was all farms, nothing but farmland clear from where we live now over to Kings Highway and back to Ocean Parkway and over to the Brighton Beach racetrack. This was all swampland, and many times the tide would come up from the ocean into the bay and then run into the meadowland and flood all the houses in Sheepshead Bay and there would be two feet of water on 14th Street. Around Coney Island it was a regular forest. Nothing but trees, and I can remember them distinctly, and the day they gave me eggnog celebrating Cleveland's election I thought it was sarsaparilla. It tasted mighty good and I got a little giddy coming home through the woods. Ocean Avenue was just a big dusty country road as wide as it is now. They used to exercise horses out there and only seven or eight families lived along the way.

"I used to drive to Wallabout Market in downtown Brooklyn with my father. He had a regular huckster's wagon for vegetables, and we used to work at night. He'd get up at one A.M. in the morning and drive to market and I would sleep in the back of the wagon. Then we would get the load and he would head the horse out on the boulevard and then I would drive home and he would sleep in the back of the wagon. I was five years old then. A few years later when they were clearing ground for the racetrack, pulling up stumps and the like, I used to go out in the evening and they would put me up on an old horse and I'd ride it in. I'd also mind cows, just sit them up on the road, take them up to Coney Island Avenue and stay out all day with them and then drive them home in the evening and milk them and deliver the milk over to the racetrack stables when they were built. My first experience at riding came from hanging around the blacksmith's shop. After the horses in the neighborhood were shod, I used to get on them, bareback, and ride them home to the people that owned them. Or when the people turned their horses out they would drift off and I would go hunting for them. That was my hobby—riding the old horses home. I would go out picking hickory nuts and shooting with my slingshot and looking for horses. I knew every horse around.

"My best friend was George Tappan. His father owned the restaurant. We called him Fish, and me and Fish were inseparable. We were kids together, we grew up together, he was my valet when I was a jockey, then my assistant trainer right up to 1956 when he died. The newspaper fellas used to call us Damon and Pythias. Well, Fish worked for a fellow named Buffalo Bill. He had a little saloon up there right opposite where the moving pictures are now. I don't know what this fella had the horses for, but around the back of this place was a nifty lot and Fish and I would go down there every once in a while when we'd get old Buffalo Bill away and get some rope and tie it on to the horses' halters and we would have a race around the lot. We were just two nuts about horses—that was all. I did anything I could that would get me close to a horse. I took any job that was connected with a horse, and it didn't take much money to get me to take the job. I was always horse-crazy. I guess I still am for that matter. I never went to school except for a few months in the winter. One thing I remember was that Harry Konohwen was one of the schoolteachers and he loved the races and would close the schoolhouse early to go over to the track and the kids would go home. I had the job of sweeping out the schoolroom while the races were on.

"My first job was as an assistant on a provisions wagon. I was the errand boy and we used to have a route around Coney Island and I worked for this man Brunner. It was like a delicatessen store on wheels, and I remember how it felt on a raw winter day, putting my hand in the pickle barrel and reaching down for those pigs' feet and the smell of those big cheeses. I got four dollars a month and my board on this job, and I would take care of the horses. Old man Brunner was quite a little gasser. He'd talk so much each place he went in to deliver, the route took all day.

"Then I worked for Ditmas. He was one of the old Dutch families that settled in Brooklyn. He owned a grocery store and I used to go out and get orders in the neighborhood. The customers all liked me, and I guess they dealt with me just because they liked me more than anything else. I was fourteen then and I can remember the Great Blizzard as if it were yesterday. I was working in the grocery at 13th Street and Avenue X and it was the 12th of March 1888. It rained all the day before and that night it stopped and started to snow and it snowed all night. The drifts came up to the door and I tried to get out in the morning and only got about fifteen feet and had to come back. It kept snowing all that day and then it froze up and got very cold and you could walk around on top of the snow. I remember walking right over the spot where the fence was, but everything had disappeared. I didn't go anywhere for a week— no one did.

"Finally I was so crazy about horses I wanted to be with them all the time and I would hang around a lot with the Brennan brothers at their stables and I got acquainted with the men. I was a little kid and of course they used to put boys on in those days. Age didn't make any difference. I asked for a job and they gave it to me, but I had a hard time convincing my mother whether I could go or not. She finally let me go. At first I did odd jobs around the kitchen, but then they put me out on the track. I could ride pretty good by this time and it was the 4th of March when I went with them and they put me on an old horse called Centennial. They just wanted me to breeze him, but when we started he ran off with me for seven eighths of a mile. I was scared to death, but I did the best I could trying to pull him up. I didn't pull him up. He pulled himself up after we got around by the stands. That was my first experience on the track.

"About a year later I was working with the horses over at Graves End and exercising this colt and went over to cool him out after his race and Hardie Campbell, who was the trainer, came over and said, 'Jimmy, do you think you can ride a race?' and I said, 'Sure.' Maybe I said sure before I thought much about it, but I thought he was talking about a race maybe next week or sometime in the future when he would give me a mount. 'Well,' he said, 'you ride Newburg today!' This was about an hour before the race, and when I came to the track that afternoon I had no more idea of riding in a race than I did of flying. The first thing I wanted to do was go to the bathroom right away. But I went up in the jocks' room and borrowed a pair of boots

from Willy Dorman. He was a good-sized boy and the boots would fit Tarzan. I didn't really want them, but I had to wear them and the pants were very baggy because I was a little bit of a shaver. I weighed eighty-four pounds that day. Well, I went out and got up on that horse and rode a pretty good race. I finished fourth. We didn't have any starting barrier in those days and Fitzgerald was the starter. I felt a little timid coming up to the start, but after we got away all I tried to do was win.

"About six months later I went to Red Bank with Hardie Campbell and his yearlings and I got very sick with malaria. I had chills and fever and an old doctor put a fly blister over my heart. He burnt me like the devil and when he got through with it, it was just an enormous water blister hanging down over my heart. It looked like a foot long and it bothered me for days. I guess my heart was affected by the trouble. But after the blister I got well and the doctor told me to go home and keep away from all excitement, never go near any more racehorses or racetracks. Well, you know I didn't take that doctor's advice. I stayed home for about three months and then I went back with the horses and I've been with them ever since.

"One dark night, shortly after I was sick, I got off the horse trolley at Neck Road and was walking home past Gus Friend's place and a huge black man walked out of the blacksmith's yard as quiet as could be. Not thinking about me, he accidentally came right on top of me and then disappeared. He scared me bad. It was so quick. I went behind the gatepost and oh, I looked down and felt my coat moving with the heart rate. You could hear it pounding and see it moving through all my clothes. Later I figured if I was going to die that's the time I would have died the way that doctor talked. I've been through everything since then in the excitement line and I'm still in pretty good shape.

"Most of my days as a jockey were spent on the track down in Gloucester, New Jersey—that was a wide-open gambling, dancehall town across the river from Philadelphia. They eventually closed the track there and banned racing in New Jersey for fifty years. The Gloucester Ferry ran from South Street in Philadelphia over to Jersey Avenue in Gloucester and the people would walk from the pier about a half mile to the track. Coming back to the ferry after the races there were many places of entertainment to make them miss the boat. Fish came over from Brooklyn to join me, and he was my valet. I rode over a thousand races there, five hundred and eighty days steady. We would race all winter long. When we had snow they would scrape the track and men would shovel the snow to the outside rail. We had small fields then, six or seven horses, and sometimes half the track was clear and half was snow. The rough days were the cold rainy drizzly days—when the sleet froze to your hands. One day like that I rode this horse called Esau and we must have waited at the post for half an hour. My hands got stiff and half froze holding the reins. I couldn't open the damn things. But other than your hands you never feel the cold when you get on a horse, the excitement keeps you warm. I won nearly two hundred races. Quite a few days I won four races on the card. There were no starting gates, of course. We would line up and we'd get hell if we broke away too soon. The starter, old man Patton, would come down off the stand and grab ahold of your horse and knock the devil out of you with the butt of his flag. He would give me a crack lots of times for trying to break away in front. Then there was this nice old English fellow named Hedges who was down the track with his advance flag. Sometimes when we broke off too soon we'd go nearly a quarter of a mile before we could pull the horse up. Then old Mr. Hedges would wave his advance flag and say, 'Pull up, boys, pull up!' and when we'd get pulled up and turned around he'd say, 'Cancel back, cancel back!' I can remember that distinctly just like it was yesterday. Now I've got Bold Ruler and Eddie. (right)

"Right near the end of my days as a jockey I was riding for Carter Hall and he had two horses, William T. and Captain Brown, and a few others. He wanted me to go to Saratoga to ride William T. in the Flash Stakes on opening day in 1893. I went and he finished second to a horse called Gallilee. Then later in the meeting I won on Captain Brown.

"Those days they would begin racing at eleven in the morning and they would be finished by about two-thirty. Then everybody would spend the balance of the afternoon at the end of the grandstand making foreign book with the wireless betting on other races all over the country. I didn't bother with that. I'd just get on my bicycle and ride up to Saratoga Lake. I can remember the pretty colors and the great lines of carriages and the people. Oh, the atmosphere was lovely. They had four-in-hands and coaches and everybody had a team and coachman. There would be hundreds of them. All the buggies going down the avenue past the old Grand Union Hotel and the United States Hotel with all the people sitting out on the wide porches.

"Years later we stayed with a family named West and we would go up to Lake Desolation and he sold me this property for three hundred dollars. It ran about four hundred feet back from the lake. Then as my son John got older and his son Jim grew up, they all built cabins and it became a real community. One day Jim put a sign up, 'Fitzsimmonsville.' I don't know how the hell they let him put it up there, but they did and that is the way our family got to go there during the meeting each summer.

"The significant thing that Saratoga did for racing was that it was there each August that a transfusion of sportsmanship took place. That is the only way I can describe it. Every person in racing that had a stable of horses that was worthwhile from Canada, from Chicago, all came to Saratoga. The great sportsmen all came there, and it was lovely. These great owners all together at one meeting was the important thing to me. It was like a meeting of the heads of state. Then they brought the yearling sales there and still more came. Each August everyone just had a hell of a time!

"Soon after that first year at Saratoga I got too heavy to ride. I had some money and I bought my first horse, a bay colt named Pat Kelly and a second one, Austrel. Fred Merrick used to ride for me. The first stake I ever won was a thousand-dollar Brewers Stakes at Pimlico, and I won it with Bartender. Wouldn't take much to win a hunch bet on that one, huh? The next was the Saratoga Cup with Star Gaze and then the Merchants and Citizens Handicap in 1915 with the same horse.

"In 1924 I started training for the Belair Stud and Mr. William Woodward, and the following year for the Wheatley Stable with Mr. Mills and Mrs. Henry Carnegie Phipps, and from there on it was clear sailing for me. The bosses made me. They would just bring me the great horses and I'd wreck 'em, but they would keep coming back." His clear blue eyes gave me a wink and he laughed. "Credit for my success goes to the bosses. Mr. Woodward, Mr. Maxwell, and J. E. Davis, Herbert L. Pratt, and Mrs. Henry Phipps and her son Ogden. There was no sacking me if the horses didn't win, so I never had to worry a bit. They just liked me and I was glad they did. Mr. Davis got me started and acquainted with Mr. Mills, the Secretary of the Treasury, and Mr. Woodward. No one could have had a better set of owners if you had your choice from a chart on the wall and hand-picked them. I never really had any favorite horses except the old horses, Pat Kelly, Electro, Poquesin, and False Pride, because I had to win a race then so the wife and the couple of kids could eat. You got a feeling for them because when they came home in front it would pick up your spirit and keep you going. They fed me when I needed it.

"Any favorites since those years would be up to the Bosses. They furnished me with some damn fine horses and they stuck with me and I was sure glad to stick with them. I had some good luck and did as good a job as the other trainers might have done. There are two elements in racing that carry the whole sport. The first is the people who bet through the mutuels. *Three million dollars a day* at Aqueduct racetrack alone last year.

"The second element is the sportsman—the people who have money and can afford to have a stable of horses and who love the sport and are willing to spend the money. Today there are a lot of people coming in racing with new silks on the jockeys you've never seen before, and they *think* they're sportsmen but they really come in to *make* money. Well, they're not going to stay very long because they are not going to make any money. The two ele-

closed behind him. As I watched his familiar figure move away from the cottage, all the names and places and the lost and lovely times gone by swirled in a kaleidoscopic maze, and the strength and courage of this remarkable man seemed incredible.

Sunny Jim paused at the end of a walk as a beautiful chestnut colt was being led along the long road to the saddling shed for the first race. The horse was before him now, towering over the bent old man, and the animal seemed to dance lightly as he walked, the white fetlocks disappearing into the soft turf. His

ments that carry racing, the people and the owners, will both lose money over a five-year period and if they break even they'll be very lucky.

"But the day of the true old-line sportsman has about had it. Racing has kicked the hell out of sportsmanship. As for the people . . . I guess they'll keep coming out to the racetrack and bet until the day the world ends."

Mr. Fitz pushed up from the chair, flipped on his bashed-up old hat and then slyly tried to hold back a yawn. He smiled. "I've been getting up before daybreak for seventy-five years and I still haven't gotten used to it."

He reached for his crutches and moved quickly to the door, went out on the stone path, and the door

legs moved in such an easy gentle rhythm that only when you saw the groom pulling heavily on the shank to hold him steady did you realize the strength of his thousand pounds. His head yanked at the chain and you could see the silken circle of his cheek and the ripple of his powerful shoulders. His flank glistened and was golden in the early-afternoon sunlight. The horse had gone past the great trainer now, and you realized in that fleeting moment what this horseman had known all his life—that the thoroughbred racehorse was the second most magnificent design in God's creation. But only the trainer's skill and caring could bring him up to a race fit to run.

Mr. Fitz crossed the road slowly and disappeared into the dark shadow of the barn.

JACK NICKLAUS

"Anybody who is successful must be a decision-maker. You've got to make up your mind on what you're going to do and how you're going to do it and then go about doing it. I think it is the positive nature of the game of golf just as it is the positive nature of life that the successful people appear to have blinkers on. Everything is straight ahead. They go forward and know exactly what they're going to do once they make up their mind to do it, and by God they don't look sideways.

"The one strongest, most important idea in my game of golf—my cornerstone—is that I wanted to be the best. I wouldn't accept anything less than that. My ability to concentrate and work toward that goal has been my greatest asset. There are an awful lot of fellows that have equal ability to mine as far as hitting a golf ball, but the discipline I've had in arranging my schedule and playing the events that I think I should play, instead of what everybody wants you to play, has been the difference. I've lived my own life and I think that is very important.

"My family is pretty darn normal and I think that's great. I've introduced my kids to golf but I've introduced them to everything else too. They play all sports. They enjoy golf but they realize that their chances of playing golf for a living are very slim. My son, Jack, wants to get into whatever will prepare him best for the business world and he's looking forward to playing college golf, but I don't think he's looking forward to golf as a career.

"I'll be forty this year and the reason I'm playing tournament golf, and the reason I want to continue to win, is that I've set a record at the present time that no one has topped as it relates to winning major championships: five Masters, four PGAs, three U.S. Opens, two U.S. Amateurs and three British Opens. When I finish playing the game I know someone is going to come along someday and break that record, but I would like to make sure that my record is as tough to beat as possible.

"That is the only goal I have left. I don't have anything to prove on a week-to-week basis anymore. I enjoy the game of golf. I love competition. I sorely will miss the day when I'm not going to have that three-footer to win a tournament.

"But the people you passed on the way up will pass you on the way down—it has all got to end one day. I just want to give them something to shoot at and set the best record I can while I'm competing.

"I built my business interests carefully over the past twelve years. At the present time, since my first venture at Hilton Head, I have worked on the new design or redesign of twenty-nine golf courses. Fourteen are complete and fifteen are under construction. In the ten years since the first course was constructed my company has expanded so that we do the community development, the club, real estate, financing and everything else right down the line. That is where my business is going. I really enjoy it very much and get a great deal of fun out of it. After the years of playing the game of golf and seeing golf courses around the world, to design and build golf courses now is a delight for me. It is a great transition as I begin to phase out of competitive golf, and I think it will be a very profitable one.

"Each golf course that we build we design for the people who will play there. Hilton Head was made difficult because it was built for tournament play. Some golf courses are built to be very easy. The challenge is to design something that fits the purpose.

"Golf is fortunate in the United States in that it is administered very well. The tour is in fairly decent shape and the entire game is in fine shape. Golf is solid.

"There is enough new blood in golf. I don't think our problem is in the number of good golfers we have coming through. We have quite a few. The problem in the game of golf lies in the fact that golf is not a sport of the masses. I don't think we're producing enough golfers of the average type. We have a sufficient number of golfers at the high school, college and amateur level to develop enough good golfers for tournament play, but we're not getting enough *starts* out of youngsters to develop the average golfers who play for enjoyment.

"Everything in sports today has gone towards an emphasis on *winning*, and not the enjoyment of playing the game. That's sad. Thousands of kids are not playing the game and missing all the years of possible enjoyment because their outlook at the start is that since they can't be a scratch handicapper, or they can't beat Tom Watson, they drop out, and I think that is a shame. Golf is something you can play all your life—affording exercise and relaxation outdoors—so many things richer than winning.

"During the first ten years on the pro golfers' tour I competed with Arnold Palmer and Gary Player a great deal and in the seventies with Gary more than Arnold. We've all been very good friends and re-

mained good friends considering the keenness of competition we've had against each other. We have enjoyed being with each other off the golf course as well, and I respect not only their golf ability but respect them as special persons. It has been a great existence especially since we are three different kinds of people leading different life-styles. I've been fortunate to know others too: the Trevinos and Millers, the Watsons and Weiskoffs and Crenshaws. Lee Trevino is a marvelous golfer and a marvelous person and a very good friend. He has always been a man of his word, that rare kind of friend who has done so many valuable favors for me and never let me do as many favors for him as I would have liked. I think the world of him. It is easy to laugh with Lee, and in golf as in anything you *need* a sense of humor.

"You learn by watching the best golfers. We all continue to learn. If we didn't continue to learn we'd be in trouble. I've learned an awful lot from playing with these men, with the exposure to them and with talking with them.

"Over the years I've had a wonderful relationship with the press, they've been very kind to me and they've appreciated the time I've given them. My press has been excellent. The fact that I've been on the cover of *Sports Illustrated* magazine eighteen times doesn't impress me. I really don't think about it. I've always assumed if my golf was successful I would see my picture published, and since the editors want to enhance their magazine I also assume they will use the best pictures they can get and make their best effort. The difference between my picture and another athlete is that I don't have a uniform or a number. So when they see me they are seeing Nicklaus the man, and over the years *that* image is what the public remembers.

"Perhaps no one realizes how important diet has been for me. I can't describe how important it is. You go along for years weighing too much, then you change your diet, then you start feeling good and you don't even mind looking in the mirror and then gradually you rise to a different physical and mental level. It reflects on all your life, not just on your ability as an athlete. It is all part of the discipline. There have been two Jack Nicklauses. The fat one and the new one.

"The standard press coverage of golf has grown through the years. It has gotten so much more extensive because of television and because of television and expanded press coverage the galleries have grown with the growing interest in the sport. Golf is more of an *event* today than it was twenty years ago when the people who came out were only golfers. Now if a tournament comes into Ohio or Carolina the people come out because it is the event to see—

not just because it is golf.

"The autograph and picture-taking furor is far more intense, especially among the younger fans, than it was twenty years ago. When I began on the tour a golfer was a golfer. The people that come to see golf today come out as a fan of the golfer as a celebrity, rather than a fan of a golfer. You must have that element to make golf popular with the public.

you can't do watching tournament golf. I think that what is missing from golf telecasts is that you go season after season without getting to know the field —just the leaders—and then not very well. The networks have got to do programming with more insight as to what athletes are all about. People are interested in people. They watch certain sports because they are interested in a certain person. People were interested in Arnold in the early sixties and

"Television does not show golf very well. You can't really see the problems a golfer has on a particular shot. You can see the golfer's swing and the ball land on the green, incidents along the fairway and the ball around the pin, but you can't see what the golfer sees in the dimension that he sees it. You can *see* space or distance, you can't read a green, you have to be told about these things.

"I think the biggest problem we have with golf on television today is the personality problem. I think that's a problem with a great many sports. Viewers used to enjoy the All-Star Golf, and Big Three Golf and Challenge Golf and the CBS Golf Classic, because those old shows created a few *real* personalities, made golfers people—got inside people—which

that's one reason the game of golf took off!

"The coverage of golf is all the same. You can anticipate what the next picture will look like on the golfer's next shot. Because of the sameness of the coverage the players are fit into identical patterns and the individual qualities of the athletes are lost. Television has to create more variety, more revealing insight to a golfer's character on the home screen.

"Golf has infinite variety. The feel of the club in your hands changes every day of your life. No two days are ever the same. I realize this. One of the things I practice and I stress it in my golf clinics is that you should try to bring what I call the *swing of the day* as close together to what is your best swing as you warm up and work on the practice tee. Then when you get on the golf course you will have a consistent *feeling* and know where you're going on that round.

"My pleasure in golf is tournament golf. It is very difficult for me to go out and play a so-called sociable round. I really don't enjoy it. The difference is in order to play well I have to shut myself off out there and let nothing affect me, let nothing disturb my concentration. You can't do that comfortably on a sociable round of golf.

"The difference between the professional and the weekend golfer is that the professional has the ability to concentrate after he hits a bad shot. He has enough savvy to go down and play the next shot and not worry about the one that's behind him. When I make a mistake on a golf course I like to know *why*. Was my alignment poor, was my grip bad, my head position wrong? Did I take the club away too fast? Did I pick the club up, did I take it to the outside, did I take it to the inside, did I sway? Did I come over the top with my right shoulder? Did I move my head? There are a million things.

"Quite often when I play a poor shot, while I still have the swing fresh in my mind, I'll check my alignments and my grip and try to find out what's wrong by duplicating the swing I have just made. And quite often I'll find my mistake. All I have to do is find it once or twice during a round and I won't repeat it again.

"Many times if I haven't found out what it is I'll go to the practice tee—and pretty soon that bad swing is going to pop up again. I may have to hit only five or ten shots; I may have to hit balls for an hour. But once I find out what the trouble is, I can make my corrections. The next day when I go out, it doesn't bother me anymore. I haven't slept with it; I've gotten it out of my system.

"No victory in golf comes easily. Winning major tournaments against the tough competitors on the tour, fifteen of whom are only a stroke or two apart on an aggregate stroke total over a year's campaign, calls for consistency of play. On the tour I believe in keeping charts of championship golf courses all over the country. I think it is essential. That's why you will see me slip out a map of the course I carry in my back pocket during a round and refer to it.

"It is important for me to keep yardage charts for several reasons. One, it eliminates an extra day's practice coming to that tournament from a previous tournament. Also, my eyes change and the light changes, and you just don't have perfect vision every day. If you're playing by sight, you've got the worst of it. I have the yardage marked

down, say from the tee on the eighth hole at Westchester to the big rock on the left of the fairway, and then from there on on extreme dog-leg left across the lake to the green.

"I feel that every club member should keep yardages on his own club course. He'd find that his scores would improve tremendously because he would learn exactly how far he hits each shot. When he goes to play another golf course, it's got to help him. When they say that some hole is a hundred and sixty, he knows he hits a five iron for a hundred and sixty yards back home, so he will feel confident that a five iron will work again.

"Golf is a funny game. It is one of the few games in the world that no one can master. Even the pros can't master it. But you sort of get the bug and you want to come back for more."

"One advantage I have playing golf is that I am almost always able to make the best of getting out of trouble. I learned long ago that in this game you're the only one that can get yourself in trouble so you darn well better be prepared to get out of it.

"The game can get difficult. Wind by itself is not too bad, rain by itself is not too bad, but wind and rain on a course are the most difficult conditions in golf. The combination of cold, wind and rain, not having any feel in your hands, not being able to keep a dry club, makes the game of golf almost impossible.

"I have been called stubborn and persistent and they have written about my tenacity on the golf course. I'm not sure if tenacity feeds on tenacity or if toughness replenishes toughness, but if it does, you can do it only up to a point. The biggest problem I have right now as I look to the 1980s is that recently I've not been tough enough on myself to work as hard as I need to work to maintain the position I've always held in the sport. I'm just going to have to get tougher on myself this year to make that happen again. I think it is a continuous struggle that we all have to fight with—complacency. You must have the edge in tournament play, you must hold the edge, and the only way to hold it is to work on it.

"This is the problem with the young golfers on the tour—they're not hungry enough to work at reaching their full potential. They've got their pockets full by May and they don't need to work that hard for the rest of the year. Instead of fifteen golfers making a living we've got one hundred golfers making a very good living. It's got to get back to the game of golf being a game more than a way to earn money. We've got to get back to the realization that anyone that wants to be the best in a sport can't play it for money alone—they must play it as a sport. If they don't they will lose sight of what they're really striving for—to be the best.

"I'm stubborn to the point where I don't ever compromise on the wrong shot. If I've got a shot that I think is the right shot then I'm going to play it. I may make a mistake in doing it but I'll come back the next day and play it the same way in the same situation because I'm just stubborn enough if I think I can do it. I think if you start compromising with yourself you're in trouble. *Confidence, concentration, and never compromise a shot.*

"Carnoustie in Scotland, Firestone and Pinehurst II were some of the toughest courses I've played, but I would hesitate to ever name a course or a hole on any one tournament as being my toughest moment in golf. There is no way you can because the conditions are so variable every time you play.

"Pressure seldom gets to me anymore. Somebody's got to win in tournament play and somebody's got to lose. My philosophy is I may as well win. In sudden death you just cut it a little finer. You figure you started the championship against a hundred and forty-three men and you've eliminated a hundred and forty-two of them. Now you're down to one man in a playoff—you may as well eliminate him. When it comes down to only one other person that can beat you I always figure there is no reason why I should let that happen."

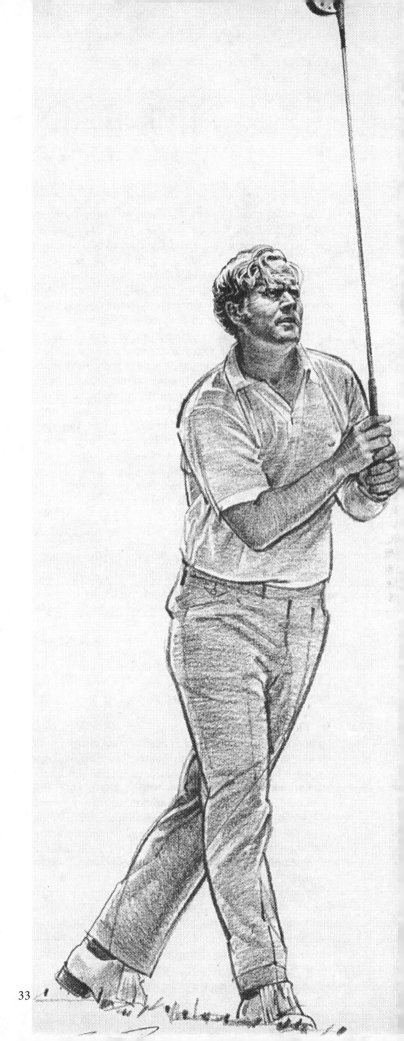

33

JIM BROWN

His locker stall in the visitors' dressing room in Yankee Stadium was on the back wall. He was the last player remaining. All of the Cleveland team had left by bus for the airport, but he had agreed to be guest speaker at a football Giants luncheon the following day. It was empty and quiet and I remember starting across the room, then stopping and half hiding behind a pillar as I watched the trainer carefully and so very slowly help him into his shirt, his vest and finally his expensive gray tailored jacket. Dressing with his soreness, with his pain, took more than *ten minutes* that Sunday afternoon in 1963.

His right arm was wrapped in heavy elastic, but he moved across the room as if his entire body were encased in plaster. (I could imagine all of the fans driving home, talking and replaying in their minds the sight of his moves, his quickness and agility and change of speed as he flashed downfield in the golden October sunlight.) This was Jim Brown one hour after the fifth game of his sixth season in the National Football League. The Browns had beaten the Giants 35–24. The Cleveland fullback had scored three touchdowns and paid the price.

"In the first half they really hit me. I'll say they did—all of them. It was just like the past six years in New York. That Giant defense busted us up good. I've always wanted to do well in New York. Today I got over two hundred yards, *but* this was the roughest, hardest game I've ever had in the six years I've been playing. As far as the championship is concerned, I'd have to say that at this point we should win it. The way I look at it, we could have won the Eastern title *each of the six years* I've been in the league if it were not for internal problems.

"The quarterback and I made some slight tactical adjustments out there and it opened things up. Early in the game I was lined up in my regular fullback position behind the offside tackle. I'd take the handoff and have to move across behind the center and Sam Huff was shooting the middle before I got to the strong side. At the start of the second half on the sideline I suggested to Frank Ryan that we run the same plays, especially our option 7, from a 2 formation where I lined up directly *behind* the center.

"Frank and I were the only ones who knew of the change. Now if Huff shot in over center I would be two steps closer to the hole and he would be a step behind me even if he came in clear. This slight adjustment made a big difference. On the third touch-

down run of thirty-two yards I ran from the 2 spot and had three options: over center, off tackle, or outside. I went outside because that's where it was. Robustelli gave it a half-inside move reacting to my start inside, then as I swung wide the tackle got him. Green put a good block on the linebacker who closed in. When I saw the outside open I knew it would go. Once you turn that end—Robustelli is the key—you know you have five yards. If your halfback gets the linebacker, you know you've got ten. I got by both of them. Now which way? I saw three of them coming across fast from my right. But behind them across the field I saw three of my own blockers. I knew if I dropped a shoulder and went straight I would get the first down, but when I turned that end I cut back because I wanted to break it all the way. I cut sharply and ran thirty yards across the field and I caught them all going the wrong way. I picked up my blockers and they just chopped the rest of that defense down as I opened up.

"This is not a planned play. I cut back because I saw the blockers across field. On an icy field or in mud you could never work a play like this. When you cannot dig in, you have no balance. Mud is no trouble for a big slow man. He runs just the same, but a bad field for a fast man cuts him in half. Mud is a great advantage to those big defensive linemen. A fast man needs a fast track, and the track was fast today. Bobby Mitchell and I used to love to play in Philadelphia. For some reason that's a fast track, real fast. Dallas is too. Love it! Cleveland's a slow track. Just awful. They have that bentgrass there and when you go to dig in, it just pulls out in a big tuft. On a fast track I can use all my speed and abilities as a runner and those big linemen are in their place. Fast track, advantage mine!

"Balance is the whole thing in running. Each situation calls for the use of a number of different abilities. To veer, slide, cut back, sidestep, spin, jump, drop a shoulder and hit, use a forearm, run all out. I must run in that balanced position wherein I can use any one of these abilities instantly. I have a philosophy as a runner. It is to advance the ball, to get to the goal. Nothing more, and you do it every way you can. Five different ways on five touchdowns. Six on one play if necessary.

"Now, I did not do very much out there today. Those blockers set it all up for me. I never was touched on those two long touchdown runs. I figure I have to bounce off and bust through two or three

defensive men and carry a few on my back for me to make a run. But I will take it this way. I have no set image as a runner that I'm trying to establish in the public mind. I don't feel that I have to run into tacklers. I don't feel that if I drop a shoulder and hit them with all my force and knock them on their backs or carry them for five yards that they are so faint-hearted that the next time I come their way they are going to step aside. You don't hurt a defensive man when you hit him. You hurt him more when he misses you. His job is to stop you, and when he comes up empty, that is where the pain is. He's got to answer for that one. It's his job. I've asked my own defensive players this, given the choice. They all agreed they would prefer me to run at them.

"When I report to camp in July I'm not ready to run. It takes me six weeks before I am ready, before my reflexes are sharp and my timing is there, and it is a matter of intelligence in running, of knowing all the possibilities of what will happen when you run inside or off tackle or outside. Running inside is what gets you ready and sharpens you. You have to be quick inside. The hole lasts but a flicker and there is no room. In the old days the great runners may have run instinctively alone, but not in this league today. You have to know where you're going, what should happen and what may happen when you get there and then what your move will be, and put them all together in a split second, until you break into that secondary and can step out."

BRANCH RICKEY

I can remember watching so many ball games with him, and the time we drove back to the big white country house set in the rolling hills at Fox Chapel. The trees were young and green and the floor of the woods was covered with a carpet of white portulaca that were pink in the sunset. The house was set under the hill beyond the long barn and the chicken houses, and across the gardens in the back there was a lovely meadow where his son had lived.

I slept in an upstairs bedroom that looked out on that meadow. I remember photographing Mrs. Rickey from my guestroom window picking daffodils on a spring morning. Their son, Branch Rickey, Jr., had lived beyond. He was a fine young baseball executive. They called him "Twig," and he had died a few years before at age forty-seven. It was the most powerful loss Mr. and Mrs. Rickey had ever endured. She called him Branch and he called her Mother and theirs was a very special relationship.

We came in from the terrace one beautiful, peaceful May evening and sat down to dinner. Mr. Rickey quietly said grace as he always does before the evening meal. He carved the meat and filled each plate. There were four of us seated at the table. "George, who do you think was the best third baseman you've ever seen?" Branch Rickey asked the question with the same enthusiasm as a young boy would have had asking it. George Sisler was seated to Mr. Rickey's left, and he thought for a moment and smiled and answered in his straightforward way, "Buck Weaver was the greatest third baseman. He could do everything. He would come in to pick up a bunt or a slow roller on the line and his nose would be ten inches off the ground."

When I was a boy growing up over the Polo Grounds, sitting on the rocks of Coogan's Bluff and watching Hubbell beat Ruffing in the rain in the first game of the World Series, or rooting for Dick Bartell and Mel Ott, I never thought I would someday have dinner with Branch Rickey and George Sisler and talk about baseball. But this evening and other evenings are realities now that I will long remember with pleasure as I worked with him late at night.

I remember when Mr. Rickey and I completed his baseball book, *The American Diamond*, there was a quiet regret because I knew I would not be seeing Mr. Rickey or the family as much as before. His book about baseball, which he called his bible, brought us together in a friendship—as all good books bring people together. It is a book that will permanently keep the trust between Mr. Rickey, baseball and the boys who love the game. It is also a book to mark the end of a time.

A strong-willed man, he loved to plan, plot, manipulate, calculate, think, argue and advise. He always had an open mind, he would reason and accept and tolerate and hope for change and advancement. Mrs. Rickey, watching her husband involved on one occasion in an urgent long-distance phone call, fisting that cigar in his mouth, remarked, "He uses that cigar to delay hasty thinking." All his answers were thoughtfully and artfully timed.

He made every day count when we worked together. He loved to laugh and fish and hunt and tell a good story and listen to a good story. He was revered by anyone he ever met, and I believe he never forgot anyone. He was always hopping on a plane and going somewhere to see someone about something. "I've got to talk to him," he would say in his growling whisper and peer out from under one bushy-white eyebrow. His face was pink and his hair was a dark, gun-metal gray and barely white at the sideburns. His strong, freckled, huge hands with their thick, bent catcher's fingers invariably emphasized every point he made in a conversation.

There is no question that Branch Rickey belongs with the sixteen immortals he chose in the pages of his book: Alexander Cartwright, Henry Chadwick, Honus Wagner, Charles Comiskey, George Sisler, Christy Mathewson, Ban Johnson, John McGraw, Ty Cobb, Connie Mack, Judge Kenesaw Mountain Landis, William J. Klem, J. G. Taylor Spink, Edward G. Barrow, Babe Ruth, Jackie Robinson. He is one of them. Mr. Rickey's criteria for selection? . . . *men without whom baseball would not be as it is today.*

There are only a few hundred Americans in all areas of public life who have lived as significantly as he has in influencing the character of other men. Certainly there are only a few who have contributed to our country's professional sports as his family has.

I tried to give a name to Branch Rickey to describe his unique contribution as a man. He has been called innovator, pioneer, preacher, teacher, horse trader, talent scout, statesman, diplomat, historian. But after seeing him in the long private hours of discussion, and meeting his friends and working with him and knowing him, battling him, loving him, respecting him, I call him *citizen*.

After all—that is what he called Jackie Robinson.

Being impatient, I would sometimes smile and he would delight in that, when I anticipated his conversation, his long talks. He would puff his cigar and look out into time, remembering moments, shaping ideas, and during this silence, he would watch me watching him before he spoke. For Branch Rickey, the spoken word was a performance.

"In the spring of 1946 the unwritten rule that Negroes could not play in the major leagues was defied. It had been upheld for over half a century. Jackie Robinson broke the color line in baseball. In 1965 there were approximately a hundred Negro players on the rosters of the two major leagues. Not only has baseball felt the impact of the Negro player, but the national problem of civil rights has been considerably affected by it. I believed that the first Negro in professional baseball should have a strong feeling about civil rights because such a person would have a comprehension of the race problem. He could not be the right person and feel only a personal problem. 'If I am treated right, nothing else matters' could and would be the complete disqualification of the candidate. He would play a game of personal salvation and let it end there.

"It was never in anyone's mind that a competent Negro player could not be found. There were plenty of them. No doubt about that, and very soon Brooklyn, having several Negro players, went out of its way to see to it that Larry Doby, a fine major-leaguer, went to Cleveland. Brooklyn needed a partner to develop the progress of Negro employment.

"The first major problem in breaking the color line was ownership. In St. Louis in 1942 and even later, a Negro was not permitted as a paid spectator to sit in the grandstand.

"The ownership of Brooklyn at the first meeting in New York approved Negro employment. That was a new day for ownership in professional baseball, and George V. McLaughlin, James Mulvey, and Joe Gillideau (the board of directors of the Brooklyn Baseball Club) were heartily in favor.

"There were many other problems. The last one—acceptance by Jackie's colleagues—could not be approached in advance, and the intervening four took two and a half years for final decision.

"Robinson was signed to a Montreal contract, a subsidiary AAA club owned by Brooklyn. After his tremendous year at Montreal, in 1945, it became apparent that Jackie was something more than a possibility for the Brooklyn club. A petition was written and signed by a number of the players requesting his nonemployment. It took considerable effort and time and many personal conferences to remove this group opposition. Several boys wished to be traded to other clubs, and the captain of the team wrote a letter requesting his transfer.

"Then came that memorable game in Brooklyn, when with Robinson at bat the most abusive vilification from the opposition was rampant, and the entire Brooklyn club, led by Dixie Walker, Eddie Stanky and Bobby Bragan—all three Southern boys with so-called Southern beliefs—protested with vigorous voice and challenge. From that moment on, Robinson felt that he had friends all about him. He belonged. That incident built a surprising fight and stick-to-itiveness in team morale that lifted the club from that time into pennant contention. The picture of Pee Wee Reese with his arm around Robinson's shoulders was greatly helpful as it appeared in the newspapers throughout the country.

"One of the most worrying of all problems was finding the man who would be all right off the field. We could know about his playing ability in uniform —but what about out of uniform? Could he take it?

attendances of his own race?

"How could a man of worth and human dignity bend enough? How could a man with a distinctive personality keep it untarnished with constant absorption of attacks calculated to destroy his self-respect? There just are not very many such humans. The trial candidate must never lose his sense of purpose nor lower his sights from the ultimate goal of making good off the field.

"I had employed scouts in Puerto Rico, Cuba and Mexico for over a year, only finally to find out that the best Negro players were in our own United States. One of the names on the list was Jackie Robinson. The scouting of the player was begun by Wendell Smith, a Negro writer for the *Pittsburgh Courier*. Then Widd Mathews followed up on him, followed by George Sisler and finally by Clyde Sukeforth. All these men believed they were scouting for

What about his habits, his associates, his character, his education, his intelligence? Could the man handle his own people? Could he handle himself? What about transportation, hotels? What about the Jim Crow customs? Could he be fully and wisely cooperative in avoiding race adulation—gifts, dinners, awards, etc? How could he oppose mass or group

the Brooklyn Brown Dodgers. Other than the reports of these very able experts, I knew nothing about the Negro player who was recommended. I simply accepted the judgment of my scouts.

"Here was a boy who lacked a few hours' credit for a degree from UCLA. He had been a fine football player and a basketball and track star—less known in baseball than in any other major sport. He enlisted in the U.S. armed services as a private. He came out an officer. If direction determines value, Robinson was on his way.

"Clyde Sukeforth brought Jackie to Brooklyn for an interview. This was the first time I had ever met him. Both Sukeforth and Robinson believed that he was to be offered a contract with the Brooklyn Brown Dodgers, a colored team. It was hard to convince the player that he was facing a job in the major leagues. At the end of a three-hour conference, Robinson showed the necessary intelligence and strength of personality, but he had more and deeper racial resentment than was hoped for or expected. I tested and probed with many questions. If he were subjected to the very lowest depth of scurrility involving him and his own mother—'What would you do?' His answer, 'I'd kill him,' showed the exact strength that was needed. But how could I bandage it and keep it fully alive?

"At this point, we spent several minutes reading a chapter on nonresistance from the book *The Life of Christ* by the great Italian priest Giovanni Papini, published in English about 1920. I just happened to have it handy in the top drawer of my desk. I thought it might become useful in the conference with Jackie.

" ' "Ye have heard that it hath been said, An eye for an eye, and a tooth for a tooth: But I say unto you, That ye resist not evil: But whosoever shall smite thee on the right cheek, turn to him the other also . . ." For an infinite number of believers this principle of not resisting evil has been the unendurable and inacceptable scandal of Christianity. There are three answers which men can make to violence: revenge, flight, turning the other cheek. The first is the barbarous principle of retaliation. . . . Flight is no better than retaliation . . . the man who takes flight invites pursuit. . . . His weakness becomes the accomplice of the ferocity of others. . . . Turning the other cheek means not receiving the second blow. It means cutting the chain of the inevitable wrongs at the first link. Your adversary is ready for anything but this. . . . Every man has an obscure respect for courage in others, especially if it is moral courage, the rarest and most difficult sort of bravery. . . . It makes the very brute understand that this man is more than a man. . . . Man is a fighting animal; but with no resistance offered, the pleasure disappears; there is no zest left. . . . And yet the results of nonresistance, even if they are not always perfect, are certainly superior to those of resistance or flight. . . . To answer blows with blows, evil deeds with evil deeds, is to meet the attacker on his own ground, to proclaim oneself as low as he. . . . Only he who has conquered himself can conquer his enemies.'

"This was, by far, the most important point in the hiring of a Negro by a major-league club. Jackie Robinson is Christian by inheritance and practice. Well before the interview ended, he was fully convinced that the Papini doctrine was necessary and acceptable. He understood that the success of Negro employment in baseball depended very largely on himself.

"This very shocking move required, of course, some Booker T. Washington compromises with surface inequality for the sake of expediency. It would require constant and completely silent reaction to abuse—oral or physical. There could be but one direction of dedication—the doctrine of turning the other cheek. *There* came in the greatness of Jackie Robinson.

" 'Punch for punch' was, by inheritance, by experience, and by desire, Jackie's quick and natural reaction to insult or attack. To self-impose control of every decent reflex was almost too much to ask for from any man, and particularly from Jackie. He was anything (one would think) but ideal for this 'experiment.' It took an intelligent man to understand the challenge—it took a man of great moral courage to accept it. He was both.

"There never has been a man in the game who could put mind and muscle together quicker and with better judgment than Robinson. No one could be heard to find serious fault if Robinson were given the second-base position on the all-time All-American club. He was not as great a right-hand batsman as Rogers Hornsby. No one was—not even Wagner or Jim Delahanty or Lajoie. But he was a skillful batsman with good power. He was a play maker—right or left. He could start and/or finish the double play par excellence. He was a fastidious roamer on fly balls—fair or foul—all over. With a call of two strikes, no man living, then or now, could threaten a pitcher with more imminent disaster. On the base paths he could turn a ball game around. He was a student of pitchers' moves and an instant learner of them—a master of commanding leads and making the daring break.

"Only Ty Cobb and very few others carried the disturbing badge of fear all the time he wore a uniform. There was concealed explosion in the relaxed and indifferent walk as Robinson shuffled along after the play was over. Don't be fooled by it. He was hard to beat. If he had entered the big leagues many years sooner, as he should have, the record books would need alteration in many directions.

"The Baseball Writers of America elected him to the Hall of Fame on merit. It is unfair to them and without due honor to Jackie Robinson to say that the vote was determined by color."

PEGGY FLEMING

"You've got to have it inside you, otherwise nothing works. I wish I was the person I am today—fifteen years ago. I wish I had the same feelings and passion when I was eighteen and competing in the Olympics that I have on the ice today. The interesting thing is I thought I had feelings then and I thought I was expressing them in my moves on the ice—but there was nothing there or so little you never see it if you look at the films or television replays.

"The men's figure skating has really opened the sport up. They have made the breakthrough and extended figure skating from its traditional boundaries to fabulous new horizons. They have been so creative, and I'm surprised that the women have done almost nothing. There have been no John Currys or Tolar Cranstons among the girls.

"The guys have a lot of guts. Tolar Cranston really had to have a lot of courage to believe in the style he was doing. They could have just killed him when he took the chance with crazy music and brought it off. The judges are so traditional that, over the years, no one has taken the risk of upsetting them. It is too dangerous. But when you really *feel* and *believe* you can work wonders.

"The homosexual skater because of his freedom to express himself is exploring new creative dimensions on the ice. It is the only area in sports where the gay person is a champion, and they deserve to be.

"The gay skater is older and liberated from the restrictions of the kind of embarrassment that immaturity brings. It is all a matter of knowing yourself at an early age, and I think the gay person has obviously dealt with that. He's dealt with it and grown from the difficult experiences. I really admire them. There are some I don't like but then I don't like everyone.

"I've worked with a lot of gay guys in their early twenties. I think you change so much between the ages of twenty and twenty-five—where you're just starting to come alive—by the time you're thirty you have it together. When you are young and being trained so severely as a figure skater you don't really understand what's happening. First of all you don't know *yourself* when you're twenty. And you don't know your real friends—who's giving you good advice.

"Why the men figure skaters are doing so well is that the gay person is so open and free to express their feelings. They are not afraid to show what they're feeling inside. The young girls are so restricted having their mothers at their side, knowing so little about life, completely regimentalized—unable to express any real feelings because I believe they have so few to express.

"I see no changes in women's figure skating. I think it will take a long, long time for the girls to come up to what the guys are doing now. It will take ten or twenty years.

"I was guilty of the same lack of feeling when I was competing, so I can't fault the women today. I know at that age I was very young and scared to death. At that age you're embarrassed to express any real feelings in front of your friends and family. When my choreographer worked up my routines in the mid-sixties and asked me to perform very expressive moves I would complain of feeling silly. It is all getting your confidence and getting to know yourself and having some feelings about it which is so difficult at that age.

"Janet Lynn was the last American skater who really expressed any feeling. But Janet was so severely disciplined by her coach that she wasn't allowed to think or do anything else but skate. I don't think she had a normal childhood. She was so geared to skating she became almost a robot. You couldn't really talk to Janet. You couldn't reach her.

"Now, unfortunately she has developed a respiratory infection that affected her breathing so drastically that she no longer can skate at all. It happened when she joined the ice show. She missed so many shows because of the problem it became a liability for the promoters.

"There was one remarkable American skater that few people remember, and that was Laurence Owen, who was killed in the plane crash in Europe with her mother, sister and the entire United States team. I've seen only two films of her skating, but she was great. Laurence really had inner feelings which show when you believe and love what you're doing. I don't think that anybody can be taught to *have* feelings or to *show* feeling. If those deep inner feelings are not there you can't bring them out. It doesn't read.

"Sonja Henie had this spirit and energy for skating, and when you study the old films you see she enjoyed what she was doing. Sonja was the real bubbler—the bubbling personality—and that was her real feeling. It worked for her all over the world, and the audience could read it. And Janet

Lynn had her feelings that worked for her too.

"I think that when Dorothy Hamill was remembered most for her hairdo—when people could not mention her Olympic skating performance without mentioning her hair—this was unfortunate. That's not what figure skating is about. It's about your performance as an athlete, not how cute your hair looks. Dorothy performed well at the Olympics but I can't remember the competition.

"As an amateur skater I was not prepared very well mentally for the transition from amateur to professional athlete. In my amateur days everyone else was thinking for me. Things began to shape in the back of my mind but everything was done for me. When I became a professional I continued this dependency. I trusted everyone. I assumed the producers and directors could do it all because they *knew* what looks best. They did OK, but as I look back now on my early television shows I really should have been more outspoken.

"I would not be doing as well now as a professional performer if I hadn't had that training as an amateur of being overworked. When the pressures increased as a professional skater I knew what it was like, and I knew I could do it. Competition was a good training ground. I worked harder in show business, although when I was in world competition it was a *terror*—but you only had to face that once or twice a year. Professional skating is not as scary as the amateur life but it is more demanding. I don't think I've missed five performances in ten years. Considering illness or muscle pulls or whatever, doing twelve shows a week, ten months a year, that the ice shows demand requires you to be in incredible physical shape for the two or three numbers required each night.

"Success comes quickly as an amateur and your perspective is such that you don't have time to think about it. I have never had any failures in my career (touch wood!). I have a great deal to be thankful for. There is no other comparable sport like figure skating where there is a job waiting for you the next day as a professional. The ice shows are *there* when you win. Sonja Henie started it all.

"I did get a few perfect marks as an amateur but I felt really strange about a perfect mark. I felt embarrassed. We wouldn't be on this earth if we were perfect. How silly to get a 6.0. No one deserves a perfect score. It should be a thrill to get a 5.9!

"Television has had an enormous effect on figure skating, and the worldwide television audience has now influenced the rule changes. In the sixties when I competed, *compulsory figures*, which were never seen on camera, were worth sixty percent of the score and free skating counted forty percent. Very soon now they will pass the final rule changes where they will get rid of the school figures completely. Free skating is just so much more enjoyable to watch, it's prettier, more of the show. School figures and those drawings on the ice are what figure skating is all about—but in competition they will soon be discarded.

"One significant idea for the future is that we will see better free skaters because they will be able to spend the full five or six hours of practice a day on free skating. I spent *four* hours a day all during my amateur years on school figures and an hour a day on my skating routines because the school figures were so important and they were so difficult to do. There are only a certain amount of hours and energy that you can give in one day. In the future the balance will be such that a figure skater can devote two hours a day to ballet and training themselves like a dancer within a certain dance or skating style.

"One of the most rewarding experiences for me was to perform with John Curry in London in his television special. We did *Afternoon of a Faun* by Debussy and it was so inspiring. I still don't really know how to express what I feel on the ice but I came closer in that performance than I ever have. The choreography was set so that every move was in great position for the skater, the line of my body was always working for me. It had nothing to do with super jumps or anything spectacular—just a beautiful chance within that music for *expression.*

"I think I go through phases of really disliking the public for intruding on me. I have to keep myself so well trained and so geared up and your energy must be directed to that. People expect so much out of you every time they see you someplace no matter how private or public the place—they feel you have to be the image that they want you to be. I now feel for a practice session that I've got to fix my hair, wear makeup and put on a nice outfit—when I should be able to look the way I happen to look that day. The children save it. They are very sweet. On their jumps they'll come up and ask me would I watch this or that—and I end up helping them.

"I do have letdowns after everything's over after a grueling tour. But I just come back here, to normal life—to the top of this mountain—and continue as a housewife and mother. I've led a very interesting life in the last ten years, sometimes too interesting.

"My life is very relaxed now. I don't get that upset or uptight anymore. Opening night used to petrify me—I still get a little nervous, I know the reviewers will be there—but it's not life or death. You're not going to die out there. The audience wants you to do well. I feel that if I just go out there —just like practice—I'll do fine. The joy now is to really express my feelings on the ice."

47

BILLY KIDD

"The major part of my career as an athlete was spent as an amateur, and if it were not for television I would not have enjoyed nor would ski racing have received the recognition it did as a world sport. Television has changed skiing in America. The 1970s showed an incredible growth in numbers and interest in skiing and the opportunities are enormous. Toni Sailer was the Austrian ace who may have been the greatest skier of all time but I never saw him win his three gold medals in the 1956 Olympics, when I was growing up in Stowe, Vermont, because the Winter Games were not televised in those days.

"You can never see a ski race very well when you're on the mountain. It took television to cover an entire race. ABC Sports positioned its sixteen cameras in the snow, lowering them by helicopter twelve thousand feet high in the Alps to follow the Alpine ski racers of the world over entire courses in the 1976 Games in Innsbruck, Austria. With this total electronic coverage of a downhill race, ABC was able to capture the emotional impact of Franz Klammer's incredible run for the medal.

"As an alpine skier I competed in all three events, the downhill, the giant slalom and the special slalom. World competition has become so specialized that very few skiers compete in all three events today. Jean Claude Killy was a competitor with me in the late sixties and with Karl Schranz, the last of the alpine skiers. I was fortunate to complete my eight years as a member of the U.S. Ski Team by winning the world championship at Val Gardena, Italy, in 1970.

"In the 1964 Olympics, when I won the silver medal in the special slalom, I was fourteen hundredths of a second behind gold medalist Pepi Stiegler. That's less time than it takes to blink your eye.

"There are two runs in the giant slalom and special slalom, each on different courses. I was eighth after the first run, one point nine seconds out. I had skied way too cautiously in the first run and I can remember standing in the starting gate, ready to begin the second run. It was snowing lightly, my folks were there and I was nervous. I realized this was my last event.

"Make no mistake; when a racer gets to the Olympic Games, everyone will be racing as fast as he can. Everyone will be going all out. You have to ski to the limit, right on the edge of control. No matter what the weather or the competition or who falls down or what number you start, you must go all out in both

runs in the giant and the special slaloms. In the sequence of four pictures (opposite) you can see clearly how I maintain contact with the snow with my ski tips and unweighting the tails, swing them over the snow to take the tightest and fastest line through a gate as I make my final run at Innsbruck. See how I take the high line, initiating my turns early, long before I come to a gate; see how I try to finish a turn right on the flag and slip downhill instantly with time to line up the next gate. The racer's upper body should be very quiet, the knees doing almost all the work. In slalom the racer's pole plant is made at the gate to get the shoulders lined up over flat skis. With skis apart, there will be better balance, better for speed and better for a recovery in trouble. Most of all, the skis must carve to hold the high line. On television you can see this, especially in the slo-mo replays, when the skis bend and the snow flies off the tips.

"Yellow goggles are worn in flat light, which is very likely in Innsbruck. When there is a cloud cover, the light is diffused and bounces off the snow and the clouds fill in all the shadows. Everything looks flat. You can't see the ruts or bumps. A racer had been killed on the course in practice and I was stiff and tight.

"The pressure in the Olympics is very different from any other ski-race pressure. You are aware of the difference when you walk through the town of Innsbruck. The welcome signs in many languages, the flags of all nations, the great numbers of foreign press all vividly convey the international feeling. You've got U.S.A. written all over you. The Olympic village is isolated. All courses are restricted. Even the racers need badges. The pressures are heightened by the fact that the Olympic competition occurs only once every four years.

"I think ski racing is one of the truest tests of the physical and mental qualities of an athlete in all of sports. It tests your balance, coordination and stamina. It tests you mentally for concentration, determination, courage and reaction under pressure.

"The three Alpine tests are all different. The equipment for each is different. The downhill event is the most dangerous. You start at the top of the mountain and you run the two miles or more as fast as you can. There are directional gates, but the racer has a wide latitude on his line. The skis are wider, heavier, than slalom skis. The racer wears a crash helmet and a skin-tight jump suit. The average downhill speed is about sixty-five miles per hour, with top speeds up to seventy-five or eighty. The course is marked by double-pole red gates.

"The giant-slalom course is about a mile and a half long and consists of a series of high-speed turns with the racer holding an average speed of about forty-five miles per hour. The racer is almost always turning. It is a very technically demanding event, and one mistake can be costly. It was my most difficult discipline.

"In the special slalom, the racer skis a series of about seventy gates over a half-mile course—a gate every second—with very quick, tight turns with a precise line where you must be within inches of the gate. The gate itself is an imaginary line on the snow connecting two matching-color flags in a blue, red or yellow series. The poles are set eight feet apart and you must pass between the poles, although you can enter from either side. An open gate stands across the racer's course, while a closed gate is one that is in line with his course, forcing him to execute sharp turns. The course is 'set' in demanding combinations of open and closed gates over a particular terrain. If you go down the course banging poles out of the way, there is enough friction on your arm from brushing against the gate markers to slow you down a few thousandths of a second—enough to lose the race. Instead of trying to bang them out of the way, you try to sneak by them, brush them up against your arms or your thighs. I knew when I had taken a slalom course well by the paint marks on the outside of my thighs where I had rubbed it off the seventy or eighty gates. The fastest time is a line closest to the inside gate.

"In both slaloms, the racer is not permitted to ski the course beforehand, but he must memorize it as he surveys it from the bottom to the top. The terrain varies, but the average speed is about twenty-five miles and the courses are icy and a demanding test on the steep sections.

"In 1964, we used wooden skis and they would splinter when you crashed. They were much heavier, they would not turn as quickly as the fiberglass skis worn today. The boots were leather then—the beginning of the buckle boot and the safety binding, but only the toe of the boot released. I used a five-foot-long leather thong to strap my boot heel to the ski.

"The combination of today's fiberglass skis and high-back plastic boots has made it possible to turn much more quickly than in the past. The boots are very rigid and cut much higher to give you more control, as is vividly shown (opposite) as Ingemar Stenmark quickly turns through a gate.

"If you stand the skis on their edges, they will bend in a slight arc because they are narrow in the middle, widest at the tip and flaring out again at the tail. What the racers do—and the reason they can turn so quickly—is press their knees forward. This pressure goes through those stiff plastic boots right on the widest part of the ski—also the most flexible part, and so the skis start to bend. Turning through a gate, a racer will keep his skis on edge without sideslipping and get a carving action in the snow. There is a bend along the arc of the turn and it's got energy in it so that when a racer goes from one turn to the next, it is not necessary to jump up and twist around—the skis propel him from one turn to the next. It is very much like a bow shooting an arrow. A racer takes advantage of this energy by simply rolling his knees over into the next turn. The skis flatten out, and since the tail of the ski was designed to shoot the skis out ahead of you, you get the impression that the skier is sitting back. But if you watch a racer right at the gate and in the most critical part of his turn, you will see he is bent forward, pressed against the front of the skis to make them come around that turn.

"A racer times his line so that he finishes the turn right at the gate, having started it ten to twelve feet before the flag. As soon as he goes past it, he plants his ski pole, rolls his knees into the next turn and lets those skis shoot. Many times you will see the skis come off the snow so it looks as if he's going to fall over backward, but he's in control, for he knows he can catch up to his skis halfway through the next turn.

"What does it feel like in the starting gate? You feel the pressure. You have so many things going through your mind. You've climbed up the course and tried to memorize the different combinations of seventy gates, how steep the hill is, where it is likely to be very icy, where the ruts are liable to form. You've got certain decisions you must make, whether to take a certain gate from the left or from the right.

"In the starting gate, you've got a countdown, you must leave on go. You've got your coach telling you last-minute instructions and advice. He's on a headset. You've gone through a last-minute checklist. Are your goggles on, are your pockets zipped. Are your boots buckled? You buckle your boots at the last minute. You want them to be very tight for maximum control, and if you have them buckled for too long, you may hamper circulation.

"You have to handle your nervousness in the starting gate. You've got an adrenaline rush. Your heart beats faster, you have more blood in your muscles. Your breathing gets very shallow and you have to remember to breathe.

"Out of the starting gate, once the clock starts, it seems as if everything moves in slow motion. It seems to take so long to get to the first gate. You

try to find your rhythm through the first few gates, which is difficult because you've never run the course before. With your adrenaline flow, your muscles overreact and the first five gates are the most difficult. The snow conditions at the Olympics will be very icy, very fast. The officials want the course fair for everyone; they pack it very hard so it won't rut up. It also makes it a better test of technical ability.

"On the way down, as you gather momentum and hit your rhythm, you must be prepared—even if you're off balance—to turn. You must start your next turn even if you're not ready for it; somehow, you must begin that next turn in time.

"You have certain trouble spots where your timing and lineup must be exactly right. I used to have trigger gates memorized to alert me to a demanding section ahead. I would divide a course into three sections. I would pick a trigger spot three gates before a difficult passage in the first section, the middle flat and the final steep. I would always be ready for these three or four demanding gates on the way down. You must not lose time in these trouble spots. There are other places where you know, with your own ability, that you can take chances and save time.

"There were close to fifty thousand spectators on the hill in Innsbruck, and it is odd but when I raced, all seemed silent. I had managed with concentration to shut out all crowd sounds and cheers. I would listen in the silence for the sound of my skis. Because I had grown up in Stowe and skied on rugged, icy terrain as a kid, I learned that you could tell a great deal from listening to the carving sound your skis made in the snow. I could tell whether I was on my edges too long and if I was making good turns.

"The finish is critical. At the end of an Olympic slalom course, you usually have four or five gates that are wide open on terrain that is fairly flat and it is here you will see the racer make his or her skating steps into the finish. A racer can make very good turns all the way down the course, but if he hasn't learned to make good skating steps, he can lose the race right there. Timing here is most important. Your rhythm must match your speed. If you make your skating steps too aggressively or too casually, you can break your rhythm and upset your speed under the finish line. That gold medal is there!"

51

VINCE LOMBARDI

"Over the nine years of our success at Green Bay, there are many games that stand out as great victories. The 1960 win over the Forty-Niners in Kezar Stadium; the big victory over the Browns in Cleveland in 1961 was a truly great triumph; and the famous 9-7 win over Detroit on our home field in 1962 was one of the classics. The tough losses were to the Eagles in the 1960 title game, and to Detroit on Thanksgiving in 1962 after having won eleven straight, and to the Bears in 1963. The two victories over the New York Giants were very rewarding. I think all championship games are. They're something special. But of all victories, it seems that beating the Baltimore Colts was the most rewarding. Anytime you beat John Unitas, that's a fine achievement—he's been such a tremendous performer in all the years, except when he was injured during the 1966 season. Those victories over the Colts were the victories I prize most.

"I found you can take nothing for granted in this league. We won all our games in 1963 except two—both losses came against the Bears—the only team to beat us twice in a season other than the Colts in 1959, and it cost us the title, but they deserved to win. I think that 1963 team may have been our best.

"I've never felt that any loss of a Packer team came because of a letdown. I don't feel we lose a game because we play badly. I always feel we lose a game because the other team plays very well that particular day.

"Of the coaches, I must say George Halas has my greatest respect. He has meant a great deal to the NFL and to me personally, and to this game of football.

"I respect all the coaches in the NFL. Any coach could beat the Packers. I would say, in all due humility, that our team has a little more difficult situation week after week because we have won and won a lot, and every team we play is up for us, and always ready to play us.

"During the years of our success I've never had any misgivings about players that I did not have. I never wished we had a player on another team. I will say honestly I know there are better football players in certain positions than the ones I have. It would be Utopia to have the best man at each position—but if I had him I still don't know whether I could win with him. I think it takes much more than ability to win. I don't know if the *best* player would fit in our system, into what we demand.

"Over the years, we have waived players or traded players or have not kept players, not because of a lack of ability but because of the lack of something else we would like to see in them. This lack is not courage or intelligence. I don't place much emphasis on intelligence; I don't think many of the coaches do. I don't think you have to. Of course some positions need intelligence.

"I think winning is the result of mental toughness. I think mental toughness is many things, and it is very difficult to explain what it is. First, I think mental toughness is humility; I think that it takes humility to realize what greatness is—really simplicity. Mental toughness is made up too of the spartan qualities of sacrifice and self-denial. Mental toughness is loyalty. You cannot win consistently without it, and as you win each man grows because of it. Losing streaks can destroy it.

"In the eight years of our success in Green Bay, there have been no broad offensive or defensive revolutions in pro football. None! I've always said, football is not formations but simply blocking, tackling and execution, *period*. That's always going to be the basis of successful football regardless of temporary fancies.

"The important thought is that the Packers thrive on tough competition, we welcome it, the team has always welcomed it; the adrenaline flows a little quicker when you are playing the tougher team that's up there with you.

"Winning is what I try to do. The years of work at Green Bay have been rewarding and I have grown with the Packers. With success a man will increase overall. Winning bears rich fruit.

"Winning isn't everything, *but wanting to win is!* That is what I'm interested in. Soon as I lose, I will probably be the first one they ride out of town. Those Green Bay fans are really something. Can you imagine? . . . They were up in arms in the showdown game one Thanksgiving against the Lions because I 'gave in' and permitted the Packers to wear white jerseys in Detroit, granting Detroit the honor of wearing home-team blue. Can you imagine anything as foolish as that, to think that shirt color has anything to do with winning or losing? It is a good thing we won, otherwise they would have blamed it on the shirts.

"Even though I played with a great line in college, it was not until I began to coach that I realized the line is everything. I was actually convinced of this

principle when I was coaching at West Point. To me, football is running. It's the contact, it's the blocking. The passing game is a very vital part—without it we can't operate. We have to have the pass. But frankly, I get a greater thrill out of seeing a well-designed running play succeed than I do with the pass.

"Now, I think everyone can be taught to block. The question is whether they *will block* or *want* to block. This is the crux of it to me, you see. Anyone can be taught, but if he doesn't have the desire to block, doesn't like to block and will not block, then he has no place on my team, regardless of who he may be. That doesn't mean to say now if I had a boy of great ability who is not physically able to block— if he doesn't have the physical ability to handle it— well, this is something else again. I would use him either as a spot player, as a specialist, or send him out as a flanker. But overall, everyone can be taught. It has worked that way in all the years I've been coaching. It is a matter of pride. A man has to feel he is making the play go with his block.

"Our blocking success on the Packers is due to endless repetition and practice with our line. We coach them so that their blocking depends on who the personnel is, who the defensive tackles are. We will handle one defensive tackle entirely differently than we handle another because of his size and his quickness. On each· play we know that our center Jim Ringo can handle certain people and can't handle others because of the opponent and the way he lines up. We know from the films what Kramer and Thurston can do, what Masters and Gregg can do. We alert them as to blocking. 'On this particular play, Ringo, this is the call. *Do not call* this type of blocking.' To me the big thing in being a successful team is repetition of what you're doing, either by word of mouth, by blackboard or specifically by work on the field. You repeat, repeat, repeat as a unit. So when Ringo comes out of the huddle he calls the line blocking assignments and he knows when he gets over the ball that against this defense, 'I'm going to make this call.' 'If it is to the left against a Stautner I can't possibly make this block—I'll have to call another. If it is to the right against a Joyce, I can make this block work.' That is why you will see him block differently going right than left against the same defense. Or differently on the same play against different opponents. Of course many of our calls are dummy calls and they don't mean anything, except to confuse the defense.

"Now if the defense shows itself the same each time we will have one type of blocking pattern and if they stunt—that is, jump around with the line-backers darting in and out—we will employ a *ding dong* blocking pattern. This is area blocking where the linemen take those who enter their area. I think

55

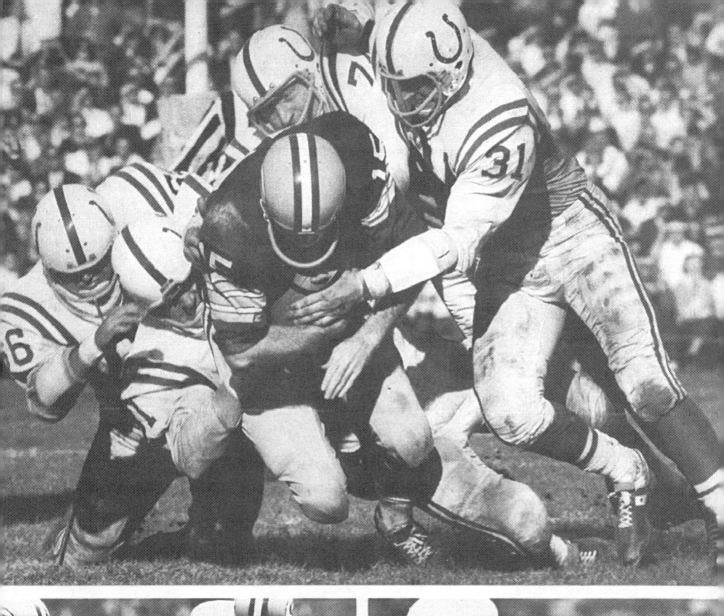

we excel at area blocking because we have a mentally quick line. This goes beyond memory of plays—memory is a simple thing. By quick I mean the lineman's ability to improvise and adjust instantaneously. This is the prerequisite for offensive play. It is more vital on offense than defense because defensive line play is more patterned. When a defensive man makes a move one way he is generally covered the other way. But he'll make the move regardless. He will play pressure. He will react to certain things depending on who is teaching him but he is patterned much more than an offensive player is.

"This is one of the real keys to offensive line play. *You know that the defensive player is patterned.*

"All of our offensive thinking is developed to capitalize on their frequencies. We tabulate and chart their offensive habits and their defensive tendencies. The patterns of their game. We take two or three games and compose a master breakdown. First of all in the games covered we find they used *four* defenses, two of which were major defenses. In the total of a hundred and ninety plays this major defense was used ninety-five times. A fifty-percent defense. Say, of the ninety-five times it was used: first and ten, thirty-two times; second and long, eighteen times; second and short, fourteen times; third and long, thirty times. Then you add their red-dog (blitz) frequencies. On· first and ten, they had three red dogs; second and short . . . and so forth. Now all of this shows whether it's a big first-and-ten defense, second and long defense, second and short, or third and long. It shows perhaps that first down becomes a predominant dog down for this ball club or that they red-dog most on third down when long yardage is needed. Which men do they dog with? All three linebackers, corner and middle, strong side corner and middle? We know and the quarterbacks know these results as well as the minor defenses used by the opponent. You build your defense to their major defense. Then you see what plays will go against their minor defense—whether the minor defense requires automatics.

"And then there are the refinements. How can you read their red dog? Do you pick it off the film, has your scout picked anything up during their last ball game or must you go strictly by the percentages— the statistical approach? When I became head coach I found there was so much dedication needed by the offensive team to our opponent's defense and by our defensive team to our opponent's offense that I had the film spliced with all the defensive plays end to end and our offense sees only this. They don't have to sit through film sessions where there are lags while the sequence of plays up on the screen refers only to the defensive men. This makes for more thorough departmental film sessions. From the

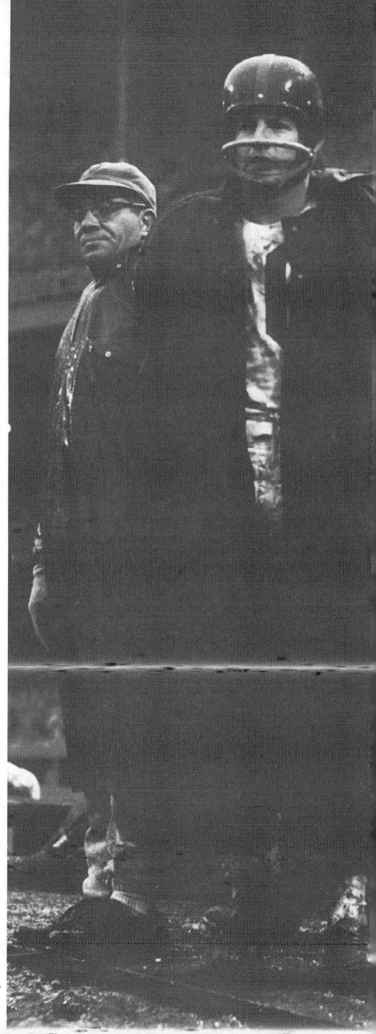

master breakdown you make a master projection first. These are the calls you will find effective against their defenses. One of the coaches will say, 'That first down looks like a good down to use the screen pass'—we have other thoughts—we agree. We put it in. We have to allow more time in practice for it. The screen requires more work than running a dive or an end run. If we figure we can sweep the ends against this club I will ask my line coach to work out a little different pattern of blocking for a sweep and we will look at what he comes up with. And we will put that play in our game plan. And so it goes.

"Offensively you do what you do best and you do it again and again. Defensively you attack your opponent's *strength*. You attack his strength because if you weaken or break down his strength everything else will break down and he will break down mentally and you will beat him.

"I think one of the tributes to Bart Starr as a quarterback, especially in the 1965 and 1966 seasons, was his ability to consistently make the third down and long yardage play—third and seven, third and nine. This success has to be achieved by a quarterback in order to win. Schooling does this. You have to know the defense your opponent may be using in a particular situation. Everybody has their own particular scheme on third and long yardage, but the pattern of success is based on a quick quarterback who can go to a secondary receiver if the particular defense you expected does not materialize. You base your assumption on past performance, but you really need a play where an optional receiver can make the needed long yardage and a passer like Bart who is clever, quick, and accurate enough to beat the coverage, by throwing to this man.

"I can remember back to the days in 1960, when I would watch from the sidelines and see Bart Starr run off a play and succeed and I would react with enthusiasm and say, 'What a beautiful call.' There's great delight in that for a coach, and I'm sorry to say that spontaneous reaction doesn't come anymore, because now we are simpatico—and I more or less expect what he calls every time.

"I feel as a coach that despite the scouting and extensive planning and preparation for an opponent, the game plan which I prepared with my staff is *not* absolute. Bart Starr has the right to leave the game plan whenever he wants. He has the right everytime, and Starr will do it. In fact, I certainly don't want anybody out on the field who says, 'Come hell or high water I'll stick to the game plan,' because if that happens we're going to get beat. If the defense takes away everything that we thought they would give us, and Bart knows another play in our system will work, then he will call it."

Over the years the Green Bay game plans have worked. Bart Starr is totally dedicated to executing the game plan when he goes out on that field each Sunday after all the work and confidence all the coaches have put into it. He has it down so well in his mind and the *reasoning* behind each play that he feels he is Coach Lombardi out on the field doing exactly what *he* would do in a given situation. "I am so devoted to this man and the way he thinks," Starr said, "that I feel if I do it exactly his way we will win." He describes this feeling with a marvelous ring in his voice. "I dearly love to go out on a field and pick a team to pieces. Actually pick 'em apart. I'm sure all quarterbacks do. Football is the greatest cat-and-mouse game in the world.

"We look conservative in our running because our basic plays are simple, but in series," Starr explained. "Our slant to Taylor starts off the same, but I can make it come out *five different ways* even though all five begin in identical fashion. Coach Lombardi likes to set up plays and then do takeoffs of what looks like the same play. These series give us so much variety that we don't need to go to extremes.

"People think when you run up a big score you get wild—why? We don't ever reach in a grab bag. We want possession. *Ideally* we just love to get that defense in second-and-three situations. We don't want second and eight. We want the pressure on them. This is what we strive to do on every down every time we have the ball. This is our offensive philosophy. What can their defense look for when we're second and three—*everything!* We can really make them sweat. We can run the gamut.

"We try to make them defense both phases of the game—run or pass—*at one time*, not play it strong for one or the other. If we put this kind of pressure on them they must divide their coverage, and this gives the Packers a decided advantage. It is like the option pass or run that Coach Lombardi thinks is the greatest play in football—you cannot adequately defense run and pass at the same time, one has to be open."

With firm conviction Starr concluded, *"We must feel to a man when we are inside the ten we are going to come away with seven points.* We have no other thought in our minds. We are dedicated to the idea that when we have the ball we have the advantage anywhere on the field. This may not be true, but I feel this way and I convey this in the huddle by looking each of the ten men in the eye on every play. We believe this because we feel we are just mentally tougher than they are—and this is where you win ball games, not physically. This is what Vince Lombardi has embedded in us. With this mental toughness we can lick any defense."

Vince Lombardi was not a complicated man; he was a gifted teacher. This is why he was a great coach. Coaching is teaching, he believed, and Vince was blessed with that rare quality of inspiring sacrifice and steadfast loyalty to the ideals, the sound ideas. "Lombardi makes you a believer," his men agreed. To everyone Lombardi's Green Bay Packers were pro football, in the great decade of the sixties. He coached one of the most amazing football teams of all time to defeat the New York Giants in the championship game in December 1961 by the incredible score of 37–0, went on to six more division championships, and three Super Bowl victories. He was rough but dignified, thoughtful and loyal and considerate, but demanding of his players, ostensibly volatile and grim-faced, but really a lovable paisano with a wonderful rasping laugh.

"I think that the balance in the league or the balance in the teams in the National Football League is coming about because they are all getting away from superstars. If you want to pick one quality of our Green Bay teams," the coach continued, "despite the great publicity that Paul Hornung and Jim Taylor received, it is that we have not had any superstars. Bart Starr was passed over for so many years. But without Starr we don't operate and everybody is

finally beginning to realize that. This has been one of the Packers true advantages—we've always been a *team*—we've always lacked superstars. I think that only the poorer teams have superstars—because of their weaknesses they must rely on singular strengths, and this constant attention to one player builds him up many times to more than he is. Of course, when the superstar has had a bad day the team weaknesses are exposed. We tried on the Packers never to let this happen.

"I'm very much concerned with the personal integrity of my players. A boy's makeup has to be considered. This doesn't mean to say that a boy who has a great ability on the football field and who is not morally sound off the field is not going to be a good football player. I would say that a boy of good moral integrity and only fair ability has a greater chance of being successful on the football field. It is easier to discipline if you inculcate moral standards into the players than if you just apply rules.

"I don't think my personal devotion to God is anything unusual. It has been a great part of my life. It has sustained me from those early days when I was an altar boy, but to me it is a part of my life just as much as eating is. I don't know if my personal habits reflect on my players. I would like to think so,

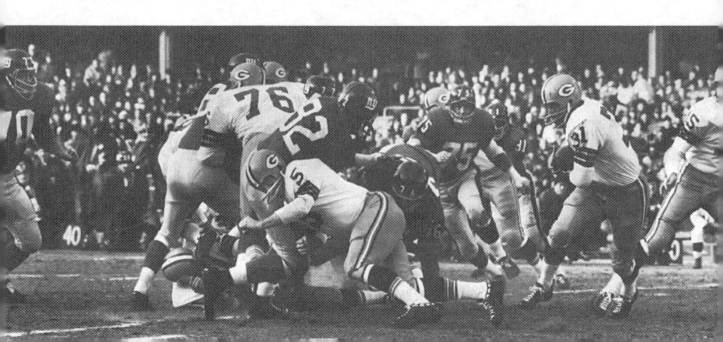

but whether it does or not, I haven't the slightest idea. That's certainly not the reason for it. I'm not trying to impress anybody. I try to live my life just the way I've been taught and I do.

"The players today are better disciplined than they were. I think they realize that professional football today is big business and they dress and act like businessmen. But discipline is specifically related to morale, and morale specifically related to play. I think the finer the morale, the finer the football team. A good player who breaks all the rules off the field is the exception. I've never had a player like that. What I would do if I had one I haven't the slightest idea.

"Of course, this·idea of discipline goes beyond the head coach. The head coach is only as good as his staff. They must carry out his ideas, but each must contribute something. It may be intelligence, planning, fire or aggressiveness, but each assistant coach *must* add. If there is a weak link in your staff, the players will realize this and will not respect that man, and if this happens, they won't practice for him or play for him.

"Then, of course, there is the consummate confidence that comes from planning and practicing well. You get ready during the week and the confidence is there on Sunday. This confidence is a difficult thing to explain, just how you get that feeling. But you do get it and the team gets it. When I'm scared, the team is scared, and I'm very conscious of this. Emotion is contagious. That is something I have to fight all the time. I am emotional by nature, and many times I try to get a quiet attitude so the team will quiet down. A nervous mother begets nervous children, you see what I mean."

The barrel-chested paisano gave it the full laugh.

There were many memorable moments in the years I covered the Packers. The 1961 NFL championship game (above, left) saw Green Bay's versatile halfback Paul Hornung (5) playing on an Army pass, score a record 19 points in the Packer 37-0 victory over the New York Giants. The following year both teams met again for the championship in Yankee Stadium and Green Bay won again, 16-7 in a brutal game. The first play from scrimmage (below, left) has Jim Taylor (31) running for daylight behind a solid block from Hornung (5) he almost scores. The wind in this game (above, right) was so vicious it killed the Giants air strength. The battles between John Unitas (19) and Bart Starr (15) were the best. The two shake hands (below, right) after a Colt victory in Baltimore.

MUHAMMAD ALI

"All people have names that fit their nation, their nationality. 'Here comes Mr. Chin or Mr. Yang, Mr. Wong or Mr. Chu.' You know he's a Chinaman. 'Here comes Mr. Rodriguez, Hernandez or Gomez.' He's Spanish. 'Here comes Maboto, Mubanda, Mr. Ghujama, Naboto.' He's African. 'Here comes O'Grady, O'Reilly, O'Neil.' He's Irish. 'Mr. Matsumoto, Noguchi'—Japanese. 'Here comes Rolling Thunder, White Cloud, Morning Star.' Indian! 'Here comes George Smith or Mr. Hawkins, Mr. Clay, Mr. Brown or Mr. Washington'—now you don't know if *that* man is black or white or American—till you see him.

"We were named after our masters. They called me Cassius Clay. That wasn't my name—*Cassius Clay!*

"How can a Chinese man with a long braid, slanted eyes, yellow skin and a little silk robe be called George Washington? Doesn't make sense. He's closer to white than me. How the hell do my black ancestors have a name George Washington? Cassius Clay same damn thing. I ain't no Cassius Clay. He' a white abolitionist.

"One day I woke up to my history, my Islamic culture. You saw *Roots*. Kunta Kinte was whopped until he said, 'My name is Toby.' They made him take that name. He would not eat pork and they made him eat it. The early slaves prayed to Allah. They were Muslims. The black man was Islamic when he first got here four hundred years ago. They were not Christians—they were *Muslims*.

"Now that I got my history, found out who I am, know my roots—don't call me Cassius Clay. My name is Muhammad Ali. Why am I such a world man? *It's the name!* Muhammad is the most common name on earth. The most popular man with the most influence on world groups was Muhammad of Arabia. He's number one. Isaac Newton number two —Jesus Christ number three. Moses number four. But the most influential man in the history of the world was Muhammad of Arabia. There's one billion Muslims on earth. *One billion.* I can take you out to the Pakistanian people, the Algerians. I'll take you to Indonesia, Syria, Lebanon, Turkey, Afghanistan, Islamabad, Bangladesh. Millions in Mecca—brothers —all colors.

"When I took the most common name on earth, *Muhammad Ali*, all those people started watching boxing. Who's the biggest black in the history of the world? Muhammad Ali. *My face!* What made me

that recognized? I declared myself a Muslim. They know me in Saudi Arabia, Morocco, Egypt, *the world!*

"Why am I fighting in Zaire? Muslim people love me. Why am I fighting in Kuala Lumpur, Malaysia? Muslims. Why am I fighting in Manila? Muslims. Why can I go to Russia? Because you have forty million Muslims in Russia! In Samarkand, the ancient city of Tamerlane, in Tashkent and in Moscow. All over Russia there are Muslims. There are over three hundred Muslim mosques in Great Britain. *Islam!*

"The biggest thing I could have ever done was accept the name Muhammad Ali. The two biggest names in the Arab world. Ali means, *the most high.* Muhammad means, *worthy of praise or praiseworthy.* Isn't that beautiful? *Clay* means dirt with no ingredient. Clay means something to white people, to the English, but Clay ain't nothin' in Africa, Egypt, Morocco, Algeria or Malaysia, but Muhammad Ali is a common name, a bond with the darker people of the world.

"Muhammad Ali. *The name!* Oh, my, that's powerful.

"Now I am beginning the plans for The World Organization. My dream, *The World Organization.* I've found out what my mission in life is. Boxing was only to introduce me to the world. Now it's time for me to go to work. Now my work starts. All of my knockouts, all that *'I'm the greatest,'* was just to get me started. Now you're going to see some real maneuvering.

"I know the people in the world believe in me. They have seen my heart. It is not the action that makes a thing right or wrong, but the purpose behind the action. What was my purpose in boxing— to hurt people? To be brutal? I'm a black man from Louisville, Kentucky. How can I be world-known if I wasn't boxing? How can I set up a world organization and go meet Brezhnev? Negro from Louisville, Kentucky, flying over to meet the leader of Russia, the biggest communist leader in the world, and him puttin' the press out, then having private meetings with me and showing me a place for my office in the Kremlin. *That's powerful!* Louisville boy! . . . Meets the President and mayor one day, then he flies to Russia with no government behind him, no State Department, and works on his own. *That's powerful!* Who can do that? What other American can get on a plane and go to Russia and set meetings with Leonid

Brezhnev? Black or white. *That* was my purpose in beating people up.

"You saw indications of how I *felt* when I was fighting Jerry Quarry. I stopped the fight. I signaled the referee and pulled him off. When I fought James Ellis, I lightened up and told the referee, 'He's ready to fall.' When I fought Bobby Fawcett—I backed off. When I fought George Foreman, he was falling and I could have hit him but I didn't. My purpose is not to kill or hurt—it's to win. God—*Allah*—knows the heart. He knows my purpose. Man judges man's actions, but God judges man's heart. Isn't that beautiful. Man judges man's actions, but God judges man's heart. God knows.

"I don't care what the press says. I don't care what anyone says. Allah, the supreme being in the Muslim world, knows that I don't want to hurt anybody. Allah knows that I don't want to give nobody a hemorrhage or a brain concussion. Allah knows the man I'm fighting has got a family—why bring misery to his wife and children just to please a damn crowd for ten minutes? No. That ain't my purpose. That's why God gives me victory.

"Do you know I'm the first black man that got out clean? Do you know that every black champion from welterweight to middleweight to heavyweight have never been able to get out clean?' *With the championship!* Do you know what I've done? Only two got out: Gene Tunney and Rocky Marciano. I've excelled them. I'm the only human to have the title *three times*. The most popular. A man who can go and talk to kings of countries. There's so many things I've been first in.

"Right now I've defeated all the critics, all the press, all those who talk bad about me. I've done whopped them all. They can't talk bad about me anymore. How many athletes can stop the press? When I lost the first time they said, 'The Greatest Is Gone.' Usually when the press says you've gone, their predictions are right. I've defeated all the Howard Cosells, the Dick Youngs, the Doc Youngs. All of them. Many times they used the sport to really get on me, to really hurt me. They are really my enemies. When I fight I think about whippin' them too. *He* can't write that junk tomorrow, *pow!* I'll whip his ass, *pow!* I'm one nigger that got out clean, *pow!* Their articles are one thing that motivated me to fight so hard, to be extra strong and to keep coming back.

"They named the main street after me in Louisville, Kentucky. They named a boulevard after me in Newark, New Jersey. They're serious even in white America. They named a sports center in Texas after me, a building in Durham, a forty-million-dollar mall in Manila with two theaters, Ali I and Ali II. In Egypt, the avenue in front of the airport is named Ali Boulevard.

"I talked with President Carter. I walked through the streets in Washington, D.C., yesterday and the traffic stopped. In the big office buildings the windows opened and all the people started looking out. What did I do? Heavyweight champion? I'm not just a boxer.

"I could run for office and be a serious candidate. If I were politically minded I would run for the President of the United States and tell all the people the truth. 'Justice will be brought to you all. Just give me a chance to show you.' I've got the belief in the people . . . I wouldn't do it, though.

"I just came back from Australia. I met with all the aborigine leaders—shook up all Australia by having them all up to my hotel room. They are not allowed in hotels. They said, 'Muhammad Ali, you are our leader. You are the black man that makes us feel so proud. You are the black man that has said, "I'm the greatest!"—and proven what you can do.' I met with the Maori people—their leaders in New Zealand all met with me. The people of South Africa said, 'Muhammad Ali, you are our leader. *The masses.*' The black people of London and Liverpool . . . everywhere.

"I'm an independent. Brezhnev said I was the best ambassador America ever had. He said no one said anything good about his country. I spoke about the good I saw on my visit. I don't agree on Russian policy. I believe in God. I ain't no communist. I just spoke of the good things I had experienced.

"Can you picture me going to Russia a couple of times a year? Get in a cab, go to the Kremlin to my office to check on The World Organization business. Russians are biggest threat America's got. The best thing is to get close to them. To know them.

"Am I thinking too big? Am I making a move I shouldn't be making by starting The World Organization? Can you imagine ten dollars from ten million people? One hundred million dollars. Whatever money we raise in a city goes to that city. I'm finding governments can't help everybody. There are people walking the streets that can't eat.

"I am heading this organization. The people know I won't lie to them. There won't be a dollar spent in this organization without me knowing about it. I'm going to be the boss. No government agency. No Muslim organization. No Catholic or Jewish organization, no Baptist. The World Organization is non-profit. The wealthy athlete has got to do something to set a good example for those who come behind him. Then it will snowball.

"I'm setting up The World Organization in sixty countries. The sole purpose is to better relationships between people on a civilian level. Our headquarters will probably be in Washington, D.C., with all the flags from every country outside my office with a

welded, winterized, eight-by-ten picture attached to each pole of the president of that country handing me the flag. We must help all the people who are hungry, flood victims, drought victims, all those who need help."

Ali talked with me in an elegant suite in the Plaza Hotel in New York, and the morning sunlight gave the room the royal mood of all the grand hotels in Europe. He wore a dark-blue suit, white shirt and distinctive tie, dressed for a morning meeting at the United Nations. His body filled the chair and he made very few moves during the hour we were alone together. We looked each other in the eye during all of our conversation. He spoke in a growling whisper. It was early and he kept clearing his rasping throat, coughing off the mucus of the night's sleep. Once he suddenly sneezed a few times and turned up the lapel of his suit jacket to cover his face. For the first half of the meeting, he kept running an afro comb through his hair. It seemed to itch, he did it so continuously. When he described the way his world organization would feed the poor by preparing great quantities of beans, he pretended to stir a huge pot with an imaginary ladle. A small dark scar on his right hand was his only mark, although the tissue at the outside corner of his right eye was lightly pulled. His face was big and round and very simple—a muted gold color. His presence was gentle with a hidden tiredness. I remembered the old heavyweights in Maine watching Sonny Liston work. I felt some strange foreboding that harm would come to him.

He seemed in between two stars on some strange odyssey, an acclaimed Odysseus searching for some new beginning. A new passage. He recited a fifteen-minute speech from memory on the heart. He said it was one of *forty-five* talks that he has memorized on the meaning of life that he delivers to young people from ghettos to colleges. He hesitated only once. He changed his voice octave entirely for the recitation, delivered with a ministerial tone. All the implications were staggering. Elemental.

"It's all in the heart. My whole motivation, my whole idea of life, all comes from the heart. Boxing people don't know me. My aim with my World Organization is to help people cultivate the loving heart quality. There's only one way to cultivate the heart quality and that is to become more and more selfless. Not selfish—but *selfless*. What prevents man from having a loving manner is the thought of one's self, and the more man thinks of himself, the less he thinks of the people that need help. In the journey of life, self will always meet you as a giant and the giant will always be stronger than you. You can't teach love, it must spring from the depths of the heart of man.

"Boxing people don't know me. I used boxing as a springboard. The real Muhammad Ali is spiritual, boxing is physical. It is money, possessions. Boxing is the bait covering the hook. People see the fighter first, but underneath there is more. The worm is the talk and the movies and the press, but the hook is the real purpose of life. *The heart.*"

PELÉ

"Soccer to me has great significance. It has been my whole life. I get everything through soccer. I make friends, I travel around the world with my Santos team in Brazil and the Cosmos team in America. I have had the opportunity to see different ways people live as I played in Europe, Russia, Korea, Shanghai, India, and in each country I saw a completely different philosophy of life. The game became my teacher and opened the door of the world for me.

"Soccer for me is the most brilliant sport in the world—there is no doubt. It is a beautiful game. It is like a ballet, you jump, turn, twist, leap, kick, head the ball and run. It demands the best conditioning. There is no rest in soccer.

"Soccer is for the poor. It costs nothing. We had no money for courts or playing fields so we played in the streets, on the beach and in the lots by the factories. I was influenced by my father, who was a soccer player, but we had many problems. He broke his knee and we had a problem with food. He had to get a job on the side because a professional earned so little money then. I had to work to help earn money, but I started to play soccer in the street with the other boys. We had no ball. We would make a ball of paper or use a grapefruit or stuff a sock with rags. I got in trouble with my father because we never could find two socks that matched in the house. The first leather ball from the store came as a gift from a friend of my father when I was sick in bed. I was ten years old. I remember the ball was all brown in color. I practiced with it every day.

"In America all sports are from the middle of the body up to the head and arms. Throw, catch, swing, hit. Baseball, football, basketball, golf, tennis, hockey, boxing. They all demand hand-eye coordination. The children begin very young in the United States with this set coordination which is much easier than eye-foot coordination.

"Any boy, if he begins young—when he is seven or eight years old—can learn to control a soccer ball in six months. It all comes with practice. It is quite easy when a boy or girl is young. You can take the best professional American football player or basketball player when he is twenty-five or thirty years old and it is very hard for him to learn the foot action and ball control so vital to soccer even though he is a fine athlete.

"The young American boys are equal on guts. I have seen some young boys in California with very good ball control. If they practice they could be very good, *equal* to any of the young players in the world. More and more the young people in the United States will concentrate on soccer despite the climate changes and so many other competing sports to play.

"The two things I have always done in the years I've played soccer is always prepare myself to be in the best physical condition and always play as a member of the team. I do everything on the soccer field as a team player. That is the way to win.

"You have many boxers but Muhammad Ali is only one. You have many soccer players but Pele is only one—as you have only one Beethoven. It is hard tò say why I was the best or what happened to me. At sixteen years I was in the World Cup in Switzerland and I made four goals in a game but always the team idea came first. No one can do it alone.

"To describe the ability that I have that has given me my strength as a player—there are two things. One is to be able to kick with power and accuracy with both legs. Then each way you turn you are ready to kick.

"The second strength is to know your position on the field—where you are—*the space*—at every moment of the game. Many players are looking only at the ball, their eyes are fixed on the ball and only when the ball comes to a player does he start to look to see where he is, does he think of what he will do, what direction he will go, what position he is in. I think he's got to know the position before he gets the ball. He has to be able to think many moves ahead and all very, very quickly.

"Everything is practice. I made a lot of goals with the head. I am not big, but normal or short. I knew it was very hard to score with the head in Europe but I made many goals because I practiced this shot. To protect myself I worked very hard in karate and judo training frequently every year up until 1970 to strengthen myself and help me prepare mentally.

"The playmaking in soccer comes down to one important idea—and that is the man who makes the pass, the man who gives you the ball, does not *make* the pass. The man who *receives* the ball makes the pass—he opens the space. This is very important to understand the game as a spectator. The receiving player makes a pass possible. If the space is not opened the pass will not work.

"You need a lot of patience when you play soccer. Sometimes you play against a weak team and your team is very strong and the goal doesn't come and doesn't come. The time passes and if you do not have patience you start to push, push, push and you are able to do nothing and you lose control and play a nervous game. You must wait. You must be patient to be ready for the right time and be prepared when the moment comes. Sometimes you wait almost ninety minutes.

"Where you have the ball you have to pay attention to the ball and to your company and to your opponent and you have to have reflection. The decisions on the field are made in parts of seconds. You watch the ball in flight and you see how it spins and then you decide, because of the spin, how you will take the ball on your foot, which foot, what side of that foot, what your first move will be and what your direction will be, because you know exactly where you are on the field at that second. You have to be very much prepared mentally. You use whatever body tricks you can, hips, shoulders, hands, moves to open your opponent's legs, but it is when you think ahead that you gain the advantage.

"The spectators see the soccer stage as very big and the players' moves look easy because the field appears very spacious and the distance between the players as very *open*. But when you're on the field of play the space is very small and the distance between players is very short and if you lose part of a second in time you can lose the ball.

"I learned a great deal about soccer from watching an old soccer player in Brazil who played in my early years, 1958–61. He was called Zeginio. I studied him when he played for Rio against our Santos team and I watched him on film and I watched him as a spectator. I learned a lot from him, how he played, his ball control, his dribbling. He taught me a great deal.

"To be recognized around the world sometimes you don't have to be a good athlete, if you have luck in a World Cup where millions see you. Sometimes there are much better players who do not have the same chance and the World Cup stage and the moment. You must succeed to be recognized around the world, and you must succeed each time you have the stage.

"As I watch soccer today I do not see a forward player who has the capacity to make a lot of goals. I do not know what has happened but in the last five years we have more midfield and good defenders than forwards. It is very difficult to understand why but when I started in 1956 we had more good offensive players—wings and centers.

"Perhaps it is because the cities are growing and the big open space to play is gone and with the small practice areas the mentality of the players changes. They think of a smaller space, blocking shots, defending the goal, short passes, *protection*. As soccer became more of a job the coaches thought more about

their job and wanted to win so they worked on defense so not to *lose* the game. They no longer thought of scoring and the capacity of the forwards' play.

"Artificial turf was difficult for me in the beginning. I would drop the ball with my foot, look to my team player and when I moved my foot to dribble the ball, the ball had rolled two feet away and I had to look down to find it. I learned to control the ball more carefully on artificial fields. When you are playing on natural grass the power of your passes is much stronger than on an artificial surface because the roll is slower on grass.

"In soccer when you are dribbling your moves depend on what you want. Sometimes moving too fast, committing too soon, will beat one man but you will lose the ball to another—where a slower series of moves will beat *two* men who may commit together. It all depends on the moment. Dribbling should be used in soccer *only if it is necessary*. This is my philosophy. If you can pass the ball or go without dribbling it is better—you go straight to the goal. Dribbling is to maneuver when you are trapped in a corner or getting into a better position to score in front of the goal.

"To kick with great power depends on leg muscles, but you must practice how to use that power best with the nicest placement of the foot on the ball. The impact position is most important. My father saw me kicking with my right foot as a boy and he was the one who taught me to kick with my left foot too, so I could kick from any position in any direction, very quick! I believed in this and I began to kick against the wall, to practice with both legs, kick and rebound hour after hour. Right foot, left foot, until I got the same power in both legs.

"As a professional I played in goal four times. The rules until 1962 prevented a team from changing the goalkeeper during a game if he was injured. A team had to move a player on the field in goal. I went in because I had played goalkeeper as a boy. The goalkeeper is the most important and difficult position on the field. Everybody can make a mistake, forward, midfield or defender, and the opponent may not score, but if the goaltender makes a mistake you lose—only the net helps him.

"The best goalkeeper I ever saw was the Russian Iachine. Then Banks from England, Barboza in Brazil, Thomashefski playing now in Poland. Loyail in Brazil. These are the best goaltenders.

"There are very few *certain* ways to beat a goaltender. But there are a few, and I practiced these year after year. Shots that are impossible for the goalkeeper to defend against.

"If you have a foul kick from centerfield with the ball on the right sideline, the goaltender will take a

position on a direct line with your shot well out from the cage to cut down the angle. As you move to kick he will edge out even more on the kicking axis and then if you kick with a nice wide curve and the ball comes in high, just inside the left post, there is no way he can defend. You will score, and I have scored a lot on that kick—but you must practice it and practice it and it must be perfect.

"This is part of the skills of the best players around the world: Georgie Best, Keeger, Garonche from Brazil, who is the best soccer player I saw in my whole life. Beckenbauer in Germany was fantastic, and now Rossie is a very good middle-field player in Italy.

"I have never seen any of these players in the world do anything on a soccer field that I could not do. Except one. One player on the Santos team, a left wing named Edu—he plays in the States now. He could do one thing I could not do in a game. When Edu was pinned in a corner, with no way to get free, he would place the ball between the heel of his forward foot and the instep of his other foot crossed behind it and with a quick kick-jump, flip the ball *over* his head and the head of the defender in front of him. Edu would then move out around the de-

fender and continue with the ball to the goal.

"I practiced and tried and practiced and tried all my life and I cannot do that. I played with him and when he would make it work perfectly I would laugh. My bicycle kick is different. There are others who try it for many years but others have not scored with it as I have. I learned it in Brazil with the Brazilian National Team, I saw a player whose name was Leonidas do it only once. I saw him do it on television. I was in a restaurant. He was a center forward in São Paulo. I worked on it. I scored a few goals with my bicycle kick. I take the ball with either foot and flip it up behind me, then turn away from that side and when the ball is still in the air kick it on goal with the other foot. It is a good trick because the defender never knows when you will do it; he goes in the direction of the first little kick and then as I turn I can kick it past him with the other foot with full power.

"When you are trying to score and you have two defenders coming on you, you go through the defenders and your mind works quickly on your two or three options—to pass left or right or dribble him. But if you come alone to the goalkeeper it is much more difficult. The pressure is greater because you

have only one choice—to shoot on goal. Sometimes you do not have enough patience. You try to go too quick.

"In my first professional game at sixteen I scored one goal. Then in my first regular-season game I scored four goals. I remember most all the games I played every year. I remember *all* the goals I scored. There are times I will watch the game on TV later and I will be surprised to see myself make a play and I can't remember how I was able to do *that*. But the goals I remember. I could talk about each of them and the last one in the rain against Tampa Bay at night when the Cosmos won at home 2–1.

"I always believe in my heart that through sport one day all the people will be together. Through the political way we can never come together. I always felt that if I were on the political side I could never get the same treatment in Russia or Red China or in Japan or South America. But as I was involved in soccer I had the open door—everyplace.

"There is great joy in soccer, a beautiful freedom. Many people don't know as they watch a game that the player has some personal problems, someone in his family is ill or some little worry or trouble is with him when he goes to the field. When he makes the goal he forgets his problems. He leaps for joy. It is a wonderful expression of release. The public goes to see the games and they have problems and when the goal comes they are free and they forget everything else for a few minutes when they are all together on the stage.

"There is no doubt there is a touching between the athlete and audience. There is love."

The two sequences on these pages are pure Pelé. Above, the largest crowd in North America soccer history watches Pelé anoint his teammate after a fine effort in 1977. As the game ended three young fans ran past police guards and surrounded the athlete before he left the field. With a move that must have been perfected with hours of practice, they held him and removed his shirt in less than two seconds. The kids escaped with their priceless trophy leaving Edson Arantes stripped and somewhat embarrassed as security whisked him off.

The sequence below is the last goal of his fabulous career. On page 71, Pelé starts upfield in heavy rain in the black night. The power kick with his cannon thigh (bottom, left) sends the ball with devastating speed into the net. The joy on this 1,281st goal matched his first goal, 21 years before.

BILLIE JEAN KING

"The first time I ever hit a tennis ball I thought I could do it, that I could be number one in the world. Then as I began to get serious, play regularly, get involved in tournaments, I realized I was a little fish in a big pond. You think then about going town to town, city to city, section to section in the nation, in the world; about being the best.

"I began to think about this challenge when I was just fourteen years old and I beat Karen Hantze, at Morley Field in San Diego. It was just a sectional junior Whiteman Cup match but at that time she was number one in the *eighteen* age group in the country, and everyone said she was to be the next world's champion. I beat her, 6–3, 6–2, and I knew then I was on my way.

"I knew ultimately that I could be number one in the world on the afternoon I lost to Margaret Court in the September 1965 finals of the Nationals at Forest Hills. I was up 5–3 in both sets and I lost both sets, 8–6, 7–5. I was furious I lost. I had her. I faltered a little bit when I realized I had a chance to be number one. I was so angry. After the match I walked around Forest Hills, went to see a movie called *The Pawnbroker,* which was very depressing, and this combined with my anger made me feel even worse.

"I said then—*that's it!* Next year I'm number one —and I was. Next time I played Margaret Court I beat her and won it all at Wimbledon in 1966. Those three moments I remember. Those three times in my life there was a different stage being set for me and I was aware of it.

"Tennis is a very difficult sport because of the precise area of play. There are no walls, your depth perception has to be extremely good in tennis, and a child without it is never going to develop the skills of a champion. I think that depth perception is the first thing I would measure in a young player—more important than the ability to run well. I think depth perception is first, and then great hand-eye coordination. Only because I had it could I develop the mobility and the flexibility to play the style that goes with my way of thinking—the way I am. What I am—*the essence*—being able to go to the net and hit the ball in the air.

"A tennis court measures seventy-eight feet by twenty-seven feet and the net is three feet high, but you've got to think of a hundred and twenty feet, because you run *behind* the court and you don't only run in it. Some people think the game is what it is because of the measurements, but this is not true. The dimensions never change on a tennis court, but each person's weight, strength, height, reach, speed and agility change. The surface of the court, temperature and wind change. These are the variables you have to handle. We all adjust our thinking from the time we start to play the game to that basic twenty-seven feet by seventy-eight feet.

"I'm always going to go to the net when I can. I love it. It's fun. Someone else who feels they don't have the mobility won't do it. It's not home for them. Home for them is the baseline. Home for me is going in and putting the ball away. I love the feeling of dancing, of lunging, of going up and back, and all the *different* movements. Many players are much more rigid than I am.

"Some players like to run to the ball, other players don't like to, other players run better to the left than to the right, some players move forward well and don't move back well, some move up and back well, so that there are no set offensive patterns or sure methods of attack in tennis—every player on any day on every surface is different. You go into a match with a plan but it all comes down to the person you're playing on execution. There are mental errors and execution errors. Position and balance are all-important. Not only does your body have to be in position, but the face of the racquet in relationship to the ball—*point of contact*—has to be exact. Whether you hit a topspin or slice there is a very slight degree change in the angle of the racquet meeting the ball to make it go where you want it on the court. That placement is everything. A person's body can be off balance when the ball is hit, but because a champion understands the face of the racquet in relationship to the ball, the point of contact will be exactly as they want it. When you watch Bjorn Borg standing on his head, going back into the corner, and he comes up with a winner, you'll hear everyone scream, 'How did he do that!' He did it because he knew where the face of the racquet was in relationship to the ball even though everything else was off balance. That part was on. That's what makes it. *Point of contact is everything*. Ideally you don't want to get yourself in that situation because it makes it that much more difficult for you.

"Sometimes you don't hit a winner when you can. Sometimes you'll keep an opponent in a rally a longer time than you need to because they're out of shape. You might lose two or three points, but because you've worked them into the ground the end result will pay off. It's called short-term loss for long-term gain. If you *know* they're out of shape. If they're in shape you better not try that. You better bag it, baby, or *you'll* get hurt.

"Tennis is like ballet. You must have great balance. In all your positions you always want to be over the axis. Chris Evert has great balance—this is her tremendous asset—and it's part of having total preparation. The reason Chris does not run is because she is so accurate. It is a matter of angles on the court. Tennis is a game of angles.

"If you want to hit the ball deep from the center of one baseline to each of the corners—within an inch—on the far baseline, you use the most demanding angle on the court for accuracy. It is the longest shot. If the ball lands on the center of the service line at midcourt, the angles for your return are increased, but your running distance drastically increases. Basically if you keep the ball deep as Chris does, you only have to run three steps to either side. When you hit at midcourt, right on the T, you have

to be ready to run at least six or seven steps either way. If you hit even shorter than that, say three feet from the net, you must be ready to run ten steps to either side.

"You never have time to figure the angles. It's *practiced.* It is so practiced that it becomes an instinct. You just know where to put the ball. You just feel it. It has been computed into your brain so many times—it is *there.*

"If a player can basically keep the ball down the middle within five feet of the center of the baseline, they're never going to get hurt. But I think that's very boring—to always hit down the middle within five feet from the baseline. For me there is not the sense of moving the ball around or changing the spins that should be the fun of it.

"Of course, as soon as you think this way you think of much greater risks. The person who can keep the ball high over the net and deep—down the middle of the court—is going to win a lot of matches, but I would say it is not as creative. As a tennis player you have to decide what your objec-

tives are. I want to make great recoveries on the court and make my opponent hit the ball one more time. That's a great feeling.

"But it is certainly not a great feeling if you're doing all of the running all of the time and they're doing nothing but running you into the ground. That is the feeling Chris Evert has given many opponents. The bulldozer service that overwhelms you causes the same frustration on a given bad day. Then you don't play tennis, you just isolate moments.

"The only way that you can combat this frustration is with *technique*. In tennis and golf and gymnastics you don't win with strength, you win with technique. This is true in any sport where timing is all-important.

"This is why in the game of tennis, if you can stay boring you're going to win more. It is difficult for me to try to find the right combination; to still have that sense of creativity and to win. Sometimes in order to win I have to pay a certain price in not being creative. So it is very difficult for me. I am very high-strung with a high degree of energy, and I love being busy and I *have* to feel creative or that's when I get totally upset.

"I see the ball coming over the net and I may want to hit a topspin on the first one, a sidespin on the second one, a slice on the third one, and on each of those three I may want to clear the net by a different margin. All those variables are going into my brain because it's fun for me, because it is creative. But there is something else that goes into my computer, and that is the knowledge that my chances of missing also go up with that way of thinking. It would be much safer to say—I'm going to hit three topspin forehands in a row, just to the backhand. *One. Two. Three.*

"Now, that may help with my chances to win the point, but it is also on the downside for my creativity. That choice has always been a difficult situation for me. I think other players like Chris Evert or Tracy Austin are the types of players that when they see the ball come over they have three shots and they hit fifteen thousand to one on the same spot on the court, and they hit the face of the racquet against the ball basically the same way every time they hit that shot. And they're going to win. That's a winning combination. However, what's winning for them may not be winning for me. Naturally I need a certain degree of both and that is a daily conflict I have. But because of this creative drive I also know that I'll have to find something else when I retire that I can get totally involved in. I don't know what that will be—I'm searching for it. Broadcasting, school, sports politics? I'm keeping all the doors open. Maybe I'll never find anything that I

love as much as tennis, but I'm willing to go search for it. Athletes take the experiences in their sport and carry them over to the rest of their lives—this is the only way they can be helpful.

"In tennis you play against the *ball*. You don't play a person, or a certain style. It is you and the ball. That's when you play your best. You are married to it. *The ball*. You consider all factors about your opponent on any given day and you know nothing will be easy. Champions never, never, *never* think that it is easy. That's the difference between a champion and someone who doesn't win. You've got to get through the first round first.

"But it's always you and the ball. You concentrate on the ball and pick out the spot on the court where you're going to hit it. *Where* I'm going to hit the ball is more important than the fact that I want to play some opponent's forehand. On a return of serve, I focus on the ball, make ideal contact with the racquet, then go for a specific spot on the court. That's what wins. In the end, of course, you're still beating a person.

"There's no time limit in tennis. That's what makes it different. Most of the players don't know when the crucial moment's there. The crowd very rarely knows. The crowd usually regards the crucial moment too late, after the fact. A great athlete knows those few times in a close match, before the point starts, that they have to win that point if they are to win the match. Most of the time the players don't know—it may only be 30–all. You must bring yourself to these key points in a match—it is most important for your momentum.

"Then you must understand that when you watch tennis the difference between a game point and a match point is enormous. A ton of difference. Even though both players know what the other will do, what each other is thinking, it comes down to *who can execute under pressure*. At the highest levels of the game it gets down to this—and to really come through under pressure is the greatest feeling in the world. Most athletes can come through when it doesn't count. Match point brings forth all my creativeness, energy and technique and will to *execute*. Match point is a love-hate relationship. The torment of, 'Oh, God, what am I doing here?' and 'This is it! This is what I've been working for.' I know this is why I pay the price. This is what it's all about if you want to be a champion. The challenge for *that* moment. Match point!

"There are no guarantees for an athlete in action, no assurance that I will not or cannot fail mentally or physically in the middle of play. It has happened to me more than once mentally and physically. There was one time in the finals at Wimbledon. Emotionally and mentally I gave up. Everything turned off.

That was in the finals in 1969 with Ann Jones. I had her a set and 3–1. Suddenly I just didn't *feel* anymore. On center court I stopped feeling and stopped caring. If I don't care and if I am not intense I've got no chance.

"I've used anger and been abused by it. I've lost matches because of my temper and I've won matches because of it. If I can direct my energies in the right direction that is when I'm mentally toughest in a match.

"I am very intense on the court and very emotional, and that's when I play my best. Especially if I keep my mouth shut. Other times physically I've failed when my body just couldn't make it even though, considering the situation, my body was still functioning.

"Tennis may seem not to strike fear into a player, but it does. You feel like the bears are running after you in the forest. But generally when I'm fearing the situation, or the other player, I do better. I perform at my best under pressure. For me fear is a positive force. I feel it and I'm afraid to lose. Most people are afraid to win. Champions are afraid to lose. That's a huge difference in sports but it is very subtle at times. People don't understand what goes on. Losing is very painful to me. I can't sleep. I walk the floors. I pay a big price. I hate losing. Others hate winning. People have the *will to fail*. Absolutely. I would say the majority of people. They will say they are not lucky, or there is no way against the odds. They can always find a way to fail. They will get to 5–3 or match point and there is no way they can close the door. The only way they can win is if the other player falls apart for them. *They* can't really win it.

"Champions win it. They make it happen. That is a huge difference. I don't know what goes on in the minds of those athletes who fail but you can just see it happen. They start to crumble. They get to the point where they can change their whole life, their career, *everything*, and they can't make it. Watching them you feel that they don't want to make it happen. I call it a will to fail.

"My career has been really an up-and-down career. I have not been as strong as a lot of players are day in and day out because I am very emotional. If I get long-term goals in my mind then I'm at my best. If there is a certain sense of drama, if it is more theatrical, I like that too.

"The theater in the Bobby Riggs match accomplished a great deal. That particular match exposed tennis to all new people. Most of the people in tennis today are new, they've just taken up the game in the last ten years or less. When I played him it bothered me that people around the country got so emotional over the man-against-woman idea. However, under-

standing human nature, it was obvious to me that it was going to happen. I told my husband, Larry, that if I signed to play Riggs I would not sleep for the next eight weeks while I trained and put up with the press. I knew that people would get very involved emotionally with the match. I knew the importance of it.

"I personally didn't feel it was any big deal to beat Bobby Riggs from a skill point of view, but I do think it helped people realize that women are good athletes and that we've just begun. No one has seen women athletes at their best yet. Twenty or thirty years from now I believe you will see women athletes the way you see men athletes today. It will show in all the measurable records. I think that single match helped women have more self-respect. And it affected men who are secure within themselves. It helped them. Men who are insecure were also affected. I think it brought a new complexion to their way of thinking. Maybe it broadened their horizons to help them think an issue through a little more objectively.

"I do know that every man and woman I've ever talked to remembers where they were that night. Where were you the day Billie Jean played Bobby Riggs? 'Oh, I was here or I was there . . .' It was an event. A social event that influenced people's lives. It *did* affect them.

"This is important because tennis is a very small sport. Of the spectatorship that we do have, most of these people are participants. I think watching tennis is one of the best tennis lessons a person can get, and I don't think a lot of participants realize that. The better tennis you watch the more it helps you. I think the people who watch good golf realize this. Tennis spectators are just beginning to understand it.

"I think of myself as a romantic person. Love is always the end result in every situation. Most people look for someone to love them more than they look for someone to love. People who are in entertainment tend to get gratification and love together as one, and where they have emotional problems is that they don't understand that you have to separate the two. When we get applause it is gratification but it is not love. When entertainers are not in the limelight, they claim they're not loved anymore. Athletes as well tend to confuse these two words greatly. That is when the disappointment starts developing. I try to separate them and not combine them. When you combine them you get in trouble.

"Just entertaining is giving in itself—which people tend to forget. The tune will go, 'Players, you owe us something!' I don't think anybody owes anything. I don't think that people that helped me owe me anything and I don't think I owe them anything.

I like to *give* to them because I care about them.

"Youngsters today growing up in tennis are given so much so soon. I can remember being number one in the world in this country for three years straight and no one knew who I was or didn't care. I had very painful, *bad* experiences with the administrators of my sport, who always tried to make me feel obligated, who always tried to make me feel guilty.

"From the time I was eleven years old—the first time I played a sanctioned tournament in Los Angeles at the Los Angeles Tennis Club, something inside of me told me that I wanted to change the *system* of tennis. That I didn't want to be chosen because I knew the right person or my father gave money to the Youth Tennis Foundation, and that the system wasn't really based on merit. That's when I really wanted to change and that's what I really wanted very much to be a part of as time went on, and I think that's been accomplished. If you're good today they can't keep you from playing in tournaments, whereas when I was growing up I wanted to go to Europe and the USLTA wouldn't allow it. I didn't go to Europe until I was number one in the *world*. Well, that's backwards. My career was all backwards.

"There is no way the youngsters today would improve their game if they were put through what I had to go through trying to improve mine, trying to fulfill my own potential. I wanted everyone to have the chance I had to experience tennis and to also appreciate tennis as an art. The fact that few people did believe in me through all these painful moments of trying to change the system, with people making fun of you while being a woman athlete, was doubly hard. My parents didn't understand what I was trying to do—in junior high school and high school—they thought I was crazy!

"A girl today doesn't have to deal with those things. I'm glad they don't have to go through what I went through. And I hope I have given something back to those who stood by me, but I know I've given most to all of them by winning—because they believed in me when others didn't. What makes me the happiest is that tennis is now appreciated as an art, as a sport, and that youngsters today want to pursue it—it's a *good* thing to pursue, whereas when I was growing up it was a *bad* thing to pursue because it led nowhere. I was trying to be a tennis bum and I was a woman trying to be an athlete, which was looked down on. Tennis in those years for a woman was *social;* they never took us seriously. I have been able to see all those things change and be a part of it. That's where I've gotten as much gratification as hitting the ball, because I *know* I've made things happen for other human beings.

"I've seen both sides. I've seen tennis when it was a dishonest sport—a so-called amateur sport, when politics played such a big role in my destiny. Children today—if they want to be good—it will be there for them.

"The athlete in American life is insulated. You lose touch with what is really going on out there, with what the real people think. But people are the ones who separate the athlete. I don't feel any different about them—but they feel differently about me, in the last twenty years. No one realized in 1966 I was even playing tennis. They think I probably made a million dollars fifteen years ago. The youngsters make more money than I do. Chris Evert made a million dollars before I did. Chris made a million dollars when she was twenty-two, I made a million dollars in prize money when I was thirty-four.

"People don't stop and think about those things, but I know how things have changed because I've gone through the transition and I know it's the generations that came before me in tennis that made me what I am and I think that each generation leaves their statement for the next generation to grow up on through your personality as well as your style of play. You look around now and all the little girls are trying to play like Chris Evert. When a new champion comes along they are going to play like her—and the next generation and the next.

"I know when I walk on the center court at Wimbledon I always think about that. Every year I think about all the great players, their little feet pittypatted along this court, their sweats on this court, their creativity's been left here for me, and that's what I've built on. And the generations after me have built on my game and what I did as far as creating opportunities. I know the younger players today have a better life because of what I did. I get a great deal of gratification out of that.

"I don't think older athletes are better than young ones today. The young ones are the best ever in the history of civilization, and the next generation is going to be even better than this one, otherwise I don't think we did a good job.

"I don't think that it is fair to think that one sport is greater than another. I just love tennis. Athletes are not objective about their sport or artists about their art. It's impossible. Athletes make me sick when they try to explain that the older athletes are better or that baseball, or pro football, is the *toughest*. No way. It depends on the person, their body types, their capacities, their mentality. Certain people belong in certain sports. Certain sports are made for certain people.

"That is why when I hit that first tennis ball I knew that's what I wanted. I knew I loved it. I get to run and hit a ball. Great feeling to hit the ball against the strings. *Great feeling!*"

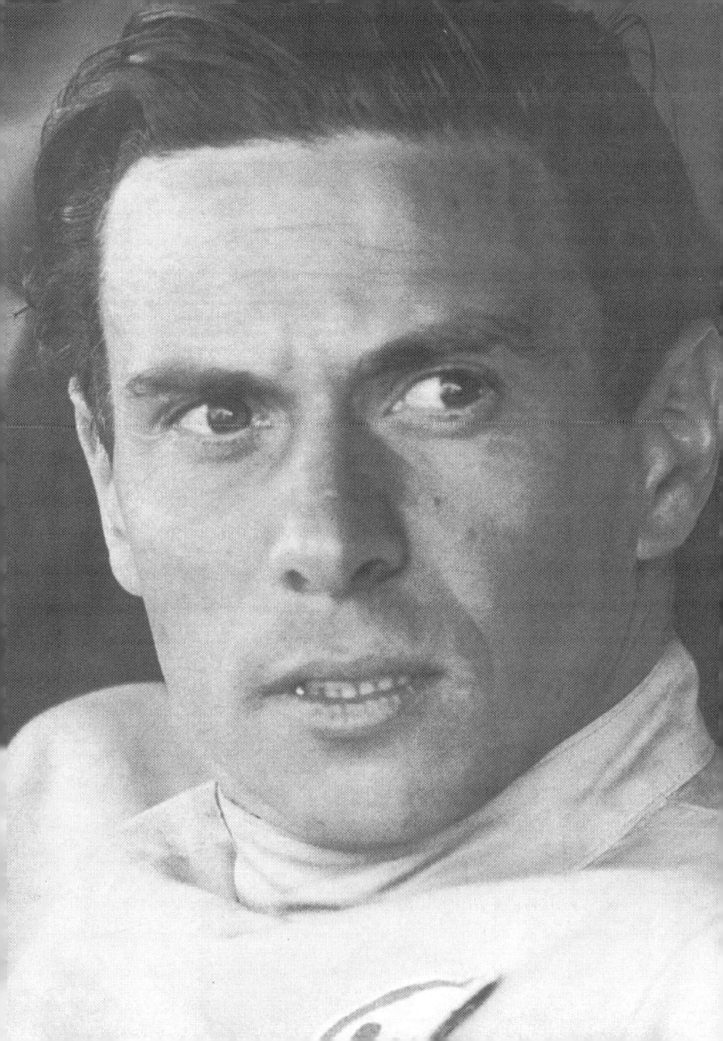

JIM CLARK

"I think for any driver to be a good driver, he must be consistent—*consistently fast!* There are many drivers who can do quick laps, but who appear to be unable to keep it up throughout a race under pressure. This is the difference between a good driver and a very good driver—the ability to go fast, and really, stamina and the power of concentration."

Jim Clark, wearing his favorite tan cashmere cardigan over his light-blue coveralls, had one leg up on a wheel of his green Formula 1 car, biting his nails. Colin Chapman, his friend and owner of Lotus, leaned against the pit counter with his clipboard, lap charts and watches. The articulate, erudite designer appraised his driver.

"Grand Prix driving is a job which needs a lot of study, a lot of application and deep understanding of the problems, and Jimmy's very good at this. Jimmy always gets the maximum out of a car. I always do my utmost to give him the best car I know how. A driver should only be asked to drive as fast as is necessary. If there is anything I can possibly do to get more out of the car so the driver can take life a little easier, then I do it. That way, the driver will be extending himself less, will be taking fewer risks and have more chance of finishing the race.

"It's very useful to clock not only the complete lap times, but also sections of a lap, because it varies through its length. Parts are straight and parts are curved, and by assessing the relative times over each section, you can see where your car is gaining. Whether you are gaining on just sheer maximum speed, or whether you are gaining in the turns, or in acceleration or braking. Of course, to give the driver the easiest possible time, you've got to gain where you can in every section, because by this means, you can allow time for him to drive just that little bit more within his capabilities, strain the machine that much less and have that much more safety margin.

"Jimmy is very quick to size up a situation," Chapman said, "to know how a car is suited to the circuit and what changes are necessary. Over the years, we've developed our own language, if you like, of explaining the symptoms and solving the problems. It only takes a few moments of conversation between us to realize just what's got to be done."

Jim Clark smiled. "When I started racing with Lotus in 1960, I didn't know very much about the suspension, design or layout of a modern car at all.

I had to rely entirely on what I was given. Gradually over the years, I've built up enough basic knowledge to know what is wrong with the car and have it put right. Since 1962, we've used basically the same chassis, with only minor modifications, and during this time, Colin Chapman and I and the mechanics have learned how best to prepare for each circuit. The car has become very reliable.

"Before, we didn't even have a seat. Recently we packed the car with clay and sculptured it out, then formed a new seat in fiberglass. The seat is a most important factor in racing so you can be comfortable and not have to hang onto the steering wheel to keep your position. Especially on a circuit like Nurburgring, where you are braking, accelerating and changing directions every two or three seconds, you've got to be wedged in, but be comfortable at the same time. Before we ship the cars, we trim the chassis here at the Lotus factory, differently for each circuit. Usually only minor things, it may only be an antisway bar, a difference of an eighth of an inch up or down. It may just be the camber setting or the toe-in settings on the wheels. Obviously, we have the different gear ratios for different circuits, even to the stage where we occasionally alter the braking ratio, front to rear.

"The preparation is a combination of a lot of effort by a great many people. The engine manufacturers and our own mechanics, who strip the cars from the last race, crack-test everything to make sure we've got as good a car as we can set up for the next race. I get a lot of the glory, but it is not a one-man effort. It is all these people working together very enthusiastically to make certain I've got the best car possible.

"One ability of a good driver is to be able to make a car do what *he* wants it to and not so much to have the car set up so he alone can drive it. I've found this at various times through the years with team drivers—one driver will come in and say the car is understeering terribly and complain he can't get it around. And yet, if I were to go out in that car, it is possible to make it oversteer and get around the track quicker: by either going into the corner very deep with the brakes on, or turning the car into the corner with the brakes on—inducing oversteering— and holding it on the throttle. If it is oversteering too much, then you must have proper control of the throttle and allow it to go through the corner as smoothly as possible. This is what makes the differ-

ence between a driver who has an on day and an off day.

"I always find it more difficult to drive the car fast downhill than I do uphill. On a very tough section of a course, a series of bends, a slalom-type section, I find I'm not particularly thinking of the corner I'm going through, but of the one ahead. I try to be in the right position for the next one, thinking of my speed, where the apex is and how I will leave it.

"I think driving is definitely a combination of things: what you feel in your hands and what you

championship of twenty-five seconds, Nurburgring is a very tough course and I found in order to get a lead like this you have to be not only brutal on yourself, but brutal on the car. I believe in winning a race as slowly as I can. I build up a lead only in case of trouble where I'm forced to save the car.

"I feel fear, at times, definitely. If I feel there is something going wrong with the car, or if something happens which I have not anticipated, then I feel afraid. But in the normal course of a race I think I have enough confidence in the car and myself

feel in your whole body. In fact, when I tried to fix the inner fiberglass seat, I found it seemed to be floating inside the car, and I couldn't really feel what the car was doing. I took it out and went something like eight or ten seconds faster. Your whole body must be part of the car—the car and driver move together. Part of it is sight, and part of it is feel: you feel what the front end is doing and the steering through your hands, you feel what the back end is doing through your back, and the seat of your pants. It's just a combination of things all being fed into a computer, as it were.

"Even though I had a commanding lead in the German Grand Prix which earned me the world

and the others around me not to be afraid. I realize the danger is there and I try to drive to make it as safe as possible. I think the others do as well. But there are occasions when you very definitely get a fright.

"The other word that keeps cropping up is this word 'courage' and that 'nerves of steel' phrase you hear people quoting. But I've certainly not got nerves of steel. I'm a very nervous person and I'm not particularly courageous. I think that these are two points that are often misused. Just thinking of drivers generally, I don't think that they're especially good qualities to have, because they can always lead to foolhardiness and possible dangers."

When Jim came home from Nurburgring after winning the drivers' world championship title, he flew alone in his own plane and landed in an abandoned RAF airstrip about thirty miles from his sheep farm in Chirmside near Berwick-upon-Tweed on the border between Scotland and England. He had learned to drive his first racecars on that same airstrip. I remember he wore a white shirt and tie as he climbed out on the wing and waved. (I was filming that week of his life. It was my first show as producer-director for ABC Sports and it was to be the prototype of a portrait series.)

I remember the grass growing up between the cracked airstrip pavement and the flock of seagulls that passed across the runway as he came in. I remember how the car felt as he drove seventy miles an hour over the twisting, narrow farm roads and how it was the smoothest ride I've ever had. It felt as if we were going thirty. I remember how the steering wheel was held between the index and middle fingers of both his hands, not between his thumb and forefinger. I photographed his hands on the wheel. I remember his tweed cap and the square strength of his shoulders, seeing him bounce down the hall stairs in front of a stained-glass window with Burne-Jones figures and edge through the narrow, wood-paneled passages of his old farmhouse. I remember him twirling his crook of a cane, his footfalls on the stone driveway. I vividly remember him stopping along the brilliant row of flower beds and cupping a rose in his hand and pressing it against his face and breathing in the life of it.

I can hear his voice as he described the two breeds of sheep in the deep shadows of the barn; seeing the glorious sunlight on the green rolling hills and watching him vault a fence to begin the long walk across the fields with the sea byeond. He recited Robbie Burns as his father had recited it to him, and it was in that tranquil landscape that he talked about courage and fear in motor racing.

We wander there, we wander here,
We eye the rose upon the brier,
Unmindful that the thorn is near
      Among the leaves;
And tho' the puny wound appear,
      Short while it grieves.

With steady aim, some Fortune chase;
Keen hope does ev'ry sinew brace;
Thro' fair, thro' foul, they urge the race,
      And seize the prey
Then cannie, in some cozie place,
      They close the day.

While on the Grand Prix circuit with our coverage I came to know the emergence of the new athlete of the sixties. The world figure. Fit, intelligent, enthusiastic, well dressed and relaxed, he managed to use all of his time. Much of it was in the business of his sport and in the case of Jim Clark it was with team manager and owner Colin Chapman (top, left) and the preparation of the Formula I Lotus (below), setting it up differently for the different demands of each of the racing circuits on the tour. Cars are set up quite differently for fast, slow or medium speed circuits.

Graham Hill was driving. A beautiful ground stewardess was holding on and laughing at the wild ride and Jimmy Clark was standing on the back holding on with one hand and carrying three heavy garment bags over his shoulder with the other. The two great drivers made the connecting flight to Nice on the way to Monte Carlo by seconds. Jimmy smiled and said, "See you soon." I remember the metal hangers digging into the red flesh of his fingers.

I thought about the pieces of the car tearing his

My life, like theirs became a ride on a dancing leaf, a fragile, unreal existence, a pattern of slow motion montages where airports and camera positions on mountains or race tracks became more familiar than the street where I lived. There was a theatrical feeling with a touring sport like racing. I can remember another happy moment when a motorized cart came careening down the red-carpeted tunnels of the TWA terminal in New York.

body to shreds as he smashed into a tree coming out of a corner at 160 mph in a Formula 2 race in Hochheim, Germany. Of imagining how everything had disintegrated into dust and silence. I remember pulling off the road in Cape Cod when the news came over the car radio one Sunday night—in total disbelief . . . of putting my head on the steering wheel for a long, long period of sadness. Dear friend.

Athletes do not die, they vanish.

GORDIE HOWE

"Hockey is legs. I think baseball is legs too. Legs and eyes. Through wisdom in hockey you somehow can get away with a little slower pace, but hockey is endurance and speed. That's what the game is all about.

"A hockey player's eyes are so important. In practice when I have my doubts about certain individuals I test them. Quite often we will be circling counterclockwise around the ice and I'll grab that puck when I'm trailing almost vertical to a player and I'll throw it near his stick. Some of the guys will pick it up immediately—when the puck's ten or twelve feet away from them—their peripheral vision is extra great. For others, it will hit their stick or hit their foot, and they won't pick it up. Then I know.

"The hand-eye coordination is everything. When an athlete is gifted I think *that* is the only thing he is gifted with. If he's got a good heart he's going to succeed in whatever he does, but I think the eye-hand coordination is the athlete's most important ability. Depth perception in hockey, of course, is very important in shooting and passing."

The older man sat on the narrow bench in front of his locker wrapped in a small towel, his silver hair twisted in tiny wet spears, his powerful sloping shoulders and biceps relaxed as his broad forearms rested on his thighs. His voice was gentle and enthusiastic as he praised his two sons who played on the same professional team, the New England Whalers, and were answering reporters' questions in front of their lockers across the room.

"I wouldn't want to bet who would be the quickest on the ice between my two sons. I've watched them skate every day for years. Skating ability requires a certain amount of quickness, a lot of power and the ability that my son Mark has to jump, to get away fast. Marty has only played defense, so there is a short stride in his skating, characteristic of a defenseman because he has to go in spurts and spasms in each direction. If you're a loose skater the opposition will figure you out in a hurry. If you're compact and quick, they can't."

Mark Howe did not look like his father—no one does. The younger son was in his sixth pro season and has scored over two hundred goals. He plays left wing. His father, during his twenty-five record years with the Detroit Red Wings, had been the league's best right-winger, alternating with Maurice Richard of the Montreal Canadiens on twenty-one all-star teams. Now, Gordie the father, fifty-one years old, had moved to center and on the final goal of a winning night played on the line with his son Mark, who is twenty-three.

"I don't know how far Mark can go," the great veteran whispered with deep admiration. "He's just a super young hockey player. He's loved it since the day he was born.

"Marty, on the other hand, loved football so much that hockey was very secondary until he was sixteen years old—then he became very interested in the game. He hasn't reached his potential yet.

"Mark always loved the game of hockey. He loved it so much that I had to keep each game fresh in my mind so that when I left the ice each night and we were driving home I could answer all the questions Mark would ask. Thousands of questions. Why did I do such and such? And I would tell him. He was a real student of the game. He had to know everything.

"What made it difficult for me but rewarding for him is that there is no set way to do anything on the ice. Whatever I would do depended on what the defense gave me—what tiny opening, what little mistake they made. I had to remember the defensive situations, moves and playmaking to make my explanations make sense to my son. I would succeed one time and then the next time succeed by doing the same thing a different way because the first way would never have worked. So much of it is instinct —drawing them off and burning it by.

"My sons did have one advantage and I feel it did help them a great deal, and that was assisting me as part-time instructors when they were very young. I ran a hockey camp, and when I had to show a kid something I would sit in front of a mirror and analyze what I did and I relayed this insight on technique to them. They knew how I did something and why I did it. As far as teaching them hockey skills directly—I did work on their shooting.

"Mark's hard shot, his wrist shot, is exceptional. I can't remember getting my shot away that quickly or that accurately. When he is off by three or four inches he is mad. He's such a perfectionist. He would come home as a boy from school and spend hour after hour shooting a tennis ball into a net he had made to develop his accuracy. I would swipe sticks and bring them home and Mark would wear them out on the garage floor perfecting his shot.

"I used to be able to shoot with either hand, but

now I shoot right-handed. I do most everything right-handed. I was most effective *moving*, taking a pass at top speed and shooting at top speed. That is the only way I played. Quickness is everything. When you shoot, *first* moves are so important. I did very little deeking [feinting]. When you're shooting on net and you get a goalie with the balance on one leg, you can shoot on that side of the net and I don't care where you put it, you've got a good chance to get in because he has to completely shift his weight and by the time he's done that it's goodbye!

"The same on the defenseman. If you come in on him and his stick's in the air, a quick release will beat him before he can get a stick on the ice. I never come right at a man but always come at an angle so he will make the first mistake. You never skate at him head on or he will keep backing up and force *you* to make the mistake. I never play for his reaction off of my action and then react to that. I come to him as fast as I can and shoot as hard as I can before he has a chance to half move or half think or see anything. I will take anything he gives me—any flaw—skate, stick, glove, head—and fire it. Gone! Quickness is everything. They can't check you with quickness. It is all quickness when you shoot, pass or change direction. That's what Mark has.

"Shooting is accuracy. I would always go for a spot *three inches wide*. That damn thing goes 120 miles an hour. You burn 'em. That puck is there! We would set pucks up in practice a few feet off the boards, a few inches from the red goal line—about twenty feet out. The angle is tough. You aim for the post and carom it into the net. That's *shooting*. You have to be dead on target. We would also play with the slot in the Plexiglas behind the net where the goal judge sits and shoot the puck through that slot —with the clearance of a dime—from about six feet out for short accuracy.

"I look back and my career was youth, maturity and old age. There's a few peaks and valleys in there but the game of hockey has remained pretty much the same up until Fred Shero of Philadelphia brought the real muscle men into the league and developed a beautiful combination of a hockey player who was very big, very tough, but a guy who could put the puck in the net too. Then the clubs answered with a big man to match a big man and this brought on the rough tactics in hockey.

"Hockey triggers tempers. It's a combination of everything, speed, hard ice, checking, sticks and *talk*. There's a lot of conversation out there. Thank God people can't read lips. I never was cool. I used to be in an awful lot of fights but now I've aged and matured.

"When I started out with the Detroit Red Wings they were struggling years for me because I was breaking into a National Hockey League that only had one hundred and twenty-one players. I had to break into a lineup with great players—but even then we had a couple of guys on the club who couldn't skate backwards. Now we have excellent skaters. I think the skating has improved because the ice conditions—the ice surfaces—have improved. The facilities have improved, the equipment has improved and the ability of the athlete has improved.

"I came into the league in 1946 at the twilight of some of the great careers of the goaltenders like Frankie Brimsek, Turk Broda and Bill Durnan. The rules in those years favored the goalie more because there was less opportunity to get open shots on net. Now they allow you to shoot through two or three lines if the puck precedes you and you catch up with it, and the goalie is now at a disadvantage. In the forties and early fifties, if your club got seventeen or eighteen shots on goal in a game we considered that a pretty good night. Now an individual player sometimes gets twelve or thirteen shots on a goal in a night. The two goaltender system was developed to take pressure off of one man.

"Then in the late fifties Jacques Plante introduced the mask for the goaltender, and thank God. That was a savior beyond everything! The delay of game to repair a goalie's face, just to stop the bleeding, sometimes took thirty minutes. The trainers would be drawn from ex-goaltenders and they would be inserted in the game—for either team—when the injuries occurred.

"The evolution of the stick began in the late fifties when Andy Bathgate began horsing around with the curved stick in New York. Stan Mikita went in and used one of Andy's sticks because he had broken a few on a road trip and he began to toy with the stick and increase the curve. Then when the other players saw the accuracy with which Mikita could shoot the puck, then everyone worked with it until Bobby Hull's boomerang became so extreme that they had to regulate and minimize the curve to a maximum of a half inch.

"Our success in Detroit was that we liked each other. Ted Lindsay, Sid Abel and myself on that Red Wing line knew each other so well, we each could carry the puck, could pass and shoot, and we believed and respected each other's ability. We would each give the puck to the one with the best shot.

"You have to know *exactly* when your line mate is going to take off and what he expects. Everyone knows what another player *can* do—you have to know what the men you're playing with *will* do. I know what my wingman wants me to do and I react.

"I enjoy playing with my sons because I know exactly what Mark and Marty will do on the ice.

"When I play hockey now after thirty-two seasons

I don't have to think as much. When I was young I thought before I tried to do something and then with quickness I made it work, but now certain things I do automatically. On the last goal tonight I was on the ice with my son Mark as he led John McKenzie in front of the net. I was going to make a play on the puck. I saw John, I saw their man make a move, and I just laid my stick on his, stopped his stick, and the puck rolled by to John and he put it in. It was instinct. If I had been a kid and excited, that would have been my goal. I would have been working at it and probably fouled the whole play up. The older you get there's less to prove, and that helps an awful lot too.

"When a player has to sit out a game on the bench, I tell him he's in the 'privileged position.' You learn so much from watching.

"People can't pick their parents but as far as genetics go when you get two strong individuals like my parents you inherit a lot of desire, admiration and respect—and Mom and Dad were two super, super people. My dad, Albert, is still alive. He's eighty-seven. Stronger than a horse. My mom died in an unfortunate accident when she was in her mid-seventies. My grandparents lived to ninety-six and ninety-seven. I feel there's longevity in me. As for size, I was two hundred and four pounds when I was sixteen years old and that's the weight I play at today. You've got one body and you sure better take care of it, and that takes sacrifice. You've got to love what you're doing. If you love it you can overcome any handicap or the soreness or all the aches and pains. Twenty-two hundred games? More. A thousand goals? More. Hockey was fun when I started and it is still fun."

Watching Gordie Howe play hockey in 1978 (right, above) with the Hartford/Springfield Whalers was just about the same as it had been 20 years before, in the old Madison Square Garden, against the New York Rangers (left, above). Gordie was full out. The intensity on the bench and the total involvement in the game was the same for him as it was for Mark Howe (below, left) and for Marty his sons playing next to him.

WILLIE SCHAEFFLER

"My competitive sport life in Germany was built around ski racing, soccer and motorcycle racing. I wanted to come to the United States in 1938. Several of my friends had already come as ski instructors, but this was denied by the German passport office, which ruled that I was ready and able to serve in a war if there was a war. Another reason I did not emigrate in 1939 was because my father was a PU, a *political unsafe,* because my family would not support the Nazi Party. Later when Hitler attacked Russia on a two-thousand-mile front, he needed everyone even the political unsafes because of his enormous casualties."

We were roommates, snowed in at a world ski championship in Portillo, Chile, when Willy's voice came down in the dark from an upper bunk as he began the story which finally ended last summer on the eve of Lake Placid as he walked the green mountain trails to inspect the women's courses for the Olympic Games.

"The physical training my parents gave me and the beliefs I experienced in childhood extended right through to the action in battle when in those seconds after being hit I had only one thing to believe in. My own body. My own strength, the conviction that I would make it, that I would hold together. There was no panic. I believed it. It came true. It was not so much a miracle to me as a gift—a return for my original faith in fitness. It always helped me recuperate faster than the average person did. The will is so strong and the body is so prepared—*that you can do it!*

"I was repeatedly wounded during the war on the Russian front over a period of twenty months. My recuperation extended to ten different field hospitals all across the occupied eastern countries and Germany as well as the underground organization in Austria. The first four injuries came deep inside Russia and I could not be taken out and had to recuperate as we went from one small field camp to the next. It was the 21st of June 1941, when I was sent to the Russian front. That summer, the long winter and late into the following summer, I fought along the front and I spent an additional four months in Russia because I had lost too much blood and I could not be moved out.

"The first injury was hand-grenade shrapnel in the right knee. Then I had a bullet wound in the side of my left knee. A tougher one was the third injury, a pistol bullet in the back of the neck between my second and third vertebrae fired from twenty feet away. It was lodged there and doctors in the medical tent on the line removed it. We were surrounded; if I stayed I would have become a prisoner. I decided to risk the loss of blood and move out. On the third day I began the journey holding a huge compress against my wound as I marched.

"The fourth injury was general shrapnel all over the body, and in the fifth injury, the most difficult, the shrapnel came between my ribs through the top of my right lung and entered the upper right muscle of the heart. The piece from a Russian panza grenade, about the size of the nail on my small finger, was lodged in the heart. The metal, I later learned, moved with the beat of the heart, and this had not been seen before. The piece of shrapnel stayed in my heart until 1974, when Denton Cooley removed it in my first open heart surgery because it had finally damaged the valves.

"Dr. Cooley could never understand how I lived with the shrapnel lodged in the heart for thirty-two years and certainly could not understand how I continued my twenty miles of skiing a day every winter and the mountain climbing in summer. The shrapnel never bothered me during those years. They would have left it in until they found that my control valve was completely destroyed and not functioning so the blood was not oxygenized as it did not go through the lung. The difficulty only first became apparent in 1973 after the Winter Games in Sapporo when I became short of breath. Up until that year when I was fifty-two, I had been doing everything my ski team racers were doing on the mountain, and with the extensive system of exercises all year long.

"When the pistol bullet hit me in the neck it was like being hit with a sledgehammer. I was unconscious for a day and a half. No one knew if there was any nerve damage. The headache was agonizing. I had to move on foot at first, later in the troop train.

"On the Russian front the hospital train was a long line of freight cars with hospital beds in it. The beds were stacked three tiers high, with a nurse or two attendants for each car. One day in November of 1943 the engine of the train was blown up and derailed. It was twenty below zero, near Rzhev, west of Moscow. Guerrillas came through the train and threw grenades under the beds or strafed the soldiers in each bed with automatic rifles, the short Russian gun that held about seventy-two rounds in one drum. They killed most all of the wounded that day. When they turned to spray my top bunk they hit but missed killing me. They then set the train on fire but somehow the car I was in did not burn and I crawled out and waited in the snow for a day and a night. The German rescue train came in and picked a few of us up and it took *five months* to work our way back to Sokolov near Warsaw in Poland, moving me from one field hospital to another as my strength allowed.

"As I recovered I was briefly trained with other wounded for the bomb detail, defusing bombs that had hit but not exploded from the heavy air attacks. From here I worked into the underground and finally up to St. Anton to train the ski battalions and ski guides. We worked to destroy communication lines and block tunnels so they could not bring in tiger tanks and 88 antiaircrafts through the mountain roads. I was happy to be back in my element again, and in a way this was my escape from the war the year before it ended.

"After the war I had run the ski school in Garmisch with the American army for three years where I met my future wife, the daughter of an American colonel. I was working with the racers for the 1948 U.S. Olympic ski team, who were chosen entirely from army personnel. It was an excellent opportunity to train the team members and to train myself, because in those days the training methods were different than they are today. The coach in teaching on the mountain would do everything *first*. Then the racers would follow. In training downhill, I would run the course first as the racers watched from points along the course, then I would go to the top and the entire team would follow about thirty feet apart on a downhill run. This was a total disaster because only the pupil who was immediately behind me could benefit. No one else learned anything—the rest were lost in snow spray.

"The coaches were very physical because everything you wanted to teach you had to do first—and *perfectly* if you wanted them to learn to do it well. There were a few alpine ski-racing events in Germany after the war and I continued to compete in the hopes of making the 1948 Olympic team, but the International Olympic Committee notified us in 1947 that they had turned down any chance for the Germans to participate in the Games. As soon as I heard this I decided to go to the United States because I would be too old to race in the next Olympics.

"I finally came to the States in 1948, was married in Washington, and took one of the many ski-school jobs offered. It was at Arapaho Ski Basin outside Denver, and as I was clearing trails alone with a horse I bought for five bucks that first summer, I was also offered the coaching job at the University of Denver. I took it and held both jobs, because of the limited salaries, for twenty-one years.

"In those twenty-one years I helped produce winning teams. My racers won seventeen national championships for the University of Denver, fourteen for the NCAA. During the first twelve years I competed myself and won the senior national championship in eight of those years.

"I was fortunate that a major series of articles in *Sports Illustrated* placed me in the sporting limelight in skiing. The story was called 'Revolution in Skiing,' and I introduced the new Austrian ski system to the United States, where the old stem christie turns were replaced with the new swing turn, called *wedeln*. The story helped recreational skiing by presenting the system in America the same year the Austrians released it, and it had a tremendous effect on ski racing. In 1960 at Squaw Valley when Jean Varnet won the downhill using the extreme tuck position of the French team, skiing had realized the two major changes that took it into the modern era of technique, style and speed.

"My involvement with the world ski organization began with success at home on the local level. As coach of the championship team each year I was responsible for putting on the winter carnival at the University of Denver. I developed my own systems for efficiency and accuracy, safety and course preparation, and each season the meet that we hosted at the university was by far the best, and the word got around.

"In 1958 I was hired by the Squaw Valley Olympic organization committee to become director of skiing and the layout of all alpine courses for the 1960 Olympic Games as well as cross-country and biathlon runs. During the twelve years since coming to the United States I had been in close contact with the ski instructors in Europe and realized how far ahead of us the Europeans were in technical skills. Skiing in America got a tremendous boost with the twenty million viewers who watched the Olympic Games from Squaw Valley on CBS television. The network paid fifty thousand dollars for the rights to televise the event. Twenty years later ABC Sports paid twenty-five million dollars to telecast the thirteenth Winter Games from Lake Placid.

"I left my coaching position at Denver to become head coach of the national team for the 1972 Olympics in Sapporo, Japan. I had served on the FIS world body since 1959 and the International Alpine Course Approval Committee, a unique job, the only one of its kind, where I traveled all over the world to inspect and advise on how to cut ski runs and how to lay them out. I advised on all safety equipment. Good racing trails are automatically good recreational trails, which is economically important with less and less real estate available. We have not established a new ski area since 1973 in the United States.

"In May of 1974 I went into the hospital for the first time since the war. I had carried the shrapnel in my heart for over thirty years but now gradually in the past two years I had experienced shortness of breath and I was very pale, which suggested an oxygen problem. They did a full exploratory, which left me very weak. They removed shrapnel from my elbow and repaired a damaged nerve. In late October, Dr. Cooley performed my initial open heart surgery, inserting a Cooley valve into the blocked heart passage, and removed the piece of Russian shrapnel.

"After the surgery I felt improved and on the 15th day of December, five weeks later, I skied for the first time and got hit on my blind side by a hot-dog skier who jumped a road and sliced my shoulder half off. I lost a half gallon of blood internally and spent twenty-one days in the hospital. Then in May of 1975 in San Francisco the mechanical valve broke up and started to drift through my system. They performed an emergency.

"I became a medical wonder because no one had survived a failure of a heart valve and lived. In the emergency operation they replaced the damaged valve with the actual heart valve of a three-year-old pig. It was a nine-hour operation, and within two of those hours I drowned in my own blood five times. I was conscious and aware of it. I died five times, it seemed, entering a tunnel of peaceful darkness, and then came out to the light and then in again as the blood took me under. I was unconscious for three days after the operation.

"When I regained consciousness I was greeted with the news that during the operation I had lost the pumping part of the original valve, a plastic disc about the size of a dime, and it was floating somewhere in my body. They could not locate it with X rays.

"Sixteen days later I flew to Texas and Denton Cooley put me back in emergency and found the broken valve disc in ten minutes using sonar instruments and said he had to operate immediately. This stunned me because at the time I was not fit nor ready for more surgery.

"The disc had been found in the aortic junction, and Dr. Cooley warned that it could be moving anywhere in the body, from the brain to the blockage point of a main artery. He set the surgery for two days later. I argued that I was in no condition mentally or physically to undergo a second open heart operation. He warned of the difficulties and the risk in delaying. I told him that I could only do it if I was in the best physical shape possible and that I would return to Denver for my downhill walks and I would decide, despite the dangers in delaying, if I could get ready physically and mentally.

"After two weeks in Denver I went to San Francisco to Dr. Frank Gerbode, who had done the 'miracle' operation five weeks before. Dr. Gerbode is the chief surgeon and chief cardiologist at the Pacific Medical Center. Three days later he completed the four-and-a-half-hour operation and removed the lost disc.

"I had started my return to fitness working on my leg muscles with the downhill walks. After the impact of the back-to-back surgery I could not risk any exercise that taxed the cardiac-vascular system. My plan was to walk *down* California Street from Nob Hill to Union Square and take the Powell Street trolley up to the top, then walk down to the bottom again—sometimes six times a day. By walking *downhill* I put pressure only on my muscles and ligaments and tendons, none on my heart. I built my body up slowly without taxing the heart, and this set me up for the operations that followed. It was all will and confidence.

"A few months later I began to ski again, but I was very discouraged. I was not doing well. I was always short of breath and lacked my real strength and agility. Dr. Gerbode did more tests and reached a decision. The pig valve that had been inserted in the second open heart operation to replace the Cooley plastic valve was too small. During my emergency they had thirteen valves available and used the biggest one they had. Their calculation figures the animal valve opening to be three millimeters too small for my capacity and needs in blood and oxygen.

"A pacemaker would probably have killed me, because when it improved the pumping action of the heart the blood would still not have gotten through. We needed a bigger pig.

"Dr. Gerbode took me up to the farm where they were breeding these medical pigs and I met *my* pig —out of a select group of boys that weighed about a hundred and eighty pounds, had the same pulse and temperature as me—but were all too lazy. The good doctor decided they would have to be moved into my active routine and duplicate my workload. They ran the pigs nine hours a day with an electric cart, and three months later they added these new valves to their medical inventory and chose the biggest one to use on my third open heart operation in August 1977. With an oink oink here and an oink oink there, I'm doing great. Full exercise program, running and skiing ten miles or more over every possible terrain every day all over the world.

"In August of 1979 I had a nuclear pacemaker put in now that the valve opening was correct, and hopefully I'll enjoy long life. There were shadows at times out of the corner of my vision, but none that I turned to face during the long ordeal. By this time I knew the feel of being ready. A few years later I realized no matter how much you think you suffer, how much you think you sacrifice, there are thousands of others who have suffered more, given more. Some men and women who have more hardships to overcome and do overcome them.

"During the last winter at the ski school at Arapaho, I was head coach of the United States Ski team but I spent enough time to work at the school especially with the Vietnam veterans. We had a special program I had developed to teach amputees and wounded soldiers, if possible, how to ski. The army colonel in charge had a conviction that the snow and the peace of the mountain setting could have a great influence on these men and help their rehabilitation, no matter how difficult, if they could learn to ski.

"When I first saw the triple amputees I thought it was impossible. I had to put three volunteer instructors on each man. We were the ones who benefited first. We were tremendously encouraged by the response we got from the soldiers. They had an unbelievable spirit. Singing in the bus when only weeks before their life had been all but ripped away in the most horrible war in Vietnam.

"One afternoon they delivered a special case, a lieutenant who was a quadruple amputee, who had asked to be brought up to learn to ski. I told the men how he had stepped on a mine and lost his arms and legs and most of his hearing and although it seemed impossible, we just had to make the effort to teach him and give him the experience he dearly wanted.

"He had never skied in his life. In the first hour on a gentle slope one of the nurses who was with him described the sky and the scenery, the terrain in front of him. It had taken hours to get him ready; we built a special ramp out of the bus. We used a bullhorn to overcome the hearing problem and attached the skis to his artificial legs. The nurse then told us we would have to guide him and hold him because he was also completely blind.

"We put a skier in front and placed the lieutenant's artificial arms on his shoulders and placed another instructor behind to guide his hips and then talked him along, describing the turns and bumps, trees and changes in the course. Each time a new view came up we described it and after a few days he could sense where the terrain had brought him and what he could 'see.' Skiing helped bring him home. Helped give him a will to live. The smile on his face as he stood in his dark world of brilliant snow was *something*, an expression of joy I will never forget. It took four men to carry him back up the hill for the four or five sixty-yard runs he insisted on making. The psychiatrists in Washington wrote us in praise that this sport had a greater influence in bringing the man back to some normal life than any other.

"I've learned again and again in so many different ways in my lifetime about the human body and how remarkable it is, especially for the athlete. There are a small number that are especially gifted—and they are usually the ones that misuse the body more than the ones who are not as gifted but *want* to be. There have been athletes that could have won Olympic gold medals for the United States but did not want to pay the price. So often the less gifted work harder than those who are overly gifted. In many cases these men and women will beat the more gifted people. One thinks with the talent they possess they don't have to work; the others know they must work to win. These are the valuable people. A coach knows this and he works to encourage each in certain ways as Honoré Bonnet, the great French coach, did to begin the modern era of ski racing.

"The decade from 1968 to 1978, launched by Jean Claude Killy and the French national team, was the television decade where ski racers became superstars. Killy won three gold medals in the three alpine events, downhill, giant slalom and special slalom, at Grenoble, France, in 1968. He came to the United States on a two-million-dollar advertising contract the following year and has grossed more than seven million in less than ten years. The honor of being a great athlete winning Olympic gold medals and being a superstar proved a tremendous incentive to young people and changed the sport of skiing. It grew from a peripheral regional amateur sport to a powerful force in all of sports in the thirty years from 1938 to 1968. In the past ten years top ski racers have become rich. In fifty years skiing has become a two-hundred-million-dollar-a-year international sport, culminating with the 1980 Winter Olympic Games in Lake Placid.

"Ski racing has given birth to a whole industry of merchandising—clothes, equipment and accessories. The racer uses various brand items to which his name is connected in all advertising and promotion and for which he receives lucrative product endorsement fees on skis, boots, bindings, racing pants, parkas, sweaters, jackets, goggles, hats, gloves, poles, skin ointment, ski wax, all of it. The equipment an athlete uses influences the recreational skier, and the safety and style factor has enormous commercial appeal—and is continuously changing.

"The past ten years have seen an explosion in cross-country skiing to where there are as many people touring the snow country of America as there are alpine recreational skiers. In some areas it became too crowded or too expensive to ski on alpine equipment and with the national interest in conditioning, cross-country skiing—Nordic skiing—was a perfect winter answer. This is very important in North America because it proves a rebirth of skiing as a national form. Slalom racing began as games played in the woods, turning between the trees on skis. Now a few million Americans every week of the long snow season are using the lightweight shoes and narrow skis for exploring and enjoying the hills and meadows and *exercising*. Cross-country is a superb conditioner for all the family from six to sixty.

"I am chief of the races in Lake Placid and FIS controller of all installations, and all safety devices, including three miles of safety nets that line the difficult sections of the courses and are capable of catching a body at fifty miles an hour to prevent injury on crashes.

"Most of my thoughts while climbing over the hills in summer setting the courses, checking the terrain at Lake Placid, were based on one premise—that unless the guarantee is given by the American government with the permanent funding to have the permanent training center there for all U.S. winter sports *after* the games we will be faced with the same dilemma there afterwards as we were in Squaw Valley, California, after the 1960 Winter games. One of the finest ski jumps in the world, the finest ice arena—all of it will be wasted. The money must be allocated for snow-making equipment and all else that is needed so the truly talented athletes in the United States have the opportunity to excel in winter sports at the world-class level."

The human body is so utterly remarkable that the stamina and strength of an athlete or any man or woman who strives for ideal physical conditioning all his or her life knows almost no limits, or so it seems as the years pass. The heart itself has to be the most amazing and incredible muscle to function without stopping for sixty or seventy years or more. Willy Schaeffler's life is a remarkable example.

Energy for an athlete is a mental energy. Desire is willed. The brain makes the spirit drive, makes the body run, climb, stretch, bend, work. The mind punishes the body of an athlete because it knows in turn a strong body will strengthen the mind. Balance is achieved. Order is gained. The great discipline demanded, however, is that the conditioning, the respect and *care* for the body *never* stop. Only in this way does the spirit stay willing and the energy flow. With the exceptional physical people it seems to flow forever, superhuman in the odds and risks, the tortures the body is made to overcome. The best athletes understand this and it is the human spirit that is praised through time, a spirit which is borne to amazing achievements by superb physical fitness. The athlete proves the human body to be the miraculous machine.

NANCY LOPEZ

"When I started out as a kid I was skinny and I could move easily. I was good in gymnastics, especially on the beam and the horse, and fast enough in track and swimming, but when I picked up a golf club I found it took a great deal more to hit a golf shot than to work on the balance beam or to swim or run. I liked that. I wanted to work hard to hit that ball because it *was* hard to hit that ball up in the air. When I finally got it up it was a great satisfaction.

"I remember playing on the municipal golf course I grew up on in my tenth year. There is this par three with a line of trees in the middle of the fairway and I had to use a driver to get over the trees. I kept trying and trying, moved up to a four wood, but it took me *two years* to finally get it over those trees. Now I can hit a wedge to that hole. I think because golf was so demanding and because I had to work so hard to accomplish something in golf was why I really stayed with it. There has always been something new, demanding and testing every day I play.

"When I had to give up swimming because it wasn't good for my golfing muscles I began to think of what else I would have to sacrifice if I wanted to keep playing golf. In the years between ten and thirteen I gave up many things so I could just play golf.

"I think that some people's muscles and bones and body are not able to swing a golf club. The coordination is not there. They may be very well coordinated for other things but they can't hit a golf ball. I *never* had a professional golf lesson, so when I first picked up a golf club I imitated my dad. Whatever I saw, I tried to do. Whether I was doing the right thing or not it was working. My dad gave me the first rule: *Always hit the ball.* When you're beginning you usually whiff it a few times or top it—but Dad said don't miss it *ever.* I concentrated so hard getting that coordination —getting that club face on the ball. When you think of that little ball and that little club head you begin to wonder how in the world do you really hit it.

"When I started to swing a golf club it was all natural. I swing in a way that felt good. Many of the professionals said it was terrible but I could hit the ball and that was what my dad told me to do. That's what I grew up doing. I hit the ball any way I could, any swing I had. I had a real bad grip but it was the best way I could hold onto the club.

"As the years went by they all said the same thing —'Oh, she should take a lesson, she should change her grip and her swing or she will never be any good.' I never listened to those people. If I ever tried to change I couldn't hit the ball. It would be somebody else's swing, not mine. That's the trouble with most golfers. They go out and take a lesson and try to imitate someone else, instead of doing what feels good to them. They start thinking about keeping their elbow straight, the right elbow tucked . . . not for me. All the time I played I just hit it the best way I could and gradually I learned to hit different shots.

"My whole swing is *feel*. When I drop in on a clinic and hear someone dissecting the various parts of a golf swing, I don't understand what they're talking about. When I wanted to hit that ball higher over those trees I just kept working to get it up. It was all feel. In the beginning I would tee the ball up all the way down the fairway. I felt the tee was going to give me elevation. It worked sometimes. For a beginner, hitting a ball that is lying on the ground is very difficult. It's much easier to hit a ball off a tee. After doing this for a year my dad cautioned that when I played in a tournament I couldn't tee it up on every shot, so I learned to get it up with my swing.

"In 1959 I had won the women's state amateur tournament. I was just twelve, and my dad introduced me to Lee Trevino when he came to play in New Mexico and suggested that Lee change my swing but he refused. 'You can't argue with success,' he said. 'Don't change it until it stops working!' This became my second rule: *Change only if something stopped working. That's what I stuck with.*

"I finally gave in to the criticism and decided to change my grip. I had a widespread grip with my left index finger down the shaft of the club. I thought I could change and bring it together all at once, but you can't, you have to work on it for years. With my old grip I was shooting 39s and low 40s. When I changed my grip I went up to 45–47. 'If you try to change that fast you'll drop back two years,' my dad warned. So I have been working on it slowly, just by feel.

"Strangely I found I was so unorthodox I was backwards. Most people roll their hand under to slice but I found that didn't work for me. I had to put my hand *over* to slice it. The low shot is natural for me, I hit it well into a wind. Now I'm getting more elevation and it is becoming my natural shot. Early on when I hit my very low shot I used to have to aim

it at the next fairway in order to place it on the fairway I was on. *I played with that!* I got to the finals playing that way at the Women's Western when I was fifteen years old and on tee shots or fairway shots I would do the same thing—face the wrong way. Of course if there were trees on the left I could go around the trees. It took me a long time to straighten out my slice. I had no lessons, so I worked it out myself.

"I like to get up early when I play so I can move slowly. When I rush in the morning I take that out on the golf course and I rush all day long. I find the way you wake up in the morning is usually the way your day is. If you're calm and normal your swing is slower and you're not anxious to hit the next shot. I find sometimes that I'm anxious to hit the next shot and that's terrible.

"Trouble doesn't upset me anymore. In the beginning if I sprayed shots I'd get scared of what was to come. Now I don't. I've made par from strange places. Anything can happen in golf. Whenever I'm in trouble I feel I can punch it out, get up on the green and get the par. You have to do that enough and succeed so that you have that confidence. Many times I didn't do it because I panicked and ended up with a bogey or a double bogey.

"Dad always told me you can make a par from anywhere. If you get into trouble, *get out.* I can hear him, 'I don't care if you have to chip out—just get out of trouble. Save the bogey if you're in trouble but *never* get into greater trouble.'

"I remember it took me five strokes once to get out of a bunker and my dad said later all he could see was sand pouring out and after I hit the fourth shot I looked over at him and he just shrugged and put his hands to the sky. When I finally got out he told me, 'Next time get out on the first shot—even if you blast it over the green!' From that day it never has taken me two shots to get out of a sand trap.

"In golf the key shot is the tee shot. That first shot determines the way the rest of the hole is going to go, mainly because the second shot is usually long. There is just not that much trouble you can get into around the green on your second shot except a bunker. But on the tee shot if your drive lands behind a tree there is no way you can get to the green. Because I hit long and straight, the tee shot is my strength.

"I feel I hit the ball very straight. When I play in tight fairways it doesn't bother me—but I still need the practice round to get my confidence that I'm still hitting the ball straight. There's more pressure on a tight golf course. On a tight course a golfer like Jo Anne Carner won't do well, but give her a wide-open course and she has the best chance to win it. She will not play at all when there are too many out-of-bounds. She sprays the ball and hits it so far that she needs the room. You tend to get careless on wide-open courses. Growing up on a wide-open course I had to discipline myself by pretending the rough was out of bounds.

"My greatest strength on the golf course is my ability to hit the ball long and straight, consistently straight. You hit yourself into a bunker because you're thinking about it. If you take those bunkers out of your mind and just *see* the green, you'll hit the green. When I was growing up anger used to ruin me. I would get very angry and I would cry. My dad said, 'You can't see the ball when you cry.' So I stopped crying when I got into trouble. My dad never forced me to play, but he showed me the way. I learned to go out and shoot what I wanted to shoot —a 39 or a 40. That made a big difference—*one shot.* When I was mad I would shoot 40. When I was cool I would shoot 39. I learned there wasn't any sense getting mad at myself when it affected my play and added strokes. You need a certain kind of *good anger* that takes away strokes in tournament play.

"If you play a course that has few birdie holes it usually means the course is long, and I like it that way because I hit long and will have a better chance of winning the tournament. When the greens are smaller I think they are better than large greens because when you're playing on a golf course with large greens you have a tendency to shoot for the safest part of the greens. Big greens make you lazy, you don't work as hard. Growing up on a golf course with small greens was an advantage for me—I always went for the pin. I still do.

"In putting you hate to leave it short. When you leave it short most of the time you're right in line with the hole, right in, that's what is so aggravating.

"The thing that bugs me the *most* on a golf course is a green that won't bite. You can hit a perfect shot

very easy. I would grab a club—the right club—hit the ball—right by the hole—hit a putt—in! Amazing! It seemed like nobody was really competing against me. It was such a super feeling to know no one was going to catch me; that the other women

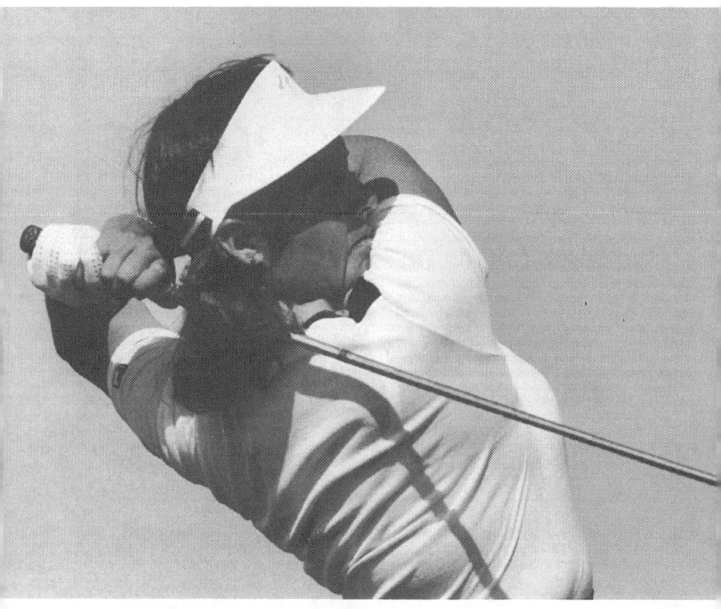

and it ends up over the green. That makes me mad.

"I have a killer instinct. I hunger for that good shot out there. When you hit that golf ball it feels good. The first year I felt sorry for some of the girls that weren't playing well when I was playing well. But when the tables are turned and they're ahead of you they don't feel sorry for you at all.

"When I was winning those five straight tournaments in 1978 it was like I was all by myself. It was

came to play to try to stop Nancy Lopez from winning instead of going out to win the golf tournament. You can't do that. You have to play the golf course and concentrate on your own game.

"After I won the five in a row on the tour I returned home to Hershey, Pennsylvania, and played horribly. Mentally I was tired, my concentration was terrible, and because I lost my concentration I lost my confidence. Without concentration you can't get the ball in the hole. A loss of confidence takes weeks to get back. It's hard to take bad shots out to the golf course. You must find out what you are doing wrong before you go out on a golf course, because you won't find your confidence out there.

"The competition with women is very good, but the competition with men is greater because there are so many more men on the tour that they have to depend on their short game to make the difference between winning and losing. We can take a bogey on a woman's round and still come back, but men, when they make a bogey, will have someone advance on them. So they depend more on their chipping and putting, and I think they're much better at it.

"The Ladies Professional Golf Tour is not normal as a life-style. A great many young girls come out on the tour for the limelight and luxury. When I was an amateur I would look at the golf bags of the professionals and wish I had a big golf bag and all those people chasing after me. It's not like it seems. I knew it wasn't luxurious, I gave it a good look and I could tell, and I'm glad I went to college for two years first.

"I think so many girls are still on the tour because they have nowhere to go. They're not making any money on the tour. You have to *average* five hundred to six hundred dollars a week to break even. That's got to be tough on your mind. I pay for my transportation, my air fare, my room and board, my caddy Roscoe, my registration fee and the clothes to wear.

"Because I won it has been great for me. Commercials, endorsements, lots of money. I love everything that's happened to me, but you have to give back a lot too, you just don't take. When I first came out on the tour I knew that's all I was going to do the rest of my life, *golf, golf, golf*. Only recently did I reason that golf can't be your entire life, because you do reach the time when you can't play well anymore. You reach that point and you're *alone*. You don't have anybody. You've wasted all those years you could have found somebody. When you're young it's easier to find somebody than when you get older, and I know many girls just stay on the tour because they don't have anybody. Golf is what they have and that's it. The hard and worn look. They don't have anyone to go home to.

"Some girls qualify and they come out for the limelight and they can't break 80. My scoring average is 70.4, and I'm making a lot of money playing on the tour. But if you look at the girls averaging 75, they're not making very much. One shot makes a big difference. The ones that are shooting 80 can't live out there.

"I feel very lucky I have a good husband and to be married at twenty-two. It is hard for a woman in sports. When they are in the limelight, they are put in a different category—where men don't ask them out. I don't think that I am better than anyone else, but the men look at us and I sense that they say, 'Maybe she's too good for me . . . if I ask her out she might say no.' Then the poor guy really feels bad.

"I know how it feels. A few guys would ask me out and I began to worry if they wanted to date me for who I was and what I had instead of asking me as a person. There is a delicate problem which we can't solve on the golf tour. We're there one week and gone the next. I think it is more difficult under this arrangement for a woman than a man. A man can go out at night with a woman and be gone the next week but a woman can't.

"Love is very important in my life. I was loved by my parents. Mom was really the lady that controlled the house. Never let me wear jeans until my senior year in high school. She insisted I wear dresses and keep a clean house. I vowed I would never be like my mother, but I am. I'm very normal.

"It is amazing the things I've learned in a few years as an athlete being approached by different people. Because I was so *normal* before I have a good perspective and I can compare now. The difference is really amazing. It makes me mad to see how normal people are treated and the way I'm treated now. I was in that *nobody* situation so now I want to give my attention to all the people that I see. I want to stand there and sign every autograph, but I can't sign them all no matter how long I stand there.

"Being out on the tour, I want to show people athletes are normal. The athletes that are very good don't snub the people that they are really like. My husband's a sincere guy and the kind of person I can live with. As an athlete I am two people. I have to keep up an image when I go out, but I love to come home and be normal.

"I'm Mexican-American. If I go into a restaurant or public place and people don't recognize me they treat me as a nobody. But as soon as someone whispers, 'That's Nancy Lopez, the golfer,' they change. They're on their hands and knees. This really turns me off. I like the respect. I like it very much, but I'm sensitive to how I was treated before, and it's too bad the situation exists. I don't know how other athletes feel but I resent it.

"On the golf course the people that come out are wonderful. The young ones, the old ones, especially the men. I like that the most. When the men come up and ask me for my autograph, I think that's grand. I'm not into women's lib or anything—because I don't really understand it—but when a man has been walking the course during the tournament and he comes up and asks me for my autograph—that's an honor for me. *That's* a great moment."

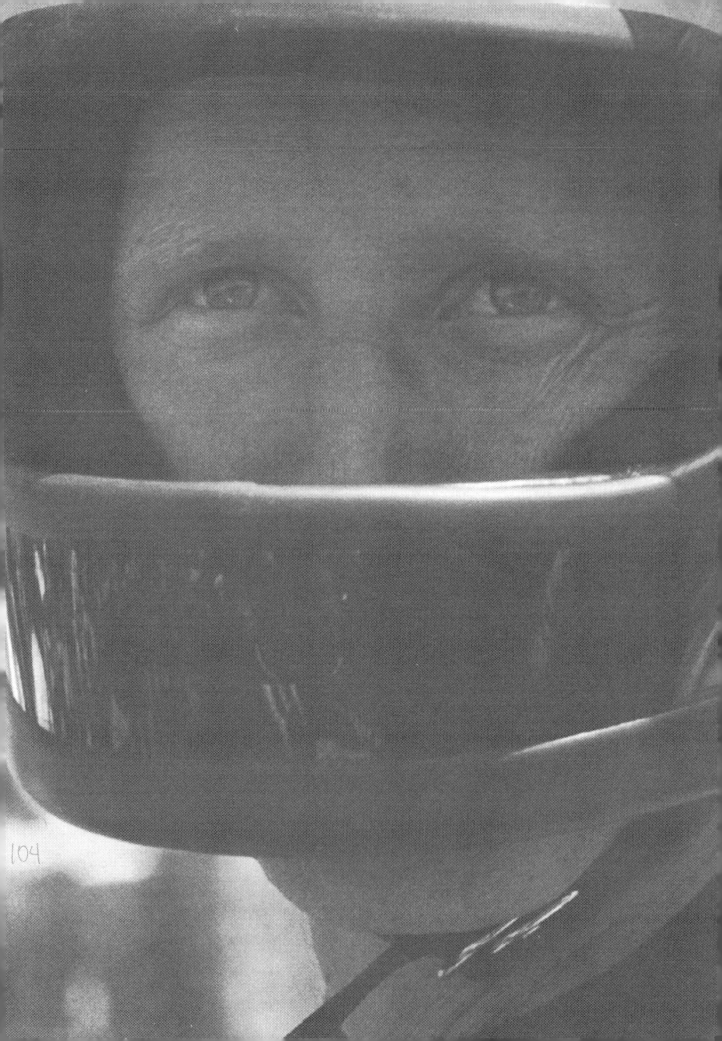

104

KENNY ROBERTS

"My whole world is concentration on one thing—making that motorcycle go as fast as I can make it go around the racetrack. *Concentration* is what makes some guys fast and some guys slow. The concentration I bring to a forty-five minute grand prix race is exhausting. I am mentally shot and can barely talk or make sense after a race. It takes three days for me to get back to my normal life-style because it drains me completely.

"Before a race I build my concentration for the start three hours before I leave the line. Concentration keeps the motorcycle on the road. If that concentration leaves me for a fraction of a second—I have traveled two hundred, three hundred feet at 150 mph, and that guardrail is only thirty feet away. If I lose my concentration I'm dead. I race my 500cc cycle aware that my life depends on it.

"You can be a little lax on a slow corner going forty miles per hour, but the S turns at 180 mph and the complicated turns, turns that set up turns that follow, demand the most accurate awareness of speed and the most critical judgment to stay alive.

"I have no speedometer. If I go through turn three too fast on some racetracks I'll never be able to set up in time for turn four and I'll be dead by turn five. If a rider miscalculates on judgment and speed—there's no coming back.

"A motorcycle is an extension of the rider. I am the balancing factor to my motorcycle. Racing is a duel with gravity—the lower you keep the center of gravity, the faster you can go around a corner. Road racing is not as rough as motocross, but when you're going 180 mph it takes a lot of balance. My bike is very light and I can do a lot of different things with it. But there is a certain technique required to ride a motorcycle—you just don't get on one and ride.

"My motorcycle is fitted to me. So much has to do with the seat height and the foot pegs and their relationship to each other. The distance from the handlebars to the seat is critical. I have to have just enough reach that I can lay down, but not too much that I can't sit up when I'm braking. The front end must be equal to the back end and the six gears must work smoothly—everything must be just right.

"You must always be perfectly under control. It takes a great deal of force to make that motorcycle do something it doesn't want to do because of the gyro force the wheels generate at that speed. The wind has got the fairing and it's got you and it does not want to be disturbed. You must have good fore-arms and shoulders to force that motorcycle where it has to go.

"When you go into an S you enter in different ways. The first thing I do is to get the bike on its right side. That doesn't take much force. You're on the left edge of the road and you lean to the right. The work comes in getting that motorcycle from the forty-five-degree angle, and sometimes more, *back* to vertical and into the opposite angle in the time I have. You can't do this without great force. I've actually picked the entire front end up at 180 mph and forced it around. I've actually pulled the bolted handlebars in—*moved them*—forcing the bike through a turn. You can bang those handlebars that are bolted to the fork with a hammer when the bike is in the pits and they won't move—but I've moved them in a race!

"It takes a fine line when you're racing through a difficult S turn at 180 mph. To maneuver at top speed means you have to go as close as you can to the guardrail on the right going in then as close as you can to the guardrail on the left and come out on the guardrail on the right. You've got about forty feet to do that in, that's how wide the racetracks are. But a motorcycle doesn't want to go right, left, right. You have to force it. If I want the bike to turn left, I'm going to push and pull on the right handlebar, then push and pull on the left one because a motorcycle at that speed doesn't react just by leaning. You have to force it somehow. If you don't force it—or you can't—you won't make it through the turn, you'll hit the rail.

"I have only *two inches* of steering on my bike. You can't turn it around in a normal strut. Any miscalculation in a turn, any misjudgment of a breaker marker—any mistake in turning can be fatal. You must have total concentration and awareness of the back tire. Going into a turn if that back tire moves one inch, I'm paranoid. I must know it moved and I must know exactly why and how—and there better be a reason. Once you lose track of what that rear wheel's doing you're on your face. To be a motorcycle rider in grand prix racing you have to have a maximum hundred percent feeling of those tires on the road to your butt. That's the touch. The only thing that keeps you going are those tires.

"The front tire on a bike is usually much softer than the rear because the rear is transferring all of the power to the road from my 500-cubic-centimeter engine. The rear tire is much bigger. I have different profiles and shapes for the rear tires depending on the traction required. I have thirty-five different tires to choose from at each track in our truck when we go racing. I have rain tires, intermediate tires, hard rain tires, hard intermediate tires, slick intermediate tires, all in different compounds and different constructions. I know which tire will be close on a given track, as does the Goodyear tire technician who travels with us.

"Accelerating out of a turn I can *slide* the rear tire three inches with the power, and that *controlled* slide is part of my style. At that speed not many can do it. This is different than the broadslide in dirt-track racing. There you slide the bike under power going into a turn to stop or you are under power exiting a turn and the bike is going sideways—a broadslide—where the back end is trying to come around and pass the front. You can do that on a dirt track because you have a lot of steering lock and you're sitting up on the bike and your handlebars are high. You've got a lot of control and you've got your foot down on the dirt for balance. In roadracing there's all kinds of traction because you're on pavement, and you're laying on the motorcycle so you don't have that flexibility. On roadracing circuits when the bike does go sideways more than four or five inches it's going to spit you off—right over the handlebars—and there's nothing you can do about it. I've been pitched over the bars and down the road because I neglected that back tire for one second. There are only two riders in the world who can control a slide in roadracing, me and Gennio Ferrari.

"In grand prix motorcycle racing we race one forty-five-minute race. Each rider on that racetrack has a different style. One rider will lean off the bike and drag his knee. I developed that style. One rider will stay straight up and down. One rider will lean the opposite way—whatever they feel comfortable with and do best for maximum speed with control through the turns. In the photographs at right you see how my knees and legs adjust depending on the lean and speed of the bike.

"The more comfortable you feel on a motorcycle the faster you go. When you start feeling uncomfortable you're going too fast. It's a mental thing. A lot of guys can go past the edge and not realize it.

"The crowds for motorcycle racing in Europe are amazing in size. We get crowds of 175,000 people at a grand prix in Ossen in Holland, the Belgium Spa, or in the Nurburgring in Germany or in the Terrane in Spain and certainly at Le Mans in France. In Sweden, Finland and England the crowds are wild.

"Most tracks in Europe are designed for grand prix racing, and the fans are dedicated. The television and press coverage is so extensive that I was twice as famous in Europe after one year as I was in America in seven years. Europeans are just natural motor-racing buffs. They don't drive with speed limits on their highways but they drive fast and safely. They know how to drive fast. They appreciate someone that can do what I can do or the other top racers and they get a big kick out of that. They know a great deal of technical information about motorcycles and that helps them enjoy racing more. There are people walking around the racetrack who look exactly like I do; they have my leathers, my helmet, and they have a Yamaha cycle. They feel like me, want to *be* like me, and it is a sport where they feel they can be.

"I also do a variety of things on a racetrack that entertain people. The Europeans didn't see 'wheelies' until the Americans came over. They had never seen a bike with the front end off the road *going at a hundred miles an hour!* In Italy there is a grandstand going into the front straightaway, coming out of a low-gear corner, that seats about thirty thousand people, just in one bleacher section. I have picked my front end up and carried it at speed about five hundred yards past that crowd and they go *crazy.* You would think from the roar there was a twenty-man pileup in the middle of the straight. A wheelie dazzles them because they know they can't do it and they don't know how I can. I pick the wheel up in first or second gear and I'll be in fourth gear sometimes when I hit the ground.

"Financially I have never had any problems on the racetrack. Yamaha has sponsored me since I was nineteen. At the end of 1979 I will have made over two million dollars. This is the first week in June and I've earned six hundred thousand since my accident in February. But it isn't that easy for all the riders. Like any sport it is the people who are really doing it that are making the money. Those in the limelight. I've never had any money problems. I've never worked for a living.

"As far as racing tactics are concerned, passing is very easy on a motorcycle because you've got a lot more room except on S turns. In an S turn you cannot pass another bike. You must clip all guardrails at each apex by a half inch. There's no room on either side. In a 250-cc race last year in Onsen my bike didn't start on the line in a drizzle rain. When I did get it started the last bikes in the field of thirty were fifty yards down the track. When I came around after the first lap of the four-mile course I had picked up twenty-six bikes and was in fourth place. I passed twenty-six riders on one lap. Four laps later I was leading. It is not hard to pass on a motorcycle, but you have to know *who* you are passing. You just don't run on the outside of somebody not knowing that he makes a late brake.

I am very mental on racing. I have improved my lap time by coming off the track and sat in the truck for an hour, covered up with tires so no one could see me, and I have replayed every inch of that course in my mind, then gone back out and on the next practice lap I've knocked off *four seconds*. It's all mental. Once I get the racetrack in my head I can 'race' on it without the motorcycle. I can improve my lap times because I know what I can do with my machine. When I went to Europe last year to face all the European riders I had to beat all of them but I had never raced on any of their tracks. We only get about twenty laps of practice—two hours—under the rules when we arrive at each track. You've got to program the racetrack in your head.

"When I arrive at practice at a new circuit in Europe I like to get off the line about fourth or fifth and follow the smart riders around the track. I follow one through turn five. Maybe he's got a better line through there than I figured and I'm going to know it. I'm going to follow him in six and seven and learn something and then figure exactly where I can make my move on a part of the course where he cannot follow me too closely to follow *my* line. Once he finds my line then I've got to fight him for every inch.

"You can bounce around in dirt-track racing but in road racing winning is a precise line through each corner. I miscalculated last year on one turn and I ended up with a concussion. I was testing tires and I tried to learn the track too quickly.

"I was going about eighty mph in practice and was lucky it was not a real fast corner. I was aware I had gone in a little too hot—too fast. I had misjudged it. I had the bike leaned over and there's nothing I can do at that point. I can't steer it or stop it when it is laying on its side at eighty mph.

"In less than a tenth of a second I decided, rather than lay it all the way over and fall down, I would pick it up and go off the track—since as soon as you straighten the bike up you stop turning and go off. Then in the next split second I was aware of trying to refocus from the road to some point on the rail in the crowd. At that degree of concentration focusing becomes a deliberate switchover—and I did not have time—and all I saw was hay bales. Now, off the road, I decided to lay it down. I hit the fence and woke up in a hospital with a concussion. Not bad.

"I raced two days later.

"In the winter of 1979 I had my most serious accident. In February I was testing one of the Yamaha factory machines, one of the five bikes they make. Their test course in Japan is a high-speed circuit and this was the first year I tested on it and I wanted to learn the course and break a lap record. I went into a 130-mph righthander a little too far inside trying to avoid a little hole in the track. At 130 mph a little bump is a big thing and if you can avoid them so much the better. I went in hot and a little low with a full lean but the engine cases were not touching the track surface. When they touch it picks both wheels off the ground and away you go. I can tell on my bike when I kiss it which will be so light a touch as not to pick up the wheels.

"I had the room so I leaned it over a little more and the front wheel washed out! The track was a little slippery just in that spot. I went down, pushed clear of the machine and went flying on my bunzie on a slide that covered three hundred yards and as I sailed over the ground I went into a rag-doll pose —completely relaxed—the only way I knew to save myself, to keep from breaking myself in half.

"As I spun I backed into the wall with my butt and I felt my back go. It smashed my eleventh and twelfth vertebrae, ruptured my spleen, paralyzed my insides, broke my left ankle and cut me up and hurtled me straight up in the air. When I landed on the road it knocked the wind out of me. It seemed forever and while I lay gasping I thought I might not get it back—this may be it. Suddenly I got it back but I had great trouble breathing. I knew then my insides were goofed up. I was conscious the entire time. I saw everything happen.

"I lay in the hospital for a month. The doctors said eight weeks before I could think about exercising. I could not be put in traction because I had smashed two vertebrae and so I lay in the hospital bed for eighteen days before I started to move. They took me to the hospital on February 3. I told the doctor that the first grand prix of the year was in Austria on February 29, I had to be there. Twenty-six days. 'No way,' was his answer. 'In three weeks you will not even be out of bed.' Six weeks later to the day I was racing a motorcycle.

"Eighteen days after the crash the first X rays showed I had healed. When they viewed the two pieces of film side by side no one could believe it. I heal very quickly—most athletes do. Part of it is condition but most of it is *willpower*. I wasn't strong, I needed three months to get the muscles in shape— but I was ready to ride.

"I rode for ten laps in the States before I left for Austria to see what the pain would be like. The next time I got on a bike was on the starting line of the Austrian Grand Prix, and I won. I finished second in Germany the next race and then won the next two races in Italy and Spain. I'm leading again and I hope to retain the world championship I won last year when I became the first American ever to win the world title.

"I'm crazy, they say, but I'm fast, lucky, and I've had a good trip."

Part 2
DOCUMENTARY PHOTOGRAPHS

The pictures for me are a breath of life. They are a tribute to the athlete and the infinite variety of his skills within the sanity of athletic competition.

They are an overwhelming tribute to his strength and the grandeur of his efforts. They are a tribute to his relationship with his fellow men within the rules of the contests he has designed, most of which have endured unchanged for a hundred years. They are a tribute to the animals he has bred and the machines he has made for his world of sport. One man alone, man and animal, man and machine, women in sports. The fusion and conflict are here.

The dedication of man involved in sport has al-

ways endured. It is the freest expression of his existence. Over the years the record of this world of action has never been explored. It has been touched on often by the painter and by the sculptor, but only as a gesture, a peripheral glance—a Degas horse, a Lautrec jockey, a Bellows fighter, or an Eakins boatsman. The pictures were often passive and somewhat distant. They were reflections of memory rather than experience. They were faithful to the laws of art, not necessarily to the forces of sport. In the first half of the century, black-and-white photographs began to search out and find the beginnings of this intimate world of dedication.

SMALL MIRACLE

The world is a great picture. The texture of each land of each day of all people moving through a moment of their lives is a great picture—if you see it just right. Photography is a miracle, a phenomenon, a delight. Photographing the drama of sports is fascinating.

To be universally understood a photograph, like a painting, must have good drawing. Drawing is the only thing I look for in a picture. If the drawing is not there I pass it by.

When I take a photograph of game action in football I am making an illustration, a representative picture of that game and of all football too. As in art, the photograph must transcend the actual fact. The universality of the picture, its intimate yet heroic scope, will give it clarity and monumental strength.

The so-called technical aspects of photography are quite simple. Exposure is a personal choice to put just so much light on the film. (This is why we squint at a choice subject—adjusting the light so it is just the way we want it. The trick is to get your camera to squint just right and develop the film to hold this light quality.) From the full negative you then personally choose that area for the print as you remembered your subject.

Pro football is my first love. I was interested in the playmaking when I started in 1950, and I established a point of view and gave order to what many people thought was a complicated scramble, before games were televised in 1956. Once I had established this order I could search out the incredible details of the game and the intensity with which it is played. When you communicate this intensity you establish great impact and drama.

Sports photography is simply a matter of marksmanship and intelligence. It demands an inordinate amount of energy and imagination. You cannot possibly photograph a sport unless you understand it completely and understand and know the men who play it.

The indefinable aspect is devotion or caring. The same intensity they have to play the game you must have to record it. Not stop it but suspend it forever in time. This is the whole art. The lens is your eyeball embedded deep in your spirit and experience. It is part of you, not your camera. It sees with you, but instead of recording the flickering images on your brain alone, it puts them on film. When you sense the pulse beat of a sport—are one with it as you shoot—then you are saving forever the significant spirit and movement. The picture has your personality and that of the game actually woven into one creative image.

Sports photography is a matter of intelligence and marksmanship. You have to decide what picture you want of Chris Evert after you watch her play, then go work on that picture. I don't go out and take a random set of pictures of an athlete and hope I get a good one. I conceive the action, set my stage and let the athlete play into it. As I develop pictures on one player or one team or one sport over the years, I change these stages or repeat and modify them. All the accidents and surprises of action happen on these stages. My old pro football pictures express this.

It goes without saying that you need the credentials to get into the position you want, the equipment that is going to work in that position, and then hit with single exposures—the moment you feel best expresses the athlete's strength.

In Chris Evert's case, her strength is her ability to be in position to return a shot, especially to her two-handed backhand.

Does this mean that a picture, using this approach, is limited to only technical or instructional values? On the contrary, with this discipline a sports photograph should offer the best design and structural strength of the human figure because of the control expressed by the athlete playing their best. It should be a synthesis of all of the action of a particular sport and best express the athlete's character—in this case the aggressive style of one of the best women tennis players in the world.

When you watch Chris Evert you see that she is in position and set for a power return, meeting the ball out front, hitting off of her right leg—whether the ball is shoulder-high, waist-high or low.

In the indoor arena you have poor light for color action so you must give away some of the beauty for action—some of the expression in a face for the expression in the body. In pictures of athletes, people care about information—the viewer feels the action and wants to study technique. But the integrity of the picture must not be diminished because it expresses a player's technique—only enhanced as a picture.

This technique must be the controlled style of a particular player. This is why I have devoted my energies over the years to filming and drawing the best athletes. *Best* in the sense of style and ability.

PRACTICE AND PLANNING

The pictures of *practice and planning* are another pattern that I have developed in photographs over the years. The long hours of drills and execution and subtle adjustments make an athlete superior in performance. They are the hours the public never sees. All the dedication and effort, the endless repetition, is what ensures the successful performance the day of the game. The men working together in their sweat suits are one image, but each athlete alone, concentrating on the perfecting of his skills in the shadows of the still and empty grandstands. These are the portraits that have always fascinated me.

The athlete is the most consistent and exciting performer as entertainer in America today. The professional athlete draws the largest audience, more than the actor or singer or musician, and with sports developing into a prime-time commodity on television, he deserves the highest salary. I think once high salaries become normal, the press will devote less attention to contractual or front-office reporting and more to the sport and the athlete's skills. This kind of reporting takes more work.

THE TEAM

Vince Lombardi was a good friend, and I was the only one he permitted to take pictures in his classroom. He was a fine teacher and he would tell you, "Coaching is teaching." On these pages are some of the faces of his men. The pictures were taken within one minute on the bench in St. Louis in 1963. Lombardi thought that this was his best team.

These are the remarkably intense, exhausted faces everyone has heard about—but under the grueling heat of battle, and unmasked for a moment on the bench, who can identify them now? These portraits were taken in the third quarter when Green Bay was leading 23–0, but there is no elation. The smiles and wisecracks and pepperpot shouts are years past. These are veterans suffering a long arduous Sunday afternoon. Vince smiled at me in the dressing room. "They're tougher and we're older."

SAY HEY WILLIE

When I first heard that name
and saw him sitting between the
New York Giants owner Horace
Stoneham and the manager Leo
Durocher signing his contract in
the picture in the morning paper
the romance began.

I would love to watch him from
the time he came down the clubhouse steps in the Polo Grounds
until he ran off. I photographed
him in his rookie year in 1951 and
took over 2,000 pictures of him over
the years. There were some athletes
I enjoyed seeing, some that made
action happen in a special way.
Willie Mays, John Unitas, Jim
Taylor, Bob Cousy and Jean Claude
Killy. I must have taken 10,000
pictures on those five. They would
never cease to amaze me.

I had a bundle on Willie even that
rare shot of a ball hit over his head
in deepest centerfield. It almost
never happened. I have a hundred
of him laughing. I photographed
him like I photographed my own
kids. Willie was a great athlete.

119

COLOR AND DESIGN

I certainly can be called the imperfect photographer. In the early years I would take photo research for my technical stories of drawings on skiing or boxing, baseball or football, and they would run about five stops underexposed. It was in Rome for the 1960 Olympic Games that *Sports Illustrated* photographers John Zimmerman and Jerry Cooke advised me, "Take a little more time—and with all your equipment you can take good photographs when you work on research." I did this, and it proved rewarding. I then began to enjoy taking photographs that were complete in themselves instead of a means to an end.

Technically my demands are quite different from those of the pure photographer. I want *imperfect* pictures, photographs that are not plastic-smooth, excessively sharp. Most of the sports photographs of the 1970s are lens work. You can call the camera and the lens by reading the surface of the picture. Trouble is that eight guys along the sideline all have the same long lens and sports pictures have an alarming sameness. The action is too repetitive, too similar.

I like cameras that are light and simple. A body and a sharp lens. I never use a light meter. I never think about the camera when I'm working. It is an extension of my eye. The current trend in photography today is the excessively sharp picture with extreme depth of field. There is very little depth of field in my pictures, whether the light is f/16 or f/2. I use the light up on the speed side, not the aperture side. In 90 percent of my photographs the depth of field is in inches and I pass this wave of sharpness through the subject's eyes or use it to define the contour of a figure in motion and so make the action of the photograph more graphic, more legible.

The color photograph has not yet arrived as a museum piece, as an exhibition piece. Black-and-white photography is still preferred by museums and galleries. The color photograph for the past twenty years has suffered from the Kodak-style advertising print of blatant clarity and obvious color. More important, color film until 1977 lacked the speed necessary for all sports action. We are entering the color-print era in photography.

In color photography the artist must choose the light for color that will strengthen the design, that will support the mood and not be seen as color applied to an object or a place or a person but color that is discovered deep in the design, as an integral part of the structure of a picture. Color that is studied and enjoyed after one feels the impact of the idea, as one searches out the texture and tones in black and white, after one enjoys the first long moment of emotional response. I feel you should not see the color before the picture. Then the key color will express the mood.

The Athlete presents a number of my early color photographs dating back to 1952 when the speed (ASA) was 10, but features the past year's color work and especially the new 400 ASA color that was introduced by Kodak in May 1977. This amazing color film has the same speed as TRI-X black and white plus a beautiful color range, rich black and only a fine grain. This fast color negative could revolutionize color photography in fine art, especially since the chemistry in color prints is now stable. Most of the engravings in this book were made from prints and not from color transparencies.

All of my recent color work was filmed on negative stock, and I am fortunate to have exceptional prints made by Quality Color Labs in New York. Most editorial magazines are geared for reproductions from transparencies, and the difficulty in shooting negative on assignment is having art directors reproduce from prints instead of the automatic color readings and engravings made when reproducing from slides.

A picture is a frame of life and it is running, always running through the projector which is the artist's being. You never can divorce anything you make from your entire self. Every word of the spoken day, every mark, makes or unmakes character.

Seeing what the other artists have done before you is a continuous river of energy that keeps reminding you of truths. You rush to an exhibit to see the original of Michelangelo's sanguine chalk drawing *Studies for the Libyan Sibyl* and look at it and squint and smile and see that the paper is ten inches high, a page from his pad that looks as if it were drawn this morning. You look at Brassis' photographs of Braque or Picasso in their studios and it *is* this morning, and then you have your coffee. You want to make pictures. *Get out and do it!*

"The greatest thing a human soul ever does in this world is to *see* something, and tell what it *saw* in a plain way. Hundreds of people can talk for one who can think, but thousands can think for one who can see. To see clearly is poetry, prophecy, and religion all in one." John Ruskin wrote today!

COLLEGE SPIRIT

There is no more endearing or enduring spirit in American life than college football. It is a remarkable phenomenon. It is so certain and intoxicating you can drink of it all your life and in any quantity, at any level of competition, at any school with any student body or alumni. It is always golden autumn, crisp and clear and somehow your school will win or at least score. The sound in a college stadium when the athletes come on the field will keep you young forever.

College football are the magic years for some students, contained and beautifully complete. For others, like Heisman Trophy winner Billy Sims of the University of Oklahoma (left) they mark the beginning of a professional career in sports. College athletes have progressed steadily toward equal opportunity, but football has become a salvation for the black athlete in America.

ABC Sports has televised over 700 national and regional college games in the past 15 years, at times to an average ten million families on a Saturday afternoon. College football is lucrative. Upon graduation, halfback Sims was advised to press for a $4.5 million deal with the Detroit Lions just 90 days before the pro season started. He had taken advances from his agent on monies not yet in. Values change for the college athlete. Life changes.

FINE WOMEN

Women in sports have always been natural to me. They were prominent in swimming, diving, track, equestrian, tennis, golf, skiing, figure skating and gymnastics. Women athletes were missing normally and by tradition in football, baseball and boxing. When they broke through to racing cars and horses I thought that horse racing was possible for women jockeys because of their touch and ability to make the weight, but I thought motor racing would be difficult. I've never seen sports as a women's rights idea but only one of rules and the quality of an athlete in competition.

The strong and vibrant faces here are Olympic champions, young hopefuls and an unknown amateur. All equal in fitness and dedication to their sport.

THE START

There is one thrill that never ceases for me in sports and that is the moment before the start. At the classic events, the Olympic games 100 meters, Americas' cup match races, a heavyweight title, thoroughbred stakes, a cross country ski run, the roar of the Grand Prix engines on the grid—the scene and the presence *at this instant* is remarkable. Still pictures can only reflect how it must be. This is when I smile, when being there is a giddy absurdity. Being *this* close, in this *perfect* position for this *event!* Then suddenly there is an instant concern; is the camera ready, are your feet positioned to make a pan, is your view assured, do you have power? In a second you lose that feeling of exhilaration and are back to the intensity of the event and your picture. The start happens quickly.

THE SENSES

When you climb the hill every step must be part of the experience of the race. Running before breakfast you hear every note of the music of the morning, see every line in the leaf. I see the surface of the frozen pond, hear the scuffing footfalls of boots, the clack of skis, the rattle of the tram. I hear the wind change as we go higher, and watch the sun strobe behind the regiment of black towering trees, see the diamonds in blown powder around a stump, the delicate loneliness of a sprig of evergreen. I wonder if any one will look at it today but me.

I watch the day take on character and let the senses feed on every sight and sound. Only then does the race have meaning, does the cold become bearable, do you become aware of the feelings of your crew. You confidently believe in D'Arcy and Peter, Avril and Joe, Harmon, Scott, Harry, David—all of them and you match your creativity with theirs and when you ask them to record some of the poetry of the place they respond.

Count down. The racer at speed. The fun begins. The spirit of a simple competition on a lonely mountain somewhere on a Sunday morning is *the* race.

The skier in your lens makes you smile and he is yours at that bump or turn. You believe it, enjoy it, understand the why of it.

You check to see the light change above the crest and see the people who have skied down to a good place and you see by their faces they believe it too.

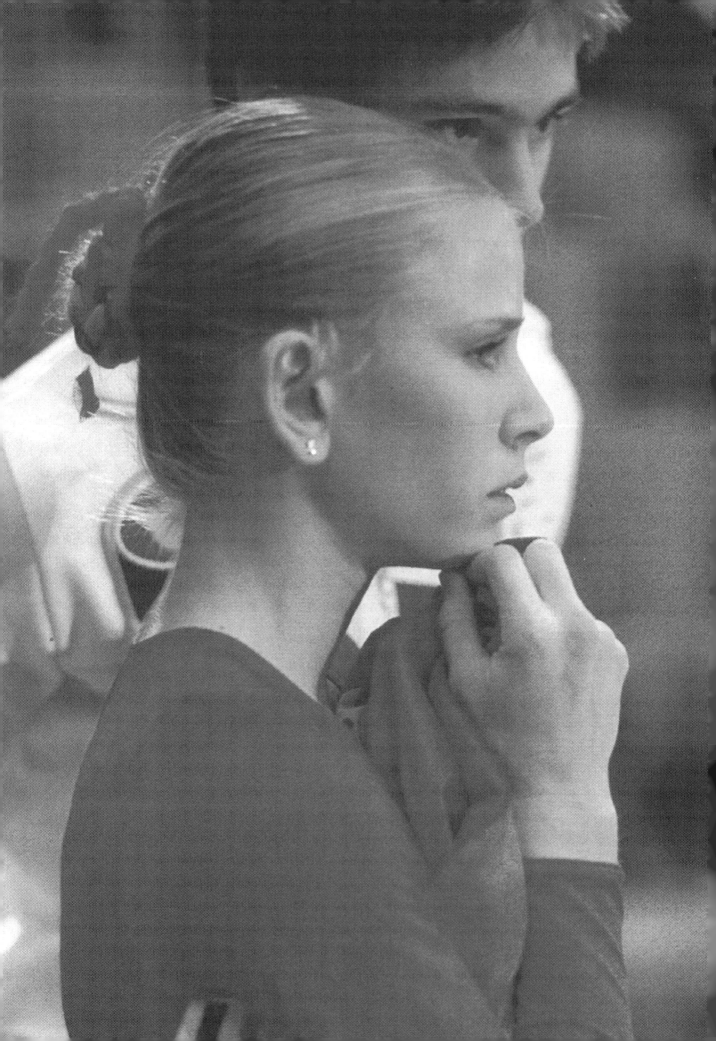

THE GYMNASTS

"My dream has always been to win the Olympic Games. When I first had the dream it didn't matter which sport I was in. I was interested in track and field and even diving, and then one day I was watching television, watching a track meet, and gymnastics came on. Cathy Rigby was performing and it just hit me that this was really a neat sport and that I loved it and I really felt that I could do it. I ran right out and started doing flips in the backyard, and about a year later I started getting into it with a little team in Florida." Kathy Johnson smiled as she fondly recalled her start, then listened to Kurt Thomas, the best U.S. gymnast.

"The turning point for me came in 1975 at the Pan American Games when I didn't even want to compete, but my coach, Roger Council, thought it would be a good meet because I had never competed internationally before. I did really well—the best of the American men—and won a few medals. I got my name up there on the scoreboard, which is important. That gave me the motivation and the psyche to keep going hard. The next summer was the 1976 Olympics, and I wasn't sure I could handle it, but my coach again thought I could make it. I really didn't think I was Olympic material. We worked on it and I ended up winning the trials and made the Olympic team. I was young and I realized I was inexperienced and I was just awed by the whole thing. You need these little builders because you really don't know deep inside if you can do it. In 1977 at the World University Games I set my goal to finish in the first ten. I was happy with the whole competition. I placed ninth, went through clean, and that's when I started seeing myself as a world-class gymnast."

Somehow over the years as a journalist you develop a perspective, a feeling when a historic time is ending, when a time is fallow or when one certain event or team or athlete triggers a new beginning in a sport. So it was with gymnastics in the United States in 1978. The world surge had begun after the 1972 Olympic Games in Munich; the American consciousness came after the 1976 Olympics in Montreal. The Russians and Romanians, Olga Korbut and Nadia Comaneci. It took a year and a half for little clubs and training programs to explode all over the country. Suddenly an American team began to flower. Kathy Johnson and Kurt Thomas were the best gymnasts on our squads, and by the end of the year they had won world championship medals in individual events, but most important, a team of excellence was maturing with them.

"There's definitely a team pride," Kurt Thomas confided. "I think that Bart Conners and I have done a great deal for men's gymnastics. We've been battling against each other for a number of years now, and I think that's the valuable idea. We're trying new original tricks and we are taking our tricks to the ultimate now, and we're starting to compete internationally and win internationally, and that is affecting the crowds and the judges. I sense the American gymnasts are greatly respected by the other countries because we're on the way up. We served notice to Russia, Romania and Japan that we may soon break into the top three world gymnastic powers. *Then* we will be respected by every country in international competition."

"Like Kurt, I set my goals on one meet at a time," Kathy said. "My first big international competition was in the American Cup in 1977. For months before it I would dream of winning that meet, go over to the gym at night thinking about what it would feel like, try to picture myself winning, go through all the routines in my head, and then when I was on the floor at the actual competition I knew I could win if I set my mind to it. I won the meet and it gave me the confidence which is really what you need in international competition. When you get that high in world competition, physically you've got it. You are ready. It is something all international competitors have. The difference is confidence. The champion knows she can do it.

"Dance is my strength. In gymnastics it's very much up to the individual on where the emphasis will be; strong, athletic moves or with a poetic grace in dance in the floor exercise. When I first started gymnastics, dance was considered my weak point and everyone was saying, 'You've got to take dance, you must study ballet.' I never had any type of dance and the coaches warned the lack of it was hurting me. So I had a crash course from a woman in Atlanta and it wasn't so much that she taught me how to dance, she taught me how to *feel* when I dance. She taught me an inner feeling has to be part of my exercise, and that's what I was missing. I had it, but it was suppressed, and she taught me how to let it out and to show how much I loved gymnastics by dancing beautifully. That is what dance is in gymnastics—it is a feeling, it is not only the action.

"Gymnastics is a very creative sport, and I think it's important that you select your moves, whether it be dance or the skills that you do in each routine, that you select them very carefully so that they fit your body type and the way you feel. There are certain moves I just love to see other people do but I know they wouldn't feel comfortable with me. I wouldn't feel comfortable doing them and therefore would not do them well. So the selection of your moves, the creativity, the *originality* is very important."

"Originality is one of the biggest parts of gymnastics right now," Thomas agreed, "because everybody can do the basics. You have to work out different variations with your coach, perfect them and try them in your routine. A move that you can capitalize on best. That is what we constantly strive to do with my routine—take what I can do best and take it to the maximum and then add different original combinations. I think that is what the sport is all about, just showing off what you can do for the other gymnasts, the crowd and the judges. Originality commands respect.

"A good gymnast can swing a lot of tricks. If a trick is executed properly you need very little strength. It is timing to have your body in the right position, to know where you are on the high bar or the parallel bars. You need strength, extra muscle, to compensate for mistakes. There are strength moves and flexibility strength moves in gymnastics, but there are also swing moves which gymnasts make strength moves by not executing them properly.

"In Olympic order the six tests for men are a floor exercise, pommel horse, still rings, long horse vaulting, parallel bars and horizontal [high] bar. My best events in my first years of competition were the horse, the parallel bars and the high bar. You cannot compete internationally with any weak events but it certainly helps to have a few strong ones. I originated a trick on the pommel horse which was named after me. They call it the Thomas Flare, and it is part of my scissor kick on the horse where I change from one direction to the other. It adds virtuosity and I feel stronger on the event. With this success the coach and I improvised and put my flare into the beginning of the floor exercise. It is more difficult to do on the floor than it is on the horse, and the crowd is really reacting to it.

"The moves in each event are set going in. I do not change anything if I'm ahead or behind in the competition. I don't change any dismount or alter any trick. I take each event one at a time. If I hit I move on to the next event. We know the combined scores as we progress in the competition."

Half closing her eyes, Kathy Johnson continued the imagery. "The four gymnastics events in the women's competition in Olympic order are the vault, the uneven bars, the balance beam and the floor exercise. The vault is an event in which I feel that I can totally let loose—with the speed of the run, the impact of takeoff, and then it's a quick action on the horse that lasts only a fraction of a second. The women's vault is a very dynamic event, exciting and fun. What is unique about it is that the dismount counts for about sixty percent of your score because it represents more than half the event, whereas on the beam the dismount may be only one part of forty moves and on the uneven bars one part of fifteen.

"The audience likes to watch the second gymnastic test for women, the uneven bars, because there are quick moves that appear very difficult. When you're working on the bars you don't move as quickly as people seem to think. You do have time to think and time to try to pick up a rhythm and a full swing—that is the feeling I want to establish, the rhythm of the swing, easily moving through the bars rather than quick, jerky movements.

"The balance beam is a very special event to me. It's a challenge. It's a discipline and I like that. When I work beam I try to get in contact with the beam—in time with it. I put myself directly over the beam and try never to move from there. Then I just try and let myself go. There is dance, creativity, balance. I can express myself. It is limited but you must not admit it is. The beam allows you only *four inches* to work with but you must use the full sixteen-foot length. The trick is to think not of the footing below but of all the space above the beam. That's what you're creating in, the beautiful space.

"The beam is really the hardest event to bring the audience into, and that's part of the challenge. You try and make people believe that you're not really looking at the beam and concentrating so deeply on staying on the beam that you can't express yourself. You must look out to the people, out past the beam, try to go out into space, try to reach the people and the judges. This dedication helps my concentration. Sometimes when I get too into the beam, thinking so much about staying on, I make the most mistakes. I make my mistake when I believe I am on *four inches*. If I can just let loose, get in time with the beam, let go and work—that's usually when I have my best beam performance.

"Finally the floor exercise is a beautiful event. You can totally let loose on floor exercise. You can't fall very easily and it has the dynamics of the tumbling and the grace of the dance and the challenge here is trying to combine them. Instead of having the dance on one side and then tumbling all of a sudden, I try and think about dancing into my tumbling and tumbling out of my dance so that it is an entire picture without blobs or brush strokes. I enjoy making the floor exercise a complete production, not just the physical aspects of gymnastics.

"I think the choreography on the floor must have significance. The beginning pose for me, which begins in the corner, I wanted it to look birdlike, like an eagle, to express freedom of the spirit, and I end my performance in the same corner, lower, head down as if the bird were folding her wings. Throughout the entire piece I try to incorporate the same feeling of the freedom of flight.

"The degree of difficulty is very important in gymnastics. The judges are very aware of what you are doing at every instant in each of the four events. A few months ago I would have said some of the things I'm doing now were impossible for me because at that time they were, but as you build in gymnastics things become easier and easier and your goals become realistic. When you first attempt something in training it is hard to believe that your body could do *that*, but if you gradually build to it, then by the time that you reach that skill it becomes easy—as long as the proper progression was used.

"There is a risk and danger in anything we do in life. That's part of the challenge of life, part of the challenge of gymnastics. You have to be aware of that risk. I had a serious accident on the vault in 1977 and it made me aware that there is a risk and I can't take things for granted. This is the only body I've got and I've got to take care of it."

Roger Council, the gymnastics coach at Indiana University, has watched Kurt Thomas from the start of his career and he has a philosophy on the *making* of a gymnast and the *sustaining* of a gymnast.

"We've been together for four years, and in the first couple of years I really feel as a coach I was very active in teaching Kurt more advanced skills and getting him started as an elite-level gymnast. However, I think one of the problems that I observe about a lot of coaches is they lack the ability as parents do with their own children to let go when an athlete gets to a certain level. I feel that when Kurt Thomas became an international gymnast with the Pan American Games, in a sense he became a child of the universe. I think that he then got the opportunity to observe and talk to many coaches and athletes from other countries and from around the United States, and every one of them has some good ideas and some good techniques to offer, and I think that one of the things I did at the right time is let go a little bit and not try to be the sole dominating force as he began to grow as a gymnast.

"I feel that it has been extremely good for him to travel in other countries and for him to travel to training camps becoming exposed to other people because of the good ideas out there. I think any coach who feels that he or she is the only one with good ideas is very naive.

"The *competition* for a gymnast is the difficult time. But not for the reasons one would believe. Meets are an interference to training. You need long periods of time if you are going to grow as a gymnast in which you can invent and perfect, and safety is a factor. You need long periods of time to live with these new elements of an exercise as you put them together. I feel that Kurt's demanding travel schedule has been a detriment to him. I feel we have to work very quickly to get new elements in and to get them to the point where it's feasible to use them safely as well as from an aesthetic standpoint.

"At a gymnastics competition there are several things to consider that make an athlete different in his sport. If the atmosphere of a meet changes you, it probably can only be to your detriment unless you can control that change, that adrenaline.

"Critical to the sport is the arena where you perform in an international meet, which is so much different, with the political aspect present and the way that it manifests itself with the judges and with the conduct of some of the athletes from other nations, than it is in a college or national competition. Some of the gymnasts from other countries can be very aloof and even appear rude during warmups. They may do anything they can to play the psychological game before the competition to unnerve our athletes. This can be a decisive element, particularly for the new gymnasts."

Kathy Johnson removed the bobby pins from her blond hair and tied a bright-red rope on her ponytail and responded to the idea of world competition.

"I'm just nineteen, and international travel for competitions has made me realize that people everywhere are different but that doesn't necessarily mean because they're different that that's bad. The Russians and the Romanians are very different people. They're brought up that way. Americans are more—I'd guess you would call them happy people. But I feel the Russians and the Romanians are happy. They might not smile in the gym and to audiences unless they win, and they are described as being rather cold, but that is just the way they are. It's not the way I would like to be. I still feel I can perform gymnastics and be at a high level of concentration yet still try and be personable and reach the audience through smiles, through tears sometimes, to show humanness. That's one thing the other gymnasts from other countries don't show really. They don't show humanness. They don't really cry because they're not supposed to, or smile or laugh, but that's just the way they are.

"We're the way we are."

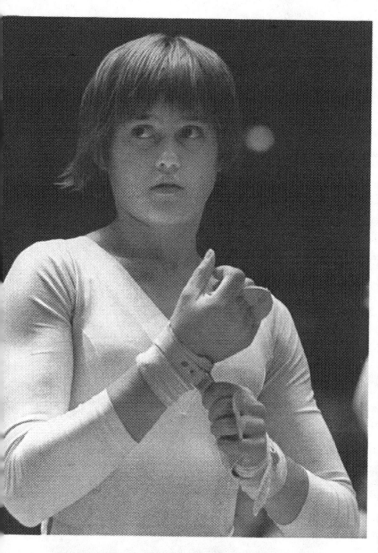

INSTANT SUCCESS

TOM LANDRY, *Head Coach, Dallas Cowboys*

"The rookie who came up in my day came to camp and was ignored. In the early fifties, when I was a defensive halfback with the New York Giants, the rookie never came in to contribute the first or second year. There were only ten teams in the league then, with more solid football players, and with the high level of talent, the rookie wasn't really good enough to step in, except in rare occasions.

"Today's rookie cannot be ignored and he is drafted with the idea that he is going to contribute right now. He's going to move into that lineup immediately and develop as a player playing, whereas in my day, we developed by exposure and in practice and waiting our turn as backup people.

"More rookies are coming through our football teams today, more rookies are making our football teams today, than made the teams in my day. In the fifties, if three or four rookies came in, that was news.

"A few seasons ago in Dallas, we had thirteen rookies make our team. I think the playing ability of the rookie today is better than it was in the fifties. The young high school and college football players are pointing to become professionals and so they prepare themselves for this career. But there is a greater turnover in players today than there ever was before because of the lack of quality in numbers in our twenty-eight teams. The top teams and certainly those who are rebuilding have many marginal players, so they continually turn over rookies looking for those players they can develop over one or two or three years.

"On the human side, the rookies are much more sophisticated, much more aware. They are exposed to the game so much more. They can see three football games on television every weekend. When they sign a pro contract they are exposed to travel, and all the outside pressures. The rookie today is in demand, and these demands, these constant outside pressures, have changed him.

"The player today is overexposed to too much outside pressure and he can't make up his mind. He's too young to really understand. An agent's telling him this, a union's telling him that, an owner's telling him this, and a writer's telling him something else. He's all mixed up. When today's rookie arrives in camp, he's basically a good athlete with fine character and a good code of ethics, but suddenly he's thrown into this big glass bowl and everyone is bombarding him with good advice and he's distracted and confused. The mental concentration needed on the field is the most difficult thing for young players today because of the distractions. When I was a player we hardly knew management existed. We were just a team, playing because we loved to play. We weren't distracted because we didn't have outside pressures on us.

"These constant outside pressures give every rookie a better out today than he's ever had before. A better reasoning for not playing well or not winning. The rookie today can rationalize why he's not playing well; management is at fault, he's not being paid enough, or he has no benefits, or too few endorsements. In his own mind, he can honestly find so many reasons why he's not winning. The player doesn't want it that way. Deep down, he wishes life was simpler—but then, so do we all. We don't particularly covet the pressures that we have on us.

"In the 1950s we were hungry and you had to play well to be successful, and our only out was to produce. You had to produce. As I watch the rookie today, he seems to be able not to produce and to be comfortable in his rationalizations to offset this. This is a bad factor, as I see it.

"As a coach I see more players than ever before, and have a better evaluation of them by carrying almost every football player in the United States on our computer. We are able to run the best in a printout, from one to a thousand. We know much more about a prospective rookie than you can imagine. We can read our information and after an hour or so of reading, I can visualize a prospective rookie without ever seeing him. This printout includes mental and physical ability and character, and it basically holds true.

"Computers can never measure a rookie's heart entirely; that's the thing you don't know until you get him out. It's the mixture within each young player that is impossible to measure. This becomes judgment.

"It is very hard, almost impossible, to arrive unannounced to a club anymore. There are no tryouts. We know every player and want only those who have come through our scouting system.

"As coach, I know that I have to understand a rookie more today. Before, it was a job and I was the boss and they had to do it. That's the way I played, and that's the way most of us played. Today, everyone is an inivdual person and you have to treat him that way. His problems are unique to him and you have to handle them if you're going to have him produce, otherwise you will not have an effective ball club."

ANDY ROBUSTELLI
Director of Operations, New York Giants

"I stand outside the stadium where people can see me after a game, and after all our losing games, I've been abused. It is hard for me as a former player to understand how people could abuse me. They do. The people are cruel, and it's part of my job to evaluate the cruelty of a fan. To them victory is something they want, and they don't care how they get it. Nothing is perfect for their team anymore.

"I understand the fans' impatience and can't deny it, but I'm convinced the deeper into losing an organization gets, the more courage it takes to stay with the building program. For the Giant management, the fan has been as big a weakness as some of the players.

"When I came back to football as director of operations for the Giants in 1972, our first draft pick was John Hicks. As a rookie, he had a brilliant year. He was the first offensive lineman in NFL history to be voted Rookie of the Year. He is an exception.

"I can't look at the game for what it is today because it doesn't really turn me on. It gave me a sense of gratitude that I was able to play and prove myself. It gave me a sense of pride. Football gave me a sense of identity. Not because it showed me who I was. I knew who I was. I was a kid that came from a poor family. My parents worked liked hell and I was

going to have to work for everything I got—and I got it—and football gave it to me. I don't honestly feel the kids today can say that, because I think that they're constantly looking for things that they're not going to get. They've already got most of what they need.

"The rookies who see me, and sign their contracts with me, know I was good. They know I was recognized as a hell of a football player and they want to be what I was, but they don't want to pay the price.

"The rookie today wants shortcuts with the same results. Today's pro football player cares only about himself. He'll find a way to rationalize, so he won't have to excel, but still get recognized and rich. The athlete has become selfish because he has grown up in a selfish society. He won't help others unless he needs help himself. The black athlete is still the greatest asset in sports—he's hungriest!

"When I was a young player, I accepted things. I never worried about my head not being on straight. These kids have all kinds of reasons why they don't win. They never look at themselves and say, 'I failed.' I have not had contract talks with one ballplayer this year that said he was part of the reason our team failed.

"From an organizational standpoint, the players are very strong. They almost have the upper hand. The game seems to be all show biz on *Monday Night Football*. Excessive flamboyance and hotdogging on the television screen have become a sham. The rookie wants the guy in the booth to stop talking about the team or the game and talk about him. When a ballplayer scores and slams the ball down in the end zone, it is his justification for his being there. 'Here I am, folks, coast to coast, notice *me!*'

"Very few young players will work extra today to achieve something extra. How can you motivate a kid that has everything? To him, leadership is junk.

"People talk about leaders in sports. There are no leaders today. It is everyone do your own thing. In our day, we motivated each other. There was a feeling of helping each other. Today, they whisper, 'Hey, man, leave him alone. He's got a problem.'

"I don't think mental toughness exists. There is a void in what we used to think of as mental toughness in the young players today because we are looking at a different kind of kid. Today's rookie only gets out of his ability what his ability can give him. Very few get extra out of themselves. I could kick lockers and punch doors or do anything to take out my frustrations for losing, because I wanted to win so bad. Today's ballplayer doesn't want to win badly enough. Today's rookie has even learned to live with failure. But sure as hell, one of these days, the rookies have to place a value on their pride and look at themselves and say, 'I'm not a good ballplayer.' Or, 'Why didn't I make the play and what am I going to do about it? How much do I want to work extra to be the best? To make the team the best?' You just don't see that attitude in today's rookies."

DON SHULA, *Head Coach, Miami Dolphins*

"I vividly remember the day I signed my rookie contract. I was awestruck. I couldn't wait for Coach Paul Brown to put the paper down in front of me; then I was afraid he was going to pick it up without letting me sign it. When I was able to make it as a rookie with the Cleveland Browns in 1953, playing in my own backyard with my friends in the stands watching me, it was a dream come true.

"We had no television to watch in the late forties and early fifties, so we would wear our school sweaters and get in to see the Browns play for a quarter. Dante Lavelli, Mac Speedie, Dub Jones and Otto Graham were my idols. I went for a Browns tryout, as a senior at nearby John Carroll University, and the next year I had a chance to compete for a position on the Cleveland Brown team with those guys!

"The rookies today are more aware than they were when I was a rookie. A young player has been recruited for high school, recruited for college, then drafted for the National Football League. Competitive bidding has placed him in the limelight, and he's not alone as I was when I came to sign. He is represented by agents and lawyers, and he comes prepared to get what he wants and to plan it properly. This change came really when I arrived in Miami in 1970. I don't remember seeing it when I

was in Baltimore. It came as a result of the protests in the colleges. When the students were more outspoken on campus, there was an immediate carryover to pro ball. When I got those rookies and looked at them for the first time with their long hair and beards and their new attitude—they were very different in appearance, and I could tell they had more confidence in themselves. They asked many more questions than I ever dared as a rookie or than the rookies I had in the sixties.

"Whenever I put things up on the board or displayed tactics in the playbook, it no longer was accepted. Today's rookie wants to know why—why are we doing it this way? I like this. When I was a rookie, I had a more inquisitive mind than most other young players and I would bother the defensive coaches by asking, "What if they do this? Then, what do we do?" This gave me the background to get into coaching. Now, twenty years later, I feel this questioning attitude of today's rookie makes a better coach out of me. It is good to have reasons why you do things, and it's good to be able to explain them. It makes it all that much more meaningful.

"The home fans and the viewers might see the rookie with his big demands, flashy clothes, expensive cars as a negative, money-based problem in pro football, but I found out that this new group of rookies, although they looked different, weren't that much different. I found, basically, that they still wanted to win, they wanted to get the most out of their ability.

"They are still interested in the team but there is much more individual awareness now. They're image-conscious. I'd rather compliment them, pat 'em on the back and have them tell me how they achieved what they set out to do. I don't spend a lot of time with players with negative problems.

"Today's rookie still has to be mentally tough. The thing our team must never do is get beat mentally. You've got to be able to win mentally and physically. I know I'm not doing a teaching job if we get beat because we don't know what the hell we're doing out there on the field. The young players who can't think in a pressure situation are going to get you beat. They're losers. You get rid of those people in a hurry. As a coach, you must see this in the rookie. You must see it early, find out as soon as you can the difference between losers and winners.

"Television has made players more aware of their individual importance. If their actions or reactions on the field are a natural thing, I don't mind it, but if it is really phony, I take issue to it. There are some real weird things going on in the end zone around the league and I will not stand for the excessive demonstration.

"Two years ago, it would have been hard for a rookie to break into our team because we were coming off of 17-and-0 and you're pretty happy with the people who got you that undefeated season. It would have taken an outstanding rookie to break into that team. But this season, we came off of an average year, and played without three of our best players. We had rookies like Freddie Solomon in key positions.

"This doesn't mean the attitude of the veteran to the rookie changes when the team situation changes. I've been around some pretty good veteran football players both as a player and as a coach, and they've been on the whole an unselfish lot. There has never been any continual harassment. On many teams, the veterans on the whole have been willing to sit down and help the rookie. I've seen a full expression of this unselfishness with my veteran football players and this makes for a good football team.

"The rookie directly or indirectly has been dragged into the disagreements that have been going on between union and management in the past few years. The important thing for him to realize is that he really doesn't have a voice until he's a player. He's got to make the team before he can get caught up in disputes.

"My door is open to all players. The rookie today demands more. As coach, I have to treat them more as individuals, but I don't hold their hands. With their new air of confidence, they stand up much more than they ever did before.

"Football is continually improving. The players are bigger, faster, smarter than they used to be. Everything is better because the rookies have been so much better prepared in high school and college and they have watched football on television for twelve years before they report to our camp. Television has been their teacher, and because of it, they are so much more specialized. They know early what they want to do. Specialization leads to a better product on the field."

CARROLL ROSENBLOOM
Owner, Los Angeles Rams

"I guess I'm so much of a fan that when I hear from other owners and the media that the players are so different today, I am afraid I must heartily disagree with them. I see very little difference in the rookie today and the rookie of the John Unitas day, with the exception that Unitas, who was a quarterback, came to us for seven thousand dollars and no bonus. The rookie quarterback today, depending on where you draft him, will come in for many, many times that money—thirty-five thousand, maybe—four hundred thousand, maybe. The important idea is that the new players coming into our league are fine young men. In the first place, the Rams won't keep a player today any more than we would when I owned the Colts if that player is difficult. We don't need troublemakers. We don't have any. Many times, when we thought we had one, we traded him and found that a change in scenery made him a very good citizen. Conversely, we have taken players other teams have said were troublemakers and they have been wonderful with us.

"It almost broke my heart to leave our close family

in Baltimore because all my guys were so great. Now, after four years in Los Angeles, we have as strong a family feeling amongst our players as we had in Baltimore, and the rookie is a tremendous part of the family. The rookie today is so much more articulate than twenty years ago that you have to be pleasured with his company.

"I have been known for being 'good' to my players. But that word 'good' is too simplistic. Most everything that a human being does in life he does with a selfish motive. My frequent giving to charity is a rewarding thing for me. I find relief in giving.

"It pleases me. It makes up for some of the evils that maybe exist in my makeup. I take great pleasure in always giving my players the dignity of my concern. I try to tell them their playing days are only a part of their productive years. My belief is that a hungry player is not your best player. A player who is safe economically is a better player because he's not worrying about paying bills. In the Ram office, we have set up a guidance and placement bureau to offer advice on business deals or any other problems a rookie might have. I feel it is important that I continue a close association with all my players, especially the younger ones. When I ran a mill, with twenty-eight thousand employees working in my various plants, I couldn't have a close relationship with all of my people except at the executive level, because I hardly knew them. But the society of a professional football team of about sixty people is manageable, and an owner must have that personal relationship, where in other businesses it is not possible.

"I don't worry about the losing teams in our league weakening the overall structure, because I have faith in the system. With our draft all teams have a chance to get the job done. It depends on top management, the best coaches, and then you have to get the players through the system in order to take a team from a loser to a winner. I've been down that road and so have the people in Miami, Dallas, Baltimore and Pittsburgh, and we all know that it works. The other organizations, when they fit everything together, will find that you can build and maintain a consistently winning team.

"The player strikes and union difficulties with management have caused no cleavage between the players and management on our football club. We do not try to guide our players in what they should do in union matters. They're their own men and we tell them to do what they think best. We did want our rookies to come to camp during last summer's strike and they did come in. They needed the work.

"If the Ram players had ever initiated the kind of wildcat action that the Patriot players did in Boston, I know I would have been completely disenchanted with my men. I don't mind what they do as a total player group across the country, but if my team had decided to strike a game on their own, acting independently of other teams in the NFL, I would have taken the most drastic action against them.

"Ed Garvey, the head of their players association, in my opinion is a destroyer. The players are being advised badly. I don't know one constructive thing Garvey has done for football or the players except to degrade them by putting them on picket lines. He has made it more difficult in every way by failing to see that excessive player demands have deprived owners of income we need when he should realize that the recipients of most of that income, in the final analysis, are the players. The players are so mature and business-conscious today in all professional sports. You've seen it in hockey, where the players themselves felt the salaries were too high—where the players felt their own salaries must be reduced. The president of their players association, Allan Eagleson, was the one who said it.

"But the players in pro football will not recognize this. If they continue to demand more and more, which they can get, the fans will become angry, because the only way management can pay higher salaries is to raise the ticket prices. I think admissions are as high as they should be. I think the networks are reaching their limit too in what they can pay for rights. I just believe that players and owners must admit that there is a limit, and if they don't recognize it, then there won't be any professional sports.

"As far as the new look to the players, well, every player is first off an athlete, but we must admit that we're in the entertainment business. People come to be entertained, and all have a common interest.

"I've seen an NFL team bring a whole town together. I've seen it in the old days in Baltimore, in Miami and in Pittsburgh when they won the Super Bowl. Television has had an enormous influence on our teams. The players do get up much higher for a nationally televised game than they do for one that isn't televised. They want to look their best and in that way they are no different than the great performers. I think one of the things that we've seen in recent years is the lessening of the role of the superstar. We just don't have them anymore, with the exception of O.J. and Joe What's-his-name. I don't think a team built around a superstar can get you to the playoffs. If the superstar fails, the team fails, and that is a dangerous disadvantage. There must be great balance in all departments, year in and year out. Television has brought all the specialists evenly into prominence, and the rookie football player is an equal on this great stage."

THE SWIMMERS

Working with the young athletes, especially at the universities, you see them as mature human beings, articulate, worldly and physically developed to the point that they are strong young men and women. You don't think of their age. You have to be around the best of them a long time before they let their guard down and you see their vulnerability and their inexperience.

John Naber and Don Schollander are two of the finest athletes I've ever met and a product of their remarkable sport, swimming. Between them they won ten Olympic medals. Together they reflected on the theme of this book from the clear perspective of their swimmers world—peripheral amateur athletes in the day of the multimillion-dollar professional gate for the boxer, the hitter and the running back each with a prime time television showcase. The shining hour for their sport comes once every four years at the Olympic Games.

"My first reaction toward swimming as an athletic endeavor was that here was a sport where I could get in the water and do something I enjoyed and with clear-cut, empirical results that would graphically demonstrate my improvement. I saw my times drop, I saw the performances get better, and I could see myself occasionally pass a swimmer who was faster than I was a week before. As I got better and better my goals began to shoot higher and higher. I started to feel competitive on a worldwide level and that began to help give me the self-confidence to address a PTA group or to do a radio interview or speak to the mayor, with the assurance that he's just another person in this world. Later I believed that if I could be the best swimmer in the world then I could treat the President of the United States just as another human being. Swimming success, international success as an athlete, gave me enormous self-confidence in relating to other people.

"The effect that television and the rest of the media has had on sports is to give it an awful easy road on which the athlete can get very egocentric. The athlete can focus on his own importance because he's on TV. Or he can look at it another way, and that is that the press coverage is a channel with which to send a message out to eager listening ears.

"America in general worships the athlete, in some cases worships him to an extreme. However, if an athlete has his head together he can use that fame and that soapbox to really expound on some of the important values of society—that are too often ne-glected when a teacher or politician or priest would say them from their soapbox. An athlete will be heard and will be respected, and so it can really be a great opportunity to be a social worker and do something specific to help the world.

"Throughout history man has always rallied around a winner. They follow the flag bearer and jump on the bandwagon. This is only natural, and it gives the nonaccomplishers, the nonachievers, a rallying point with which to look at themselves and say, 'At least I'm backing a winner.' It gives them an attitude of optimism. I think that as long as people find something to make the world look a little better—I think that's great. I think that when people think the world's rotten and things are going poorly, that attitude will manifest itself in actions. So that if they admire good people and they start patterning themselves after good people it may have a sincere effect on mankind in general. There is that possibility.

"The sum of the whole is greater than the sum of its parts. This is taught in team sports, where the individual has to sacrifice his own ego and his own glory for the perpetuation of the team ethic. The championship teams are the ones where the individuals gladly step back and let the team take over. I think this is a significant educational experience for the individuals who want to eventually land in business with a strong interrelation of people.

"I think the only thing the athletes are gaining now as we begin the new decade of the eighties is a lot more *money*. That's bad news. Sports are not a livelihood. Athletics are a hobby which promotes character development. The athlete who's out for money and his own personal glory is cheating himself of the best thing the sport can offer, the education on which you cannot place a price tag.

"For every winner in America there are thousands and thousands of losers, and I find that that has to be an unrealistic role. Ten years before, the winners and the losers were dreaming of being winners only. The emphasis is placed on result and not on character development which is a shame. Ideally, you can achieve both.

"I think that in this point in time swimming is the only major amateur sport around. If I had my way I would definitely promote athletes who love competition to get involved just for the competition. When the emphasis gets placed on money the sport no longer becomes a sport, it becomes a job."

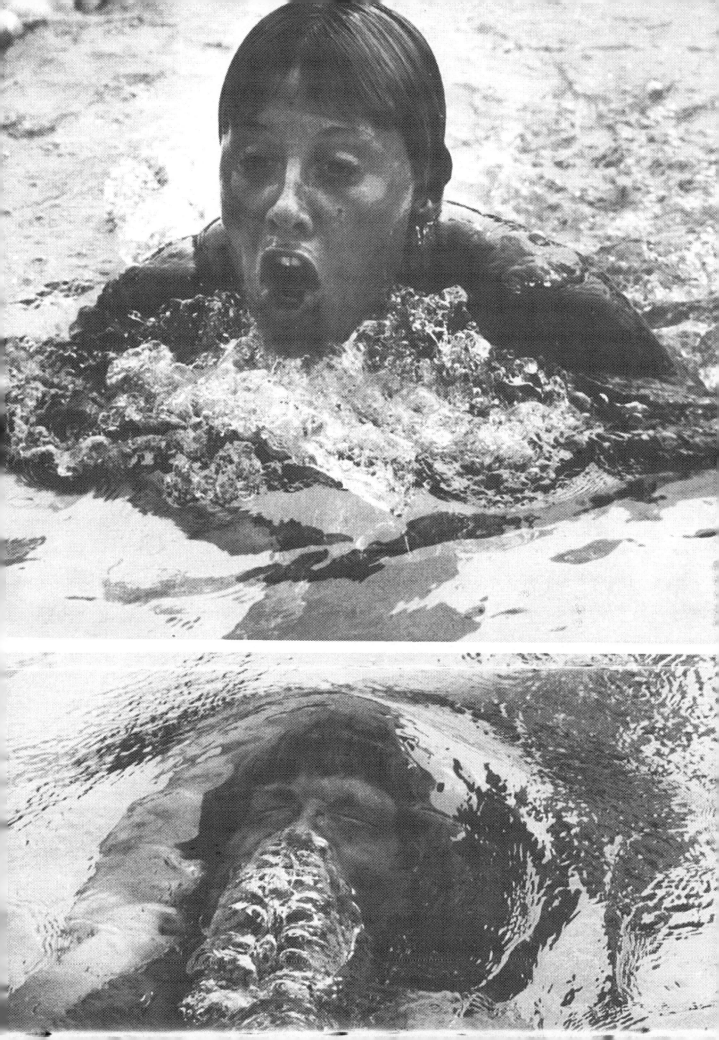

"One of the most difficult things we have to deal with in American society is the *success syndrome*—walk out successful into the sunset—I did that at *seventeen*, because at that time there were no further opportunities for a woman in sports. I often wonder what would have happened if there were.

"I had to make a tremendous adjustment when I completed my competitive swimming in 1964. The adjustment was to the world that isn't black and white. Sports is a world that is black and white—you accomplish a time, you win first place, you know what your goals are and what your rewards are. When you get out into the marketplace and the real world, the things you want aren't as easily defined. Sometimes they are much more complicated to attain, and when you have achieved success early you expect it of yourself in every other area. The thing that I did not have time to understand is what your impact on the world was as a sixteen-year-old. I don't think that I ever comprehended that I was the best in the world or that I was working on network television the following year. I had to wait until I learned all of that. My perception was that of a child in the world but not really understanding it.

"The lessons I learned through sport and the pride I had in myself as a woman strengthened me to survive in the struggle and become successful in television. Those are the values that kept me going and believing in myself when the industry did not find a place for women in the area that I wanted to travel in. I was thirteen when I made my first Olympic team, I was first to win the individual medley in the Olympics, and now I've developed the courage to know that I can be first in my area of broadcasting.

"In 1964 I had a wealth of expectations when I went to Tokyo for the Games. I always said that expectations can take the joy out of victory. I was expected to win my race. I had been on the cover of *Sports Illustrated* twice. I was a celebrated and acceptable woman athlete. It made some impact in the mid-sixties, but it has had even a greater influence in the seventies for the rights of women.

"As far as my role as a professional host, I find the pressure now is as great as it was when I was an athlete. As a woman I sense the hope and expectations of many other women who want to fill that role someday. I also feel a very strong obligation to do the right kind of reporting with women athletes.

"I think the greatest frustration I had when I was swimming was that I wanted to be recognized as a great athlete. I broke eighteen world records as part of the U.S. swimming power in the 1960s, but I found that I was continually described for my physical characteristics only. There were three or four years in my life when I rebelled from that. I signed a swim-suit contract, but I refused to do the mannequin poses. I also didn't sell my soul to a great many advertisers who, in those years, only looked at a woman from the glamour point of view. To help me avoid this exposure I gained weight. I called it my great escape. Then people didn't approach me on that level anymore.

"During this time I worked to develop my writing skills which would help me in broadcast journalism. I worked hard to understand the politics of sports and became a special consultant to the U.S. Senate, which, to me, was the proudest moment of my contribution to amateur sports. This and my contribution to Title IX. These gave me the same feelings of victory and accomplishment as those I had as an athlete. Title IX was a milestone for women in sports. In 1972, the Equal Education Amendments Act passed Congress, and Title IX was part of that act, which stated that at any federally funded institution you cannot discriminate on the basis of sex. That meant that sports programs at schools had to be open, and equal opportunities had to be provided for men and women. This hit the big traditions of the major sports. In 1974 the President signed the guidelines, and in September 1979, the federal government acted to prosecute those that are not following the mandates of Title IX.

"When I realized I had a responsibility to look good and be fit because I am an athlete, I decided to drop the weight. I train at the Nautilus training center. I push weights three days a week, I run two miles a day, I swim when I can, and now this strength takes me through a twenty-hour broadcasting day when the pressure is maximum. I am in a man's world and I have to be able to compete in a man's world. This strength and energy is very important to me—all the more as I get older.

"Television has had a tremendous psychological impact on young girls who see Olga Korbut and Nadia Comaneci, Tracy Austin and all the others, and see the dignity of the young woman athlete.

"In the 1980s the athletes must begin to share in the incredible sums of money being paid for rights fees such as the two hundred and twenty-five million dollars ABC paid for the rights to the 1984 Olympics in Los Angeles. Our athletes are still being forced to labor under an unfair competitive situation. An athlete who performs for his country on television in this kind of financial structure must be compensated. *They're the show!*

"If we take advantage of the amateur athlete, especially the Olympic athlete, if we abuse him and misuse these men and women, they will be embittered and will not thrive as champions and certainly will not stay with their sports and replenish their sports as coaches and teachers of those athletes coming after them."

"I would take a position that the athlete does not influence American society but rather is influenced by American society. I view sports as a changing evolution. When I was growing up in the 1950s and looking at the stars—the so-called stars—in various sports, the theme that was emphasized again and again in the media was the theme of the *All-American*. Growing up, I tried to pattern myself after the ideals of the athletes that were the best. I'm not so sure that those athletes really influenced society and influenced me as much as the media reflecting on that athlete influenced society.

"When I was old enough to hit my stride in international competition I became aware that society seemed to be wanting an anti-hero and so we went through a period in the 1960s where so-called anti-heros like Joe Namath were paramount, the new star thrust upon the public. I know for myself it was difficult, having grown up in a situation where I thought the idea was to be clean-cut through healthful living and spartan training—it was difficult for me out in Oregon to look at Joe Namath in New York and understand how the public respected him. I didn't know then what kind of a guy he was—it was just the image that was portrayed, and I think Mark Spitz to a certain extent was the last of the anti-heroes, the image of a real swinger.

"When they interviewed Mark and asked him what he thought about when he swam, he answered, 'Beautiful girls.' Mark didn't think about that—it was just an answer he thought he was supposed to give. In 1976 Bruce Jenner became the example of society's changing whim back and away from the anti-hero to the clean-cut family man.

"I saw this immediately when, after winning the decathlon gold medal in Montreal, he ran over to kiss his wife for a world audience. This was an important statement. Jenner was saying, 'Hey, world, I'm not the anti-hero. I'm the clean-cut American male. I'm the family man.' Bruce has marketed this. He and his wife had a child and then spent the last three years making television commercials together and writing a book called *Family Fitness*. His *exposure* has been enormous.

"I feel that most athletes, like most actors, are basically very insecure and that they adopt roles or images that they think will make them more acceptable to society, and the only difference today from fifteen years ago is that we're more sophisticated. The American athlete today in 1980 is much more sophisticated in adopting a role and merchandising that role.

"Sports has come down to individual role-playing. I personally feel that the effect the individual athlete has on society is negligible. Teams and sports and games and the popularity of those games and

the popularity of the teams influence American society strongly, and I suppose it could be argued that the teams are made up of individuals, but the individual athlete no longer has pure goals, and this is the weakness.

"I look at the athletes in amateur sports and no longer are they content simply to be the best and to try and accomplish for self-fulfillment. Most amateur athletes are looking for any possible way to *capitalize*. Professional athletes are looking at ways to increase their revenue, negotiate better contracts or get better endorsements at the end of the season. Most of the professional athletes that I know are very insecure people because they know that their playing time is limited. They either try to hoard their money or they are worried about the investments they should be making because people are taking or will take advantage of them. I think this greed that many athletes exhibit now is having an influence on American youth and maybe teaching them wrong ideals. But I'm not so sure that American society isn't greedy in general and that everyone isn't going around trying to get theirs. The compound effect of greed is disaster. Disastrous inflation. I think American society is forcing the athlete's hand.

"One difficulty in American sport is the idea of fragmentation. As a swimmer I am acutely aware of this. Football players are not going to listen to Abduhl Jabar. Swimmers are not going to listen to Fran Tarkenton. Track people are not going to listen to me. There is no one leader in sports, and so you can't *feel* any federation, any single strong organization. The hero now is the one who makes the most money. He may or may not be the best athlete.

"Television has had the most influence on young people from the standpoint of opening their eyes to other sports. Television has opened their minds to other possibilities, like gymnastics, skiing, swimming and diving and equestrian competition. Television particularly through the exposure at the Olympic level has really helped swimming and gymnastics. There is an enormous amount of teaching possible from the television screen.

"Through television sports the public is more aware of the athlete, the individual mannerisms of the athlete, but that doesn't necessarily make that athlete more important. Sometimes familiarity breeds a common denominator. I think one reason Babe Ruth was such a hero is because the public really didn't know him. He was a god up there on the pedestal. We all know Joe Namath and we all know Reggie Jackson and I don't think they're placed as high on the pedestal as Babe Ruth because we are more familiar with them."

147

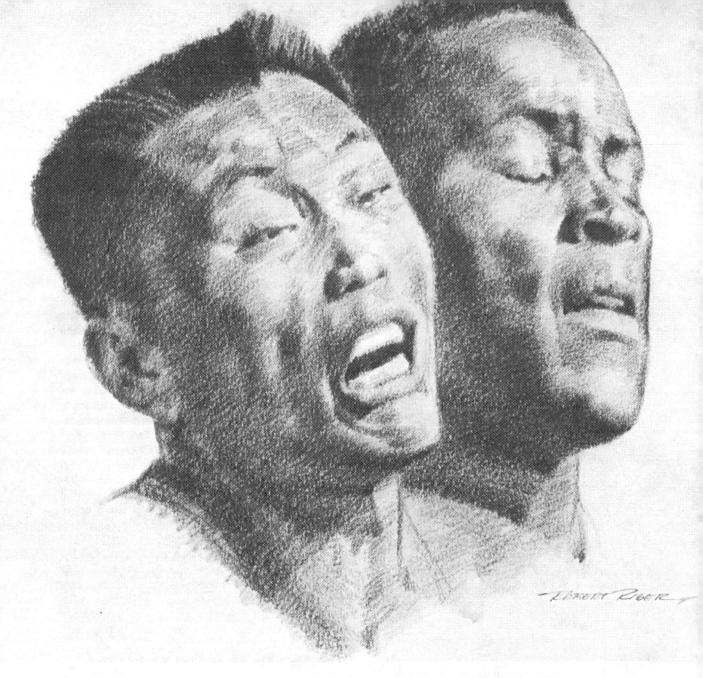

OLYMPIC DECATHLON

As they ran the decathlon 1500, theirs were like two great stone heads carved out of the mountain of darkness—contorted with the agony of their infinite ordeal. Yang's head swung from side to side those last forty meters—his exhaustion was absolute, his torment unbearable; for in running to win he drew Johnson on and on with him, a shadow he could not erase. He was the hare and Rafer the greyhound. He won but lost.

But they seemed to me, as I watched in awe, to be the symbol of each athlete's complete and total effort in the Olympic Games. Regardless of race or creed or country. To see them was to understand the devo-

tion and the sacrifice and the pain of victory.

Bob Mathias had won the Olympic decathlon medal in London in 1948 and Helsinki in 1952. He stood near the finish of the final event in the dark stadium and shook his head. "I met Yang five years ago in Formosa—we are the best of friends. I wanted him to win out there tonight. I think he should have. He beat Rafer in seven out of ten events, and if they had run the 1500 in separate heats, Yang would have won the medal. He lost because his pace drew Rafer on. Rafer never ran that time before in his life."

I made these two pictures in Rome in 1960.

During the course of my years of work with athletes and the analysis of their technical skills, there have been two radical changes in style that I remember, and each one seemed preposterous when the athlete first presented it in competition. They were both in track and field. Parry O'Brien changed the shot put at a meet in Texas in 1955 by facing *away* from the direction of the throw, and Duane Fosberry went over the high-jump bar head first—on his back—in 1969, creating the classic flop. The shot put and the high jump were changed because of the inventiveness of one athlete in each sport.

Track and field athletes have interesting heads. Someday some enterprising scholar will do psychiatric probings into the minds of the track and field people. They seem abnormal. Quirky. All of them. In some it is subtle, very subtle. Others are apparently peculiar—except, maybe, the decathlon man. All of the athletes who compete in the ten tests of this event seem nicely balanced. Or maybe it is just my hunch, but in my travels I have found that track athletes in most cases and the field-event athlete in almost all cases can destroy themselves in competition with their mental condition.

When John Thomas went to the Rome Olympics in 1960 they were going to give him the gold medal *before* the event. I saw him in his room the day before he competed. He was catatonic. He was the only athlete who ever refused me an interview or ever refused to talk about his sport, his style, his technique. He sat there in total silence until I walked away. The Russians beat him easily.

One of the most articulate athletes I've ever worked with, a man who could verbalize on all aspects of his track skills, was the Olympic medalist Dwight Stones. Dwight uses the same energy and force and thought for everything he does and he appraised the idiosyncratic nature of the track and field people.

"I would agree that because of the diverse events in track and field with the sprinters, the middle-distance runners, the pole vaulters and the weight men and naturally the high-jumpers, track and field tends to produce an assortment of *strange* people. None of us are super-stable.

"Pole vaulters are basically the kids who would take any *dare* and do *anything* when they were growing up. High-jumpers are very introspective and go through a great deal of thought process. It is the shortest event in track and field—just ten steps

swelled head because of who he is and what he done, but week in and week out you are toiling a hard as any professional athlete and you are *unpaid* Because of the back seat we take financially, some o us make up for it by being highly vocal.

"As the 1980s begin there are certain rule-inte: pretation changes taking place and I do not believe they are just a coincidence of time. I feel the stan I took in track and field on *payment for perform ance* and my suspension from the sport has had lot to do with these changes.

"Many of our amateur athletes in the Unite States are not allowed to seek out corporations ar businesses that will join the fold as sponsors f national teams and Olympic teams. The athlete : this association will be permitted to receive fees f advertising and consulting. I have to feel I was part responsible for this new direction in amatei sports. I made a stink. I made it known that tl athlete does not get what he deserves. In the pa the governing body in sports, the AAU, had tl brutal concept to use and abuse him. To ignore he

"I have always been very outspoken about thin; I feel are wrong. My mother taught me that—sl was a crusader. I always try to steady a situatio When the President's Commission on Olymp Sports came out I claimed it was a total whitewas It proved to be just that. But I'm only one person one sport—track and field—which is not regarded televised as much as in Europe, and I'm only o person who performs one event and has a big mout I've had a popular five years in my event but r time is short-lived, so all you can hope to do is ha an influence while you are in the limelight.

"I feel that track and field and amateur sports general have enormous potential for the kids to g both the respect they deserve, the support they ne and some kind of reward for their efforts. I don't s that happening. I see people being taken advanta of. I see a network pay a quarter of a billion dolla for the rights to put on a performance—the 19 Olympic Games in Los Angeles—but what will t performers get? Young people who are the best the world. The governing body, the Olympic Co mittee, should get a good percentage of the advert ing and television revenue, but as agents for t athletes they must get what is a fair agent's p centage and share the rest with the athletes.

"The rules governing the amateur athlete have be relaxed in the next three years. There must be open door for more athletes to do more endorseme: for more corporations to attract them to supp amateur athletics, bringing more business i: sports and keeping the best athletes in their resp tive sports as teachers. Only then will America re as the best nation in the world in amateur sports.'

150

swelled head because of who he is and what he's done, but week in and week out you are toiling as hard as any professional athlete and you are *unpaid*. Because of the back seat we take financially, some of us make up for it by being highly vocal.

"As the 1980s begin there are certain rule-interpretation changes taking place and I do not believe they are just a coincidence of time. I feel the stand I took in track and field on *payment for performance* and my suspension from the sport has had a lot to do with these changes.

"Many of our amateur athletes in the United States are not allowed to seek out corporations and businesses that will join the fold as sponsors for national teams and Olympic teams. The athlete in this association will be permitted to receive fees for advertising and consulting. I have to feel I was in part responsible for this new direction in amateur sports. I made a stink. I made it known that the athlete does not get what he deserves. In the past the governing body in sports, the AAU, had the brutal concept to use and abuse him. To ignore her.

"I have always been very outspoken about things I feel are wrong. My mother taught me that—she was a crusader. I always try to steady a situation. When the President's Commission on Olympic Sports came out I claimed it was a total whitewash. It proved to be just that. But I'm only one person in one sport—track and field—which is not regarded or televised as much as in Europe, and I'm only one person who performs one event and has a big mouth. I've had a popular five years in my event but my time is short-lived, so all you can hope to do is have an influence while you are in the limelight.

"I feel that track and field and amateur sports in general have enormous potential for the kids to get both the respect they deserve, the support they need and some kind of reward for their efforts. I don't see that happening. I see people being taken advantage of. I see a network pay a quarter of a billion dollars for the rights to put on a performance—the 1984 Olympic Games in Los Angeles—but what will the performers get? Young people who are the best in the world. The governing body, the Olympic Committee, should get a good percentage of the advertising and television revenue, but as agents for the athletes they must get what is a fair agent's percentage and share the rest with the athletes.

"The rules governing the amateur athlete have to be relaxed in the next three years. There must be an open door for more athletes to do more endorsements for more corporations to attract them to support amateur athletics, bringing more business into sports and keeping the best athletes in their respective sports as teachers. Only then will America reign as the best nation in the world in amateur sports."

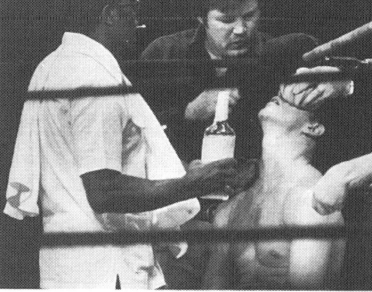

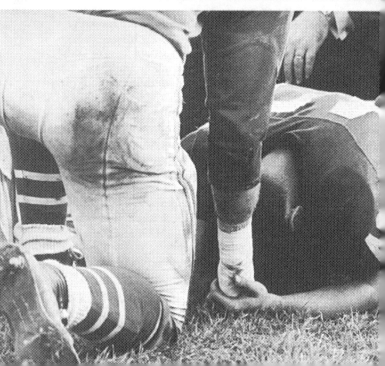

PAIN
AND FEAR

All of the great athletes I have known have an almost unlimited horizon for pain. Pain is their enemy, but they never admit it, never discuss it. Athletes at the height of their power must endure pain beyond their imagination and what they thought was their capacity for suffering in order to achieve their maximum performance.

"Your stomach feels as though it's going to fall out," Don Schollander said. "Every kick hurts like hell—and suddenly you hear a shrill internal scream. Then you have a choice. Most swimmers back away. If you push through the pain barrier into real agony, you're a champion."

The dry fire in the chest is the painful price the distance runner must pay. Roger Bannister, the first man to break the four-minute barrier in the mile in 1954, described his strength against pain as the peculiar capacity for "mental excitement" which enables the runner to ignore or overcome discomfort and pain. "It is this psychological factor," Bannister agreed, "beyond the ken of physiology, which sets the razor's edge between victory and defeat, and which determines how closely an athlete comes to the absolute limits of performance."

Cus D'Amato, the fight manager of the fifties, said, "Fear is a powerful natural force, and the great athletes use it, control it, and they make it work for them. Fear gives the athlete that extra strength. The adrenaline makes the heart pump faster, which brings more oxygen to the body, then more energy. But fear is like fire. If you don't control it, it will destroy you and everything around you."

Athletes suffer in silence.

153

DANGER AND DEATH

In these 25 years I've never, *never* seen an athlete flinch. I've never seen a physical admission of being afraid. I've read awareness of fear in the eyes of an athlete but none have ever turned away scared from any test. This may speak more for their pride than their courage, more for instinct than discretion. In total involvement and absolute concentration there is no time for fear. Luck and quickness get them through.

The portrait, at right, is Austrian Niki Landa, Ferrari's top driver after his fiery crash in a Formula I race. He hit the curb on the apex of a turn at 200 km an hour in Nürburgring. His Ferrari broke away at the back. Suddenly the car made a violent move crashing through the catch fencing, bouncing off an embankment back .to the track and caught fire. A pole took his helmet off. He was pinned in the flames. Four brave men rescued him. Pulled free, his head, face and hands were burned but breathing the burning petrol was mortally dangerous. The heat was 800 degrees centigrade. His lungs were scorched and his head swollen to three times normal size. There was physical and psychological recovery. Skin was grafted from thigh to face. Niki got well in six weeks. Saved by doctors and the steel frame of the Ferrari, Landa raced 47 days later at Monza. He crossed the fear threshold that day. Won again and again but one day years later he stopped his car in practice on the circuit, got out and walked away from the sport forever.

Lorenzo Bandini in my 1967 Monaco Grand Prix film was not so lucky. He gave his life (right). I've seen great horses fall at Buches Brook in the Grand National and an espontaneo jump the barrier in the bull ring in Madrid and seen his face an instant before he was gored to death.

154

ONE MAN ALONE

It seems most of us are suspended on the tedious hook of indifference. Nothing happens. There is little time, little chance, little energy, little reason, little *feeling*. There is no room for us to maneuver into the one day of adventure that would change our lives. The temporary pressures and little problems keep us swinging, but we can't get off the hook. The battle lines are indistinct and we're not sure where we are going. There is a numbness, and against the soft edges of inaction we make no crucial decisions because there are none exciting enough to make. For many of us, most things in a day just happen.

The athlete is blessed. His line is clear-cut. The time of decision for him is absolute. He faces it again and again, and his feelings are real. There is a total awareness of the full scale of emotions all of the time. No one tells him what he should feel. He experiences it! This experience, this feeling, is worth all of his brutal effort and concentration. His mornings begin just as slowly as ours, but his imagination and purpose fire his dedication and desire, and he is rewarded. What is more, most of the way he goes it alone.

I welcome the long late hours of work on this book when all the vivid action of the years in pictures is selected and arranged and I see again the easy patterns of a day somewhere in France or England or California. As I fit the photographs and drawings to the layout of these pages, I am there again and I remember exactly how it was.

Strangely, now, it is like a Cocteau film. All is silent—still—no wind is blowing. I can feel myself moving with the camera and see the particular color of the light and see the faces of Billy Kidd or Arnold Palmer and feel the crowd surging and see the contour of the land. I am enveloped in this dreamlike vacuum and I smile as I remember exactly how it was when I took each picture and how that moment will never come exactly that way again.

This collection is a tribute to *one man alone*. The athlete—alone in the field or before a goal, alone on a sled, or car or horse, alone as a golfer is, or a long-distance runner, alone as a tiny gymnast is on a bar. Alone as all men and women are each day—as they make it on their own—if they are afforded that privilege.

No athlete comes suddenly to the test and is by some magic a match for it. The gifted athlete is able to perform at the apex of the drama because he is a known quantity. There is no sudden metamorphosis in sport. Not for the champion.

So it is with Jim Clark or Niki Lauda before the start, Billie Jean King and Chris Evert at match point, Ingemar Stenmark and Anna Marie Proell at the final gates, Nadia Comaneci and John Naber achieving the Olympic medal or Robinson, Unitas, Ali, Nicklaus, all of them in this book. In an uncertain world, their strength sustains us.

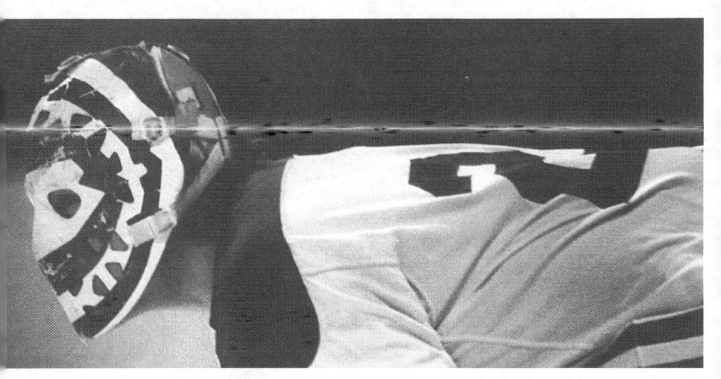

PICTURE STORY

It was like the old days at Ebbets Field, those glorious, mild, brilliant, sunny days when the World Series began on the first days of October and baseball was a magic game of peace and poetry and boyhood. It was like the Dodgers waiting for the Yankees, in their gray road uniforms, in that little green-painted ballpark in Brooklyn. It was a special day when everything looked and felt exciting and you knew everyone in the United States would be watching or listening or caring about this baseball game.

It was Fenway Park in Boston, and when I stepped out on the field I smiled. The little park, the immaculate green grass, the Sox in the cage and the sounds of the bat hits and the hiss of the ball and far off the hollow whoops of kids with gloves catching foul balls in the seats. It was two hours before the game and Ted Williams was in the dugout talking baseball with the same energy and conviction he had expressed in the last American League playoff game against Cleveland thirty years before. The somber face of Luis Tiant, who had pitched a two-hit shutout to force a playoff, the pepper games and infield drill and the batting cage with the Yankees' awesome hitter, Reggie Jackson, displaying his power, it all made you feel comfortable.

Now it was the New York Yankees and the Boston Red Sox. Both teams had played an entire schedule, each had won ninety-nine games and finished the season tied, and today was the quest for the hundredth victory. "The ultimate confrontation," Carlton Fisk, the Red Sox catcher, called it the night before when the Sox had won their eighth straight game to catch the Yankees, who lost to Cleveland on the final Sunday.

The drama is unmatched in this complete society of the ballpark. One team must win. The best players, the two best pitchers, one pitching against his old teammates; the home-team crowd that would give anything for the win, the fans that have traveled and sit behind the visitors' dugout. The drama has a beginning, a middle and an end, and to the final moment no one can predict victory, and when the end comes it comes quickly and the curtain is drawn.

On this stage the veteran comes to the plate and receives a tumultuous ovation. It lasts for three minutes and the crowd with their voices and their faces and their bodies thank him for the thrill he has brought each of them with his brilliant play over the long season. He is deeply moved, smiles and shakes his head in disbelief, and then hits a home run, and the expression of sheer joy that explodes in the sunlight of those stands is something you will never experience again in your lifetime. Yastrzemski hit one! The expression of feeling of five thousand standing, waving, screaming, happy people—or all the eye or camera can see at one look—is dreamlike when you are there. In the deep shadows of the grandstand people are hidden and you feel only their collective force. In the bleachers at Fenway every single face is a mighty individual in the blazing sunlight, come to be heard, reborn, or die. Nothing in between.

Ron Guidry wore no sweatshirt, and the sunlight defined every muscle in his remarkable skinny arm. Mike Torrez shut out the Yankees for six innings. He knocked their shortstop down, then made one bad pitch to Bucky Dent. Jackson homered big. I saw the ball in the kid's hand in deepest center field.

This is a picture story. A picture story in journalism must extend beyond coverage of specific events. In a few pictures the photographer must sense the history and hold forever the character of the sport, the game, the players, the people, the true dimension of what he sees and feels by being there, and the physical and deeply personal tone of everyone involved. Then you have a microcosm, in a few pictures, of one classic game and of all of baseball, of the influence of the athlete on American life.

The paradox of still *pictures* is they allow each beholder to better understand and appreciate the vital missing dimension. Voice. The real power of moving pictures or television is sound. But that sound is recorded, transmitted sound. Only in the live presence does sound become a true and magnificent experience. The throated roar of joy in sports, like pain or happiness, can never be exactly remembered. It fades to silence deep in your brain.

You are left with quotations. Since sport mirrors life there is the bitter and the sweet as the *Chicago Tribune* reporter asks the exhausted Red Sox catcher in the clubhouse when the game is over and lost, "Is it poetic justice that the Yankees won?"

"This isn't a game of poetic justice," Carlton Fisk said. "Some guys seem to be poets of emotion when they're pitching or running or hitting or catching or whatever they're doing. But I still don't think you can look for any poetic justice in this game." Or in life.

STEELERS

At its best the Super Bowl is a celebration, a festival, a Mardi Gras of power. A battleground for old pros. The victory for the Pittsburgh Steelers in Super Bowl XIV, in January 1980, under a blazing Pasadena sun was a golden 31-19 win, over the Los Angeles Rams, their *fourth* Super Bowl championship in six years. The Steelers are the best of all time.

The pictures here are a kaleidoscope of action, from Lynn Swann (88) missing a soft, wind-blown pass in the frustrating first half from Steeler quarterback Terry Bradshaw, to the Ram runs by elfin Wendell Tyler. The intensity in the eyes of the defensive linemen, Joe Greene and L. C. Greenwood and the first of the big plays, Swann's catch of a 47-yard pass to put the Steelers ahead 17-13 in the third quarter. The lead changed hands six times with McCutchen's scoring option to Smith, Vince Ferragamo's cool game for L.A. at quarterback.

The Ram's terrific defense held the Steelers to 84 yards running, so Bradshaw threw perfect passes to John Stallworth for 73 yards and another for 45 yards to set up the final score. Steelers number one!

The rage of Coach Chuck Noll with 1:40 left in the game and the Steelers ahead by 12 points, was to his defense as the Rams were driving. "Don't give anything away." He screamed. "Nothing, *nothing*!" Just like Lombardi at Green Bay.

THE RACE

Affirmed/Alydar, Belmont Stakes, Thoroughbred Racing Triple Crown, 1978

The poetry of sports is based in part on the seasons. Down off the mountains and the world of the alpine skier, out from the ice rinks to the blossoms of springtime and thoroughbred racing. It happened every year for so long and lovely a time. The Kentucky Derby was like my birthday, and all the racetrack people were the finest people I met in sports and the racehorse the most magnificent animal in the world.

The head and face, the color and grace, of the great racehorses are as clearly remembered as any athlete I ever photographed. Nashua, Swaps, Bold Ruler, Gallant Man, General Duke, Kelso, Secretariat, Forego, Seattle Slew, Affirmed, yes, and a horse called Alydar. Alydar reminded me of General Duke —like all the big Calumet horses. That's the way racetrackers talk—owners and trainers and the knowledgeable people around the track. Every great horse reminds them of another great horse in a certain way, and so the bloodline is continued in the eye and heart of all of us who love the life of the racetrack and all the spirit that keeps it alive, which seems so far away from the bettors and the mutuel tickets, so far away from the odds—as far away as the grandstand appears from the last barn in the stable on a spring morning.

It was seven A.M. and Affirmed's trainer, Las Barrera, was laughing in the bright California sunlight. Steve Cauthen leaned on the rail next to him. It was an interesting contrast to see the young jockey sip his coffee and study his hands, strong and angular

with distinct veins; Barrera's were pudgy and smooth. The traffic on the track was heavy at morning work, and Cauthen wore his gray exercise helmet and a heavy olive drab jacket, his stick tucked under his arm. The two men were talking in confidence. They were the hot team in thoroughbred racing in 1978. The best team with the Big Horse— *Affirmed!*

"Stevie Cauthen has worked wonders with Affirmed," the trainer said in his clipped Spanish accent. "He's been with the horse from the beginning in Saratoga last year. He work with him in the morning, he love the horse and he know everything what the horse do. He can race the horse and bring it from behind and do anything with the horse that he wants to do, and I think it will be no problem for him to handle the horse on the lead or from behind. When you work with a jockey like Steve Cauthen a trainer can go to sleep on the night and relax because you know if something is wrong with your horse you're going to find out the next day. Stevie will tell you.

166

"In our workout, Affirmed went the first quarter in :25, the second quarter in :24 and then he got the third quarter in :22.3. When he comes back to me in the morning he holds his fingers up—middle finger to thumb in a circle of perfection which means, 'We got 'em!'

"Steve Cauthen, for his age, he do most everything right on horses. He make a mistake like every human being but he's a smooth rider and if we are lucky to keep him around we're going to see one of the greatest riders the United States ever had. He gets out of trouble very well, he's very alert. Stevie see trouble happen before it get to him. Sometime you can't avoid trouble in horse racing because you have to make a decision so fast—that you have to be lucky sometimes to get away from trouble, but Stevie believes he's got the 'gift of the gods' that was born with him—that he can see the trouble coming.

"Affirmed is a tall, good-sized horse but he's not too heavy. Affirmed is very light on his feet, he hit the ground and bounce back right away. He don't stay too long on the ground. He fly. He hit the top of the turf and go, and that's what makes him such a good horse.

"He watches everything during the race—it looks like he enjoys himself running. My horse has no worry—the guy that has to come from behind has to worry."

I watched Steve Cauthen through the window of the station wagon as he came back to the barn area after he'd worked another top horse, J. O. Tobin, on the grass. He walked with a quick stride but did not look at many of the visitors. He gave a half-nod and a little crooked smile to the racetrackers that he knew and who gave him a word. Cauthen slipped into the back seat to talk on the eve of his first Kentucky Derby. He wasn't giving the press a word. Nothing. Their stories were all the same, the *kid* from Kentucky about to ride to glory in the big run for the roses in his own backyard. It was the sure road to the triple crown: the Derby, the Preakness and the Belmont Stakes.

The best American jockeys in California at the winter meeting had cramped his style. He wasn't the leading rider—frustrating for Steve, who had been the nation's biggest winner the year before at age sixteen with horses that had earned more than $6 million in purse money on 2,075 mounts. Cauthen scored 487 victories, 345 seconds and 304 thirds, finishing in the money better than 50 percent of the time.

Cauthen was a quiet young athlete who never seemed to laugh or take much joy in what he said about his horses. He spoke in a squeaky monotone, with a "ya know" inserted in every phrase. Cauthen

never looked you in the eye much. Sometimes not at all. He reminded me of Bill Hartack in manner and mood. I was certain he would act the same if he was a big winner or a big loser. And for some strange reason that April morning I thought that like Hartack he would know both worlds. He began to talk about race riding.

"I always try to have good position. I always look at a race, the horses in the race, the horse I ride, and compare that horse with the main factors in the race; where I think the good horses will be most of the race, the jockeys that ride them and what I think they'll do. I get the race up in my mind and I know it all can change if there is some unexpected incident coming out of the starting gate or going down the backside. Many times something happens that you can't control that changes the race, but riding as many races as I have I know what to do when the situation changes—and I do what I feel is right.

"Everybody gets in trouble sometimes. Nobody can say they never get in trouble. I can see trouble coming. I think I've had experience in most of the situations that arise in a horse race.

"My horse Affirmed is very intelligent. The start can be important, especially in a big field. Affirmed is well schooled and he always breaks very good—no matter what. Then you can ride away and do whatever you want with him. You can take him back, you can go to the lead, whatever you decide to do at that time. He's a very willing horse and he's very easy to get along with. He reacts to the gates opening. He's a very quick horse. He can be standing nice and square and the gate opens and he breaks alertly all

the time and then you can take him back or go to the lead—whatever you want. The danger in the gate is to have him standing wrong and when he breaks, if he breaks hard, he stumbles because his feet aren't under him and drops his head and the other horses will outrun him as he loses his momentum. If a horse is jumping around in the gate, the assistant starter will work to set him right, but I have to see that my horse is ready to break.

"Heavy-headed horses or lumbering horses don't usually break very fast. Some horses just aren't good gate horses. They always come out of the gate slow. If you get them to break fairly well you've done your job. Those kinds of horses are tough, it's like trying to get a fat person to move quickly.

"I feel I have a good sense of time. That's one of the things I worked on very hard before I started riding. My father helped me with it a lot—he made sure I knew it was very important, and I worked on breezing horses in the morning, and I became very good with a clock in my head.

"I could tell, usually to within a couple of fifths of a second, how fast I went, or if I wanted a horse to go in a certain time—if he had the ability—I could pretty near do it. I became very good at *time* and in a race I usually know the pace and if there's a fast pace in front I will know within a few fifths of how fast they're going. Different racetracks work differently. This track at Santa Anita is a very fast race track, yesterday they went the first quarter in :22 and change—at Aqueduct in New York that would be very fast because the race track is slower. Your sense of pace changes with the horse and the track.

168

"In the Kentucky Derby nothing happens until you get there and you work with the trainer and I set up the plans—I decide what I'm going to do. When the overnights come out and I see the horses in the race, I'll decide where I want to be in the race, where I think everyone else is going to be, how fast I think they're going to be going, then I'll decide what I should do.

"Mr. Barrera never tells me anything. As a trainer he trusts my sense of timing. He trusts my sense to judge the race. More or less he might tell me, when different races come up, what his thoughts about a race are, but he leaves it up to me usually and that's the best way because as long as he's got faith in my judgment, it's better for me to have a free conscience so that I can decide at the moment instead of having the weight of something in the back of my mind that the trainer wants me to do. This way I can decide what I want to do, which makes it a lot better.

"I don't get in habits necessarily doing anything. I don't have a rule for everything," Cauthen whispered. "Sometimes, *sometimes* I do things out of habit, but I don't try to do 'em because of habit. I have used the whip on Affirmed but it's been in tight races and strong finishes. When he's head-and-head with a horse I'm not sure he needs the stick that much, maybe just to keep tapping him to make sure he's got his mind on his business. But when he's in front then you've *got* to keep his mind on his business for sure because he tends to wait on horses if he's all by himself. It would be a shame to get caught right on the money for no reason.

"Affirmed and Alydar have completely demolished their competition, and when they come together it's always a very good race. Since I've been riding Affirmed, I've beaten Alydar three times and with Jorge Velasquez riding him he beat me once as a two-year-old. In the stretch I've had my horse both inside or outside. In the Belmont Futurity I was inside of him, in the Hopeful I was inside, in the Laurel Futurity I was outside.

"Being inside or outside of him if the track is even doesn't make any difference to my horse. The Calumet horse seems to like to be outside.

"Affirmed is a long-striding horse. He's got a really great stride when he levels off and gets down head-and-head with another horse—he's got a tremendous stride. He hits the ground very lightly. You have to be on him to know the real feeling. I can't say Affirmed and Alydar are totally different. Affirmed is a lot more versatile than Alydar. Alydar seems to have one punch. I've never ridden the horse, so anything I say is only from what I see. Alydar's a nice-looking horse. He's big, he's well proportioned, but the two horses have different running styles.

"They're both game colts and they're both very consistent all the time. Affirmed's got great ability, that's the one important thing about him, but when you come down to race and there's two good colts and they both have great ability, then you look for something else. With Affirmed it is his *versatility*.

"When Affirmed is head-and-head and fighting out he's as game a horse as I've ever ridden and he fights to the end. That's a sense you instill in a horse

169

through your hands when it comes down to the stretch and down the lane, when you really start asking him through your urging, through your hands. The horse understands it's time to fight, it's time to run. I can't tell you how he knows it, but they know it and you know they know it and when you get that feeling together it's a great feeling.

"My horse has speed, he can go to the front. He's the smartest horse I've ever been around. Nothing bothers him. He likes to run. When he gets in the heat of a race he tries his heart out all the time. He

white hoops, and took Affirmed along the rail at Pimlico and beat Alydar again in the Preakness by a neck. This time Velasquez, wearing the devil's red-and-blue silks of Calumet Farm, owned by Mrs. Lucille Markey, began his move earlier, but Steve Cauthen drove his horse a little harder and won again quite easily. (bottom, page 166)

John Veitch, Alydar's trainer, decided to make two changes in strategy for the third and most demanding race of the Triple Crown—the Belmont Stakes. Veitch was determined that in this classic

fights to the finish. After a race he plays in the barn —he's never excited, never tired. He's a super champion sort of horse."

Steve Cauthen gave Affirmed a nice ride in the 104th running of the Kentucky Derby. The kid from Kentucky won his first Derby on his first try, beating Alydar, ridden by Jorge Velasquez, by one and a half lengths, never bothered by the late surge of the Calumet three-year-old colt. Affirmed's time of 2:01⅕ was fifth fastest in Derby history. Secretariat set the record of 1:59⅖ in 1973. (top, page 166)

Cauthen slipped his ninety-seven pounds into the flamingo silks of Harbor View Farm, owned by Louis E. Wolfson, with the bold black sleeves and

test at a mile and a half Affirmed would not have it all his way on the lead, set a slow early pace and save it all for the stretch run. The fear was another runaway that began with a gallop. "The one thing I don't want is a slow pace," he told his Panamanian jockey. "If the pace is too slow for the first half mile, go to the front, but stay with him, shadow him all the way." The second move by the trainer was to take the blinkers off Alydar in the hope of making the horse more alert and so able to use his speed to stay closer to Affirmed.

There is that unending challenge in sports when champions meet in a series of tests. Each time the strategy changes and each time the caring of the people changes, and with horses as with athletes there is a deep affection that grows, even love. Each time in the game or the fight or the race it comes down to speed and heart. No one will ever forget the 110th running of the Belmont Stakes. It was a magnificent horse race. Was it the greatest race of all time? Close to it. I'll bet on that.

I came to the track that day with my oldest son, Christopher, lugging the big sequence camera that I had done all my horse action research with, and placed him at the quarter pole where I had spent so

with Cordero. It was vivid and I photographed it—an amazing preview to the battle to come, but no one will remember that excellent race. Cauthen won it.

When the gate opened Steve Cauthen took Affirmed smoothly to the rail on the lead—an artful move, since Alydar broke inside of him in the number 2 gate position. The lead horse sets the pace; it was Cauthen's horse race. As they came by my camera, it was smooth and silent. I see the hoofs flashing but the animals seem to flow inexorably into position. The first time they go by all my attention

many afternoons covering Eddie Arcaro twenty years before. Chris had never used the camera, but we worked on the viewing and pan during the early races. He did fine and recorded the sequence above.

In the sixth race, while I was working with my son, I saw Steve Cauthen locked in a duel with Angel Cordero, Jr. It was an exceptional race, a tough physical race that I believe readied Cauthen for his battle with Alydar in the eighth race on the card. Cordero was outside and tight on Ruffian's half-brother, Buckfinder, and Steve in Harbor View Farms flamingo was riding Life's Hope. Cauthen was forced to whip left-handed, to ride the same lane, to fight in tight quarters, shoulder to shoulder

is to a peripheral vision, a numb awareness—only that the race is on. I see no detail, hear no sound. I think I hear the hoofbeats but it probably is my imagination. I squint and watch the flamingo color in the sun on the rail slide into the first turn. Steve's got good position. I smiled and all my senses switched on. The sound began.

Cauthen set his clock at :25 for the initial quarter of a mile. The first half mile was run in :50. It was just what Veitch had feared, a slow start that would save Affirmed for the final quarter. Cauthen was running his race for his horse. Velasquez had to move early, and he brought Alydar up on Affirmed's shoulder to shadow Cauthen at the head of the back-

stretch. The two horses were lapped with a mile to go. They ran that way for a mile to the wire, stride for stride, and this was the remarkable nature of this race. Those six and a half furlongs became the truest "test of champions" in Belmont history.

The closing mile was run in 1:36⅘, the fastest time in the history of the sport. Remember that! In a shade over a minute and a half as I watched the two horses make their run down the backstretch I learned how the human spirit, free and happy, can speak *together;* the more than 65,500 voices and hearts reached out in the most exalted sustained roar I had ever heard. A free people, present to cheer for their horse, their rider, this lovely day in June. The sound that day made it the greatest horse race ever run for those of us who were there.

Cauthen, racing near the rail as usual, kept Affirmed in front, leading by a half length in 1:14 for six furlongs and by a head after a mile and one quarter in 2:01⅗.

The horses entered the stretch a quarter of a mile from home, head and head, so close together that Cauthen had no room to whip right-handed. Velasquez, whipping right-handed, finally brought his horse even. The roar became cataclysmic, a human sound no one will ever forget.

Steve hit Affirmed once with the right hand, then switched the stick and cracked him from the rail side with his left hand. He had never hit the horse left-handed before. Affirmed responded with just enough speed and heart.

My camera was in a good position as the race started, but during the run over a hundred photographers had edged way out on the track and shut off my view. I saw only the sixteenth pole, the white rail and the flower beds through my viewfinder as the earth seemed to shake with the roar. I focused on the pole and set the frame and in a blinding instant they were *there.* The picture matched the sound. I started to fire in rhythm with their stride— two chestnut colts radiant in the late-afternoon sunlight, closer than any horses I've ever seen in the stretch, head and head, stride for stride. Velasquez raised his right arm as Cauthen raised his left. They were a mirror image as they came down the lane, as an eagle over the river, their arms whipping as wings, as they swooped to the prize at the wire. It was a lasting image, those magnificent animals, the two jockeys, their heads buried, looked as one horse, one rider, the entire crowd one heart, the world of the racetrack in those final seconds—one voice of supreme urging, caring and joy.

Affirmed outgamed Alydar again. Cauthen won by less than a head and with abandon stood in the irons and waved his whip just past the wire. Affirmed had won it all.

The two horses finished 13¾ lengths ahead of Darby Creek Road, the third choice, 21½ lengths ahead of the fourth-place horse, Judge Advocate, and 22¾ lengths ahead of the last-place finisher in the five-horse field, Noon Time Spender.

This Triple Crown was history, demanding because it is contested on three different tracks at three different distances in less than six weeks. In fifteen starts Affirmed had lost only twice, both times to Alydar at Belmont Park. The winning purse of $110,580 raised his total earnings to $1,-133,807.

Young Steve Cauthen was so happy when he came back. "When I won, Jorge called over, *'Congratulations!'* I thanked him and said it hadn't been easy. We were going nice and slow early. Alydar was running with me, but it was a slow pace. I kept Affirmed in front without pressing him down the backstretch and kept him slow with me. Alydar came to us on the turn and we let out a bit. Going into the stretch Jorge was riding tight on my side and I had to change the whip, but after he took one stride in front at the three-sixteenths pole, Affirmed came back again. *This* was a horse race."

THE FIGHT

Muhammad Ali/Joe Frazier Heavyweight Title, Madison Square Garden, 1971

The facts of that Monday night come back in a blur. Joe Frazier won his twenty-seventh professional fight, and it was the first defeat for Muhammad Ali in thirty-two bouts. The crowd in Madison Square Garden in New York was a record 19,500, and the *New York Times* front-page headline read, "TV audience of 300 Million Around World Views Fight," certainly one of the most amazing headlines in sports history. The record live gate was $1.25 million.

Referee Arthur Mercante called it 8–6–1 for Frazier; Judge Bill Recht ruled it 11–4, Frazier; Judge Artie Ardala 9–6, Frazier. A unanimous decision over fifteen rounds.

Muhammad Ali, who had embraced the Muslim faith and changed his name from Cassius Clay, was returning from a three-and-a-half-year exile for refusing to fight in Vietnam, quietly avoiding jail and waiting in vain for reinstatement of his heavyweight title that he had won from Sonny Liston. He had prepared for this battle with Frazier, the champion, by beating Jerry Quarry and Oscar Bonavena.

Ali appeared in a red velvet robe, red trunks, white shoes with red tassels that danced as he waved to a thunderous ovation. Joe Frazier was in a green-and-gold robe with green flowered trunks. He looked grim and solid and tough. It was going to be one of the great heavyweight fights. I was nervous as hell.

I had two cameras and ten rolls of black-and-white film and I wondered as I watched the two fighters climb into the ring if it would be enough. I was sitting in the twenty-sixth row of "ringside" with Jim McKay and Roone Arledge and Frank Gifford. I had been asked to come to the fight at five o'clock that afternoon and had bought the film in a drug-store in Greenwich Village. U.S. network television was barred from the fight, and I was going to pre-pare a technical report on the outcome with my sketches and photographs. It never happened. A legal hassle on my fee for my special report aborted the assignment and five years later 340 of the 360 negatives were lost or stolen. The pictures on these pages are some of those I salvaged. So I remember the fight with a mixture of haunting pain and deep nostalgia.

Muhammad Ali won the first two rounds, and at the end of the second round he waved his right glove in derision at Frazier and put both arms over his head in victory. But I sensed that perhaps he had gotten a message in those two rounds. He stood in his corner for sixty seconds between rounds, as Joe looked across at him from his stool with Yancy Dur-ham bending over him. Ali came out early, before the bell starting the third round, and stood at ring center.

Joe Frazier charged out at the bell and won the next five rounds. He won them by being stronger and never slowing his forward charge. He moved Ali to the ropes at will, and he seemed to have a savage strength and thumping power that electrified the arena at the end of the third round, when he smashed Ali in the face at the bell.

Frazier bullied Ali relentlessly, charging out of an impossible low crouch. Muhammad began to lie on the ropes. He choreographed that slow rhythm of defense, moving his elbows and shoulders, his hips and head, blocking, slipping, countering punches, being hit harder and harder and showing his tired-ness. Ali came out very slowly for the fifth round. Frazier spat his mouthpiece half out to jeer like some crazed wolf and continued his inexorable for-ward bulling force. Joe started to go for the body. He began to dig in short, murderous hooks to the belly—but landed the big punches accurately to the head and face, again and again.

Ali began to hang on, wrap his arms around Joe's neck to try to avoid the deadly hammer of Frazier's big punches. Exhaustion began to seep and crawl around the ring like the spread of germs. Both fighters tasted the pain of exhaustion, Frazier from the attack, Ali from defense.

Clinches seemed unendurable. From the slow tiredness of a slow-motion embrace, Ali would tap out a rhythm of stinging punches, hitting Joe three

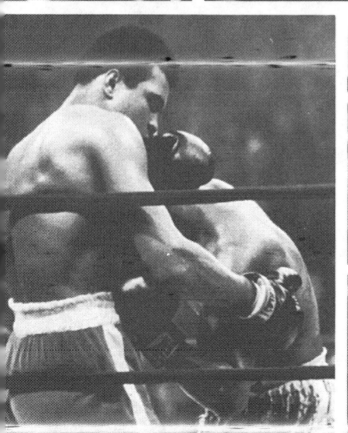

and four to one, but they had no power, they were at times almost a ritual flailing, a hapless faltering in a lost rhythm of little moves as he fell back and pretended to play along the ropes. Frazier had landed twenty powerful punches to Ali's head and face in these rounds, and rocked Ali with a brutal left to the head to end the eighth.

The classic part of the fight began in the ninth round. The crowd knew Joe Frazier was ahead. The champion climaxed his deadly attack to Muhammad Ali's body. Frazier kept storming in, relentlessly charging, cutting off all the circles of escape Ali could make. Ali backed without circling. Deadly game. There are only the ropes left for a fighter who does not move laterally, does not circle, does not dance away. Joe hooked short to the waist, pummeled the hipbone, the gut, the ribs; he appeared grotesque in the extreme crouch. Ali looked down and saw the top of Joe's head and all of his back. A fighter can't punch down, can't hook or jab down with any effectiveness, or shoot uppercuts when an opponent's that low. Can't tie his man up, either.

Ali has always had a childish streak in the ring. Rather than look ineffective or be made to appear ineffective by another fighter, he will ride with the current and take punishment on the ropes. He will turn the opponent's strongest moments of attack into a rope defense, proving he can take relentless punishment, and so slowly turn the aggressiveness of his attacker into a weakness by his playful, insulting clowning and superb disdain of his attacker's power by *enduring* on the ropes. A dangerous game for most fighters, this night wasteful for Muhammad.

The blows that Ali landed over the first eight rounds were abrasive stings to Joe's cheekbones and face. Now in the ninth, Joe straightened up, his face swollen red from the licking jabs of the man he still called Clay. The fighters twice leaned against each other, and Mercante had to pull them apart. I sensed that Ali was feeling the load, measuring Joe's tension, his tiredness—probing to see if Frazier was punched out after winning the previous five rounds. Ali read it that way and came alive thirty seconds into the ninth round. There was a surge of crowd energy. Everyone thought the fight would turn right here. Ali's jab began to sting and snap. He landed leverage, landed right hands, twisting his mouth in that mean grimace as he hit Frazier again and again. The photograph (upper left) shows that fierce expression of Muhammad and his power.

Ali hooked hard, danced and circled, gathered points and for the first time hit with speed in combination. His left-right rhythm came in threes, and they stopped Joe's charge. Frazier wobbled for the first time.

180

Sensing the danger of turnabout, Joe Frazier stormed out of his corner for the start of the tenth round. Ali boxed slickly to start the round, but Frazier landed a hard left to Ali's head and moved in. Ali caught him with a left hook to the head, which Joe took to counter with a straight left to Ali's nose. Muhammad, violent, unleashed a left-right-left to Frazier's face, his most damaging blows of the fight. Ali landed with another left to Frazier's face and Joe's charge slowed again.

Ali had put two strong rounds together, won them both as his strength and hand speed had returned after the long agonizing early rounds. The next few seconds were so intense because you knew, if you believed in Joe Frazier's storming, relentless power, that he would get to Ali as if his life depended on it and bull his way back to land the killing left hook or long right hand. If you believed in the wonders of Muhammad Ali you knew his magic and speed and boxing skill would slice up the rugged champion. The kill would come soon.

The eleventh round proved memorable. It was a round of champions, one of the best single rounds in Joe Frazier's career, the one round I believe where Muhammad Ali took his worst punishment. Ali began by stabbing with his left as Joe tore in. He missed with a left and Ali bounced off the ropes and slipped to one knee. Joe bulled Ali into a neutral corner and mercilessly hit him with two left hooks to the head. Frazier landed two more lefts, then Ali in desperation countered with a left and right to Joe's face. Frazier then shook the ring with a deadly left to the head and Ali went reeling around the ring, nearly knocked out on his feet, at one instant both gloves down, his feet spread, his eyes rolling back in his head.

I saw his eyes roll back through my long lens and was amazed. I fired and my trigger jammed. This instant was one of about ten pictures I took over a twenty-year period on the thirty-seventh frame of a thirty-six-exposure roll. End-of-a-roll luck—and in this fight it was to happen twice. I used two cameras to avoid running out, but both cameras came up empty at critical moments under the excitement of the night.

Ali looked helpless, just standing there hanging on. Frazier won the roaring crowd then with a thunderous punch that sent Ali to the ropes virtually out on his feet. He staggered back to his corner at the bell. Gone.

Dr. Harry Kleiman, who was the ring physician with Dr. Edwin Campbell, climbed quickly into the ring to ask Ali if he was all right, then let the fight continue. Joe Frazier attacked like a savage beast to open round twelve and cracked a left hook off Muhammad's chin. Joe bulled him to the ropes and then half destroyed him near the corner post with three lefts to the face, and Ali fell in on Joe. Frazier tore free and caught Ali as he was moving back and twisted him with a painful left to the jaw. Muhammad tried to fight back. It was the only moment, the only image of Ali in all his fights, where he looked helpless, where he cried for sympathy. But even as the crowd reached out, his great pride and heart served him and he forced Frazier to the ropes and smashed a right to his jaw as the round ended.

At the bell for thirteen the crowd was amazed. Ali came out *dancing*. It was incredible to watch. He whipped and stung jabs to Frazier's head, pushing it down to throw Joe off balance. They wrestled and clung, but Ali drove a fine combination to Joe's head and almost won the round. It was critical—because referee Mercante and judges Aidala and Recht gave Muhammad Ali the fourteenth round.

Ali won it with nasty whiplash slices with his gloves around Frazier's eyes. Ali kept holding Joe's head, Frazier trying to get him off for punching room. Frazier took a hard right, then landed a good left, the left hand that would remain the indelible weapon of this battle. Ali got in three quick lefts to Frazier's face and then took a numbing blow, another left on the head and another to the face. Ali ended strong, so strong with a combination to Joe's face that you wondered if he by some miracle of style and strength and courage would come back and win the fifteenth. Referee Mercante and judges Aidala and Recht gave Muhammad Ali the fourteenth round.

As they came out for the fifteenth and final round, Joe Frazier had nine rounds. Ali had five rounds, and two of those could have gone to Frazier. Ali would have to knock Joe out to win. It was not to be that night—in fact, Joe Frazier came close to knocking out Muhammad Ali in the fifteenth round.

The fighters touched gloves as they began the final round. I forgot to check my film between rounds, or misread the counter on one camera, and thought in the excitement I had reloaded the second. What had happened was that I had rewound an expended roll but had not reloaded. I finished one camera quickly as Ali landed his opening combinations, then was *out of film*.

I cursed and stared through the viewfinder to see Joe Frazier unload one of the mightiest punches in ring history, a savage left, a long, wild, magnificent left to Muhammad Ali's jaw that sent him dead dizzy on his back, *Ali down*. A hammer blow, a heavyweight champion's punch, and only a heavyweight champion could endure it and get up as Ali did after three seconds of the referee's count. Ali took the mandatory eight count and I reloaded frantically as Frazier charged in for the kill. Frazier

drove a right to the jaw, then hooked a left and right to the body to try to finish Ali. Brutally, he smashed two more lefts to the jaw, a right on Ali's chin, a wicked left to the body. Ali clinched for his life, hanging there as Joe Frazier almost sent him down again with another screaming left. Ali's legs were gone, and another clubbing left sent him into the ropes. The right side of Muhammad's face was swollen as if his jaw was broken. Suddenly through the frenzied roar of the crowd came the final bell. Ali stood there two feet away from Joe, face to face, as Mercante came forward and Joe Frazier smiled with joy—and held up his glove in victory. Muhammad stared at him like a child in disbelief. He had lost.

My last photograph that night was Muhammad Ali, his face swollen, sad and alone, being led by police through the floor crowd to his dressing room. His words in the next hours were whispered without remorse or regret and in praise of the man who beat him. Ali had fought with the spirit of a champion and spoke like one.

"So I lost. You see any marks on me? A little on this side. I did my best. So I lost. So I'm human. I don't cry. I hit him so many times to his not hitting me—but I made the mistake. A fellow could be intoxicated with his own ability—the next time I won't play around on the ropes. I'll show the people.

I'll learn. I caught a couple of hooks, but I got up and fought to the end.

"He hit me punches that would have stopped others. I was under tough pressure but I kept moving and sticking my jab and faking. He had me out on my feet a couple of times. He really shook me. He had me gone. I told myself, 'You are hurt,' but I stuck in and knew if I'd get to the corner on the stool I'd be ready for the next round.

"He hit me harder than anybody I ever fought. In the fifteenth the hook that knocked me down—I saw it coming and figured I'd ride it back, I don't remember going down. I was down when I looked up. Boom! I didn't know it happened until I got up. He really tagged me. When a man gets me going, when I'm wobbly, that's a punch. When a man drops me, that was a helluva punch. I didn't give the fight to him, he earned it.

"There was no physical pain, I was just numb. You just realize that you've been down. You realize that you can be beat. It's good in a way. You learn through losing. You see how things look from the other side. It sets an example of how to take defeat by those who follow you. They see how cheerful I am and they are able to accept defeat better. A man with pride is an honest man.

"There'll be another day, I'll get him."

football game where everything was very clear and visible, a game where you remembered every play.

Pat Summerall gave the Giants a 3–0 lead in the first quarter, but the Colts made the Giants gunshy with a long pass to the dangerous halfback Lenny Moore, and immediately New York assigned two men to him, sometimes covering Ray Berry with only one man.

In the second quarter, Gifford fumbled twice and the Giants' superb defensive tackle Rosey Grier was too lame to be useful. Unitas scored on a two-yard wedge over the left side to Ameche and a pass to Berry. Colts 14, Giants 3 at halftime.

seeing Gino Marchetti shut off the end, he cut back inside. Marchetti lunged awkwardly away from Jack Stroud's block, got his hands on Gifford and slowed him. Big Daddy Lipscomb, the awesome Colt tackle, piled on to shut off the first down, and the impact broke Marchetti's ankle. That play stopped Gifford inches away from the vital first down. The cutback by Gifford (16) seems certain (top, below) but the tackle is made (below). I can remember Gino sitting on his stretcher. He refused to be carried off the field until the field goal tied it. Later, reflecting on the biggest day of his life, John Unitas said, "You have to gamble or die in this league.

The third quarter saw a heroic goal-line stand by the Giants which denied the Colts a touchdown in four tries from the Giants' three-yard line. That was something!

The Giants' tough defense continued in the fourth quarter, and quarterback Charley Conerly scored twice on key passes. Kyle Rote took a long pass over his shoulder only to fumble on the twenty-five yard line, but Alex Webster, running on bad knees, had trailed the play for sixty-two yards and the Giant halfback picked up the fumble and carried to the Colt one, setting up the first New York touchdown. Then Conerly, throwing off a fake reverse, hit Schnelker for forty-six yards and followed with a pass to Frank Gifford for the touchdown on the next play that put the Giants ahead 17–14.

The Giants were inches from victory! With third and four and the clock running out they needed only a first down to win late in the fourth quarter. Conerly called a sweep to the right, and Gifford carried on the crucial play. He ran in his brilliant style, and

I don't know if you can call it controlled gambling, but that's how I look at my play-calling. I'm a little guy, comparatively—that's why I gamble. It doesn't give those Giants a chance to bury me."

Carl Taseff took Don Chandler's punt on their twenty-yard line as the sudden-death series began for the Colts. Unitas chose his plays deliberately. "I wanted to move on the ground to minimize loss of the ball. I didn't give a damn about the clock. It was our pace to set. I gave the ball to Dupré on a sweep to the right, he carried to the thirty for a first down. I intended the second play to end it. Remembering the long bomb to Moore in the first quarter that had missed by inches, I sent Lenny deep and Crow barely tipped the ball and Moore was going so fast he couldn't recover to handle it. The third play

was a surprise—a special play for this game—I had been saving it. Sam Huff at middle linebacker had been following Ameche everywhere. I sent Ameche outside and pulled a draw to Dupré that took advantage of the hole Sam left.

"An inch or two and he might have broken. The fourth play was just a flare pass to my fullback. Svare forgot to pick up the flare man, staying with Berry, so I just hit the Horse. The fifth play was a good first-down call—it was the same play as the first, but this time Dupre cut inside. They hadn't adjusted too well to our running stuff. So we stuck with it. Now we're on about the forty-six-yard line and I decide to pass again, but Modzelewski slipped a block, ran by Moore and wrapped me up for a loss back to the thirty-eight. It was now third down and

fifteen. Big play!

"I would say this play, lucky seven of the sudden-death series, was one of the game-turning plays, giving us a valuable first down. I called what was a new formation for this game—a slot right formation, with Moore the slot back. Our steady slamming into the line had helped set things up. I saw Moore on the right side was covered, so I rolled out to my left; there was no one near me. The Giant line had swung away to the other side for Moore. I saw Carl Karilivacz, a substitute defensive back for New York, covering Berry and he slipped, so I stopped and waved Raymond deeper. When Ray shook loose I unloaded. He caught the pass for a first down on the Giant forty-two-yard line.

"The next play worked to perfection. Modzelewski was playing his heart out—blowing in too fast to suit me. I think this play sealed the Giant doom. We had run it once before in the game. Usually we figure it for four or five yards. Huff had been playing to his left and back. This made him an easy blocking assignment for our tackle. Sam was playing for a pass, and the way Moe had been crashing I figured they were right for a trap. I hit it big. Art Spinney cut across behind center on a great trap block to cut little Moe down, and George Preas shut off Huff, who

was playing too deep. I gave the ball to Alan up the middle and he ran all alone on that chopped-up stadium turf for twenty-three yards. All alone. Karilivacz and Huff just made the save. We had another first down on their twenty.

"The Giants stopped Dupré into the line for no gain, and then I hit Berry on a plain old slant pass over the middle. We were inside the ten. On play eleven, I figured Ameche would carry it in. He went off tackle but cut inside. Huff was waiting and just closed Alan off. The next play was criticized as an unnecessary gamble.

"They were playing for the run, one on one on Moore, the linebacker head-up on our other end, Mutscheller. I told Jimmy to get out by the flag real quick. All I had to do was flip it up in the air and have him catch it. We missed it.

"Thirteen. Our only call, a power play. We got the halfback blocking ahead of Ameche with a double team on the tackle. When I slapped the ball in Al's belly and saw him take off I knew nobody was going to stop him with one yard. They couldn't have done it if we'd needed ten yards.

"I left the field quietly. We had beaten a real good team and won it 23–17. I never expected they would make a fuss about the game."

192

Robert Riger

Robert Riger

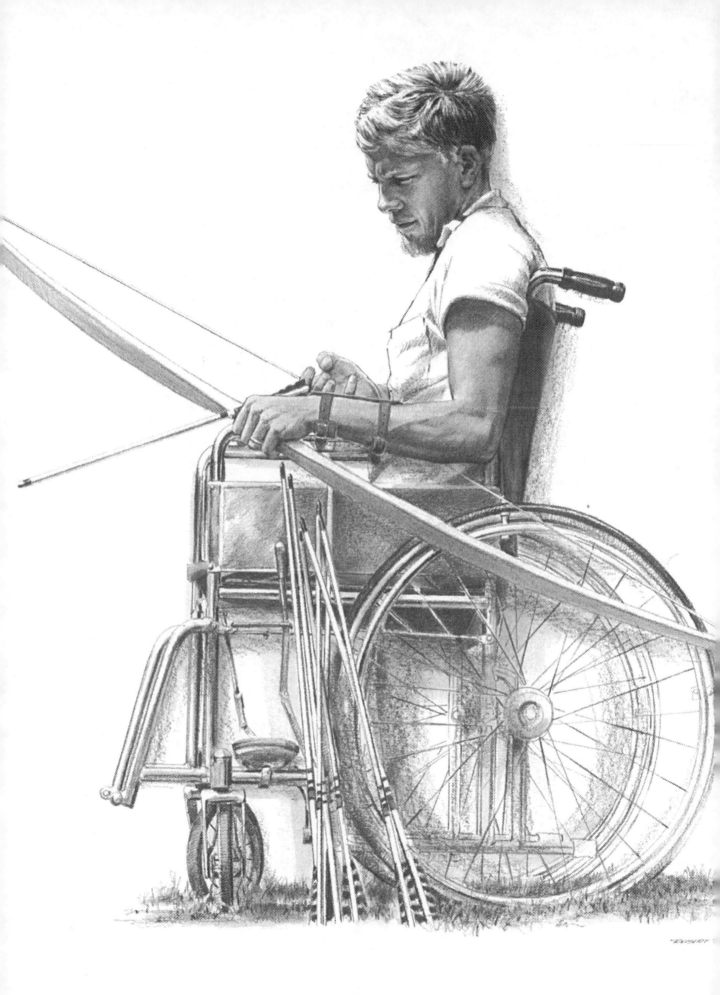

Part 3 TELEVISION SPORTS

TELEVISION AUDIENCE

There is strong evidence that television is not only influencing the life of the average American, it is shaping it. Not only in its role as an exciting medium of news and entertainment, but as a whole environment. A one-way flow of sound and image, full of facts and reflections, interpretations and analyses, attitudes and distortions, going directly into our homes—into the eye and sometimes heart of each member of the family—with an enormous and continuing impression that is left and developed by an entire audience, an entire country.

No one as yet has explored the effect that the largest area of live programming has on the greatest audience—*sports programming*. No one has examined the influence of the athlete on American life through the explosion of sports television in the United States in the past twenty-five years.

There are 130 million TV sets in our country, covering 97 percent of American homes. The average person watches four hours and five minutes of TV per day—between twenty-one and thirty-five hours a week—more than half of which is sports programming. In 78 percent of the homes, no conversation takes place during the viewing of a TV program except during commercials. In 36 percent of the homes surveyed by CBS, TV viewing was the only all-inclusive family activity. In 1985 there will be 234 million Americans in 85 million homes watching even more TV than they do today.

The growth of sports programming in the United States in the past fifteen years has been amazing.

THE INFLUENCE OF
THE ATHLETE
ON AMERICAN LIFE

There is strong evidence that television is not only influencing the life of the average American, it is shaping it. Not only in its role as an exciting medium of news and entertainment, but as a whole environment. A one-way flow of sound and image, full of facts and reflections, interpretations and analyses, attitudes and distortions, going directly into our homes—into the eye and sometimes heart of each member of the family—with an enormous and continuing impression that is left and developed by an entire audience, an entire country.

No one as yet has explored the effect that the largest area of live programming has on the greatest audience—*sports programming*. No one has exam-

When I joined ABC Sports in 1963, their advertising billing at the end of their second year was just under $2 million. In 1976, after the Montreal Olympics, it was $160 million. In 1970, the combined networks sports programs totaled 787 hours. In 1979 it was 1,356 hours, *with women constituting over 40 percent of the total television sports audience in the United States.*

The monumental plan by NBC Television Sports for world coverage of the 1980 Olympic Games from Moscow called for 150 hours of programming; more than 65 hours to have been aired in prime time. This staggering total, in which a commercial minute of advertising would have cost $150,000, is more than

ined the influence of the athlete on American life through the explosion of sports television in the United States in the past twenty-five years.

There are 130 million TV sets in our country, covering 97 percent of American homes. The average person watches four hours and five minutes of TV per day—between twenty-one and thirty-five hours a week—more than half of which is sports programming. In 78 percent of the homes, no conversation takes place during the viewing of a TV program except during commercials. In 36 percent of the homes surveyed by CBS, TV viewing was the only all-inclusive family activity. In 1985 there will be 234 million Americans in 85 million homes watching even more TV than they do today.

The growth of sports programming in the United States in the past fifteen years has been amazing.

double the amount of air time ABC Sports devoted to the coverage of the 1976 Olympics from Montreal.

CBS Sports paid $50,000 for the right to televise Squaw Valley in 1960. ABC Sports paid $41 million for the right to televise the Montreal Games. NBC had signed to pay $100 million, including the rights payment to the Olympic Committee with $15 million more for the crew of six hundred that NBC would have sent to the Soviet Union had not the world political situation changed everything. The daily U.S. audience would have exceeded 100 million.

This is the stage for the athletes in America. How they conduct themselves, the excellence of their performance — is having a powerful influence on the spirit and conduct of this television sports audience. The tone of the country is fitness. A young boy runs a marathon. Women joyously *participate* with the men.

When one considers that there are thirty frames per second to a video signal—that a viewer is exposed to 1,800 *pictures* a minute or about 250,000 pictures of an athlete during a televised pro football game in one hour—you may realize the visual saturation of only one sport on television in the course of a year.

The retentive powers of today's television sports viewer, if not of all viewers, is enormously acute when you consider that a sixteen-year-old has grown up and been educated by television and his ability to retain the quickest look or gesture, or hand or leg action, has been sharpened to an incredible degree. The viewer is inordinately perceptive to everything on the screen, even when the action is in fractions of seconds. The imagery presented is observed and remembered during the program time, and if electronic devices such as slow-motion replay are used on the simplest of acts, like leaping and catching a ball, the memory patterns—the information, enjoyment, impact and stimulus—are unbelievably intense. They amount to an experience that is, picturewise alone, twenty times more impressive than the response received from hearing an event described on radio or in conversation or reading about it in a newspaper account. One only has to listen to a radio broadcast of a football game or a horse race in this electronic age to realize how limiting this imagery is; how much less is the emotional response.

In television sports in the last decade the language has been powerfully graphic. Victory now becomes a shared experience. Defeat now becomes a shared experience. Error, failure and indecision are exposed. Composure and assurance are evident. Strength and tiredness, sportsmanship and misconduct, team fitness and team togetherness are apparent. Jubilation or dejection are obvious no matter how subtle. Spirit is read on the screen as accurately as a cardiograph. Anger is shared, arguments and brawls are so intimate as to be at times uncomfortable or repugnant.

The drama is so real and pointed that the impact of a sporting event has ten times, or one hundred times, the effect on the viewers' emotions of an incident within the family or the routines of the job.

There is no other visual experience that can match it. Not the television reports of the affairs of government, or achievements of science, or of comedy.

The understanding and awareness are due to the basic American belief that sports belong to the people. Most all of them have participated in sports, and so the experience shared is that much stronger.

The athlete thus is exposed upon this electronic stage, and his strength, intelligence, excellence, and example, his success and failure, and his sympathy

for both become a vital part of this shared experience for the American audience.

The incredible visual magic of television sports is that the cameras record continuously at an event and the choice for the director from his many cameras, and the pattern of the selections he makes, can combine the scenes of panorama and spectacle with the most powerful and revealing closeups. A picture in which 100,000 people lose their individual identity, as seen from a blimp, to become specks in the furor of a stadium, is juxtaposed with the strong portrait of the furtive glance of a linebacker.

One man alone. One woman alone. The skier is alone on the mountain, or the golfer, the tennis player, or the boxer is alone in a one-on-one battle. A pitcher alone in the ninth with the bases loaded and the winning run at the plate. You feel, in the privacy of your home, the challenge of those moments made so intimate and visual through the camera's eye. The television viewer shares the impact of the competition and understands the challenge for the athlete; this was never possible for millions of viewers at one time until television sports covered the action as it was happening. This is why the emotional involvement is so great.

The American society in the sixties and seventies has come to thrive on watching top athletes in risk-taking competition. A university study by Bruce Ogilvie of California State University on athletic motivation draws the conclusion that the finest athletes are *stimulus addicts*. Stimulus addiction implies a need for repeated exposure to situations where the balance between fear, danger and anxiety remains within the boundaries of personal control. The cyclical need to extend oneself to the absolute physical, emotional and even intellectual limits is the striving to escape from the bland, tensionless feelings associated with everyday living. In interviews with three hundred athletes, chosen because they had attained the highest levels of achievement in their respective sports, it was found that these men and women experience little joy in life when their true ability remains uncontested. They much prefer to have the odds against them, because they find it impossible to invest their egos in pursuits that do not require the best they have to offer. It is the performance of these athletes that makes watching fascinating.

In the past twenty-five years the individual men and women champions—the leaders in American sports—in all areas of competition have had an overwhelming influence on family viewership that has extended to all areas of their lives. The fervor of regional team rivalries and the pageantry of nations coming together in friendly competition have had an equally significant effect.

PAT & TOM

Pat Summerall is a solid gentleman. After a fine career as a player in the NFL and fame as a field-goal kicker with the Giants, Pat entered broadcasting on a fluke and long since has transcended the term "jock" to become one of the three best sports announcers in our country. Many think he is the best. Summerall has continued in the great tradition of broadcasting and has brought dignity to the business of commentary. An imposing figure, when he hangs on the good threads he looks as if he owns the network instead of working for it.

Pat Summerall and Tom Brookshier teamed together at the end of their first full year to telecast Super Bowl X. It was a choice assignment—seventy-eight million viewers. The sunshine boys' basic philosophy was to enjoy the game and make sure the viewers did too.

Summerall began in broadcasting by not even trying. He was sitting in the Hotel Manhattan waiting to play a Friday-night exhibition game in Roosevelt Stadium in 1960. His roommate, Charlie Conerly, had made arrangements to audition for a radio job—a show that Phil Rizzuto did for years on CBS—and Charlie was in the shower when the phone rang and Pat answered it. It was the man from CBS calling to remind Conerly to be on time for the audition that afternoon. As Pat was about to hang up, the man said, "What are *you* doing this afternoon?" "Nothing but sitting here sipping beer," said Pat, and the CBS man suggested he come along to the audition. Pat got the job.

He did the show while playing with the Giants and then went at it as a career in 1962 after he retired, working with Chris Schenkel on the Giants games for two more years. Pat has been fortunate in having worked with the best.

Tom Brookshier is tough, quick, smart, with a puckish sense of humor and a ready laugh. His gusto, conviviality and enthusiasm for the game of football match Pat Summerall's.

Brookshier laughed. "When I started," he said, "I broadcast just about the way I used to play, which was overplaying it: late whistles, always trying to steal the ball or the mike." Tom shook his head, his voice a gravel paste, half words, half laughter. "I really had an awful time. A few years ago I thought I was going to get out of it, because I knew I was never going to make it. Then the call came to team with Pat. He would move over from color analyst to play-by-play and I would do color.

"When Pat played with the Giants and I played with the Eagles we didn't like each other. We didn't like each other as competitive color men either. Then we began to work together one day a week in Philadelphia on the NFL Films highlight shows. He'd have a New York hangover and I'd be laughing about the Monday-night game or something. It worked well and a friendship began."

Tom Brookshier was injured at the height of his career as a defensive halfback in 1961. They carried him off the field on his shield with a broken leg and into a long stay in the hospital. Tom Swafford of Philadelphia station WCAU called Tom in the hospital and asked if he'd like to start doing radio. Brookshier was young and immobile and figured he would give it a shot.

"I started doing reports from the hospital bed," Tom recalled. "It was a morning programming and I would talk about the games. I was so bad but the fans were so patient—they sat with me for eight years.

"I came to the big time with the help of Jack Whittaker, whom I respected and tried to emulate, as a color man on regional football games. In the beginning the brass never really dug my act."

Pat and Tom work together in the broadcasting booth the way two athletes play a precisioned secondary or an offensive line. Their timing is effortlessly precise, a flawless fit, considering the continuous flow of complex action and the instructions and cues coming through their headsets. They seem to have a natural compatibility when they work together.

"We're good friends," Pat says. "That means a lot. One play-by-play announcer I worked with for three years I'm certain never listened to what I said as a color man and in all that time we had dinner together only once. With Tommy, we enjoy each other's company, and I think that comes across.

"After my first six games last year as an analyst, our new director of Sports, Bob Wussler, reacted when I casually remarked, 'For a long time I've wanted to do play-by-play.' He quickly said, 'Let's get on with it. Try it next week. Who would you like to work with?'

"I told him Tom and I had worked together on films and I know that he likes to laugh and I like to laugh and that I would like to work with Tom.

"I'm much more fatigued now after a game doing play-by-play than I ever was as a color analyst. But I'm having much more fun. When they say go, I'm the one that's got to crank it up. I've got to get the show on and off the air, lead in and out of commercials, do the update when we come back at halftime and the rest. The additional responsibility is something I enjoy.

"The electronic devices enable us to do a much better broadcast. We have done away with tape in the remote truck. The slo-mo disc takes care of all our replay needs. We are capable of replaying every play from two angles. Tom and I sit down with our director, Sandy Grossman, the day before so he can orient his shots. We tell him our thoughts and checkouts. We have our own game plan of the way we're going to televise a game. We have code words and idea checks during commercials."

The Super Bowl is a special showcase. "I've done six," Summerall continued, "but never as a play-by-play announcer. You must guard against repeating what everyone has heard in all the buildup."

Some announcer teams sound like a dull monotone, others are inane, innocuous and inept. They don't realize the variety of people in their football audience.

Tom Brookshier smiled and said seriously, "I used to see two imaginary viewers watching me. A pretty good-looking middle-aged woman with her son—about fourteen. Now I see a whole family. I see the old man maybe with a beer in his hand. The kids have grown up—the mother is still good-looking—and now there's a whole group there watching and listening.

"I think the people are tired of having to figure out double zone defenses all the time. I'm tired of it myself. I think we've gotten too clinical in TV analyses. I think football is a fun game. Tough fun. The players know and like that, and when it's over all the toughest, meanest guys go over and have a beer with the other guys. A game is three hours of unleashing yourself. I try to add personal experience for that audience.

"In the Redskin game, I watched the Giants hit Bass and leave him for dead. When there's an injury on the field it really scares me. We ran the replay and I said, 'When you get hit that way it burns clear down to the bottom of your feet.' I've been hit. When you really take a shot on the head that is the way it feels. The bottom of your feet burn, nerve endings and all."

With the intimacy of the sideline camera the humanness on the field comes across much more. There are very few words that are needed. Silence from the booth is. This discretion is one of Pat and Tom's strengths. They know distracting remarks will ruin a fine piece of video. The improving audio of the stadium presence is enough; they let it play.

At times Pat will break Tom up with a smooth retort to a playful question which eases the tension of the game. At other times, Tom will fracture Pat. In a tight game Los Angeles is locked in a battle at Minnesota. Things are not going well for the Rams, and their quarterback James Harris, his defensive

unit on the field, sits on the bench with the phone in one hand, his other arm out on the backrest, his legs crossed. The picture comes up on the screen and Tom says, "I hope Harris is not calling the airport."

Oakland is six ahead on Blanda's two field goals. Tom asks Pat, "Did George Blanda ever break any of your records?" There's this little pause and Pat says, "He broke all of my records in one day."

"He keeps me on my toes, that dirty rascal." Brookshier laughs. "I was about to stick it to him and he lays it right back on me, without putting me down."

Tom laughs again as he remembers. "Another time, we hear the hectic screaming in our headsets from the truck as they're getting ready down there and the countdown begins. Then the director tells us to relax. We almost broke up as we came on the air. Here's a guy who's kicked fifty-yard field goals in the snow, they're standing on their heads in the truck, and they're telling *us* to relax. Believe it, we're *always* relaxed! That's *how* we do it."

Pat Summerall concluded, "Many of the viewers, so many, are knowledgeable enough so that if you make a mistake somebody is going to pick it up. Unlike many broadcasters that I worked with, neither Tom nor I is afraid to say, 'Hey, I made a mistake.' We've done that, and one thing I've learned is the viewer appreciates it when you admit your mistakes.

"We're not as regimented as play and color announcers used to be. Years back the play-by-play man would set the down and yardage situation and the formation every time a team came up to the line, and every so often the color guy, an ex-athlete who was supposed to predict every play, would say something short and appropriate.

"There was a stop and go. We don't do it that way. If Tom is talking as the play starts, he keeps talking and does the *play*. If I'm talking on an analysis of play-making or on a player's moves—I do the *color*. This makes it comfortable and very easy. We have no hand signals, no tricks. We just recognize each other's strengths and weaknesses. I know he's not going to leave me hanging and he knows I'm not going to leave him hanging. Tom *listens* all the time. So do I."

Maybe that's why the viewers do.

ELECTRONIC REMOTE

Time! Time is the absolute criteria and control in electronic broadcasting. In no other of the media does time have the significance, the believability, the emotional impact on the audience that live performance, *the event seen as it happens,* does in television.

Electronic Field Production was born during the political conventions and NASA's space program coverage but more than anywhere EFP—the big electronic remote—was pioneered in sports. The three major events for the sport road circus at the networks as they display people and hardware across the country and throughout Europe is the Super Bowl (right, above), the World Series (center) and the Olympic Games (right, below).

When Green Bay scored against Kansas City in the first Super Bowl in 1966, 75 million people watched as the game was aired by CBS and NBC. ABC's telecast of the World Series in 1977, brought us Reggie Jackson's three home runs in the final game. The third one (right, center) was instantaneous to the entire nation as it was for all of us in Yankee Stadium. The faces and flags of the athletes of the world are seen live at the Olympic Games at different hours depending on time zones, and recorded and played again in prime time in different countries. At right is the flag ceremony in Grenoble.

Over 640 million people watched the first decade of Super Bowl action, and the greatest audience ever to watch a sporting event in America viewed Super Bowl XII. 101 million homes! For Super Bowl XIII (see pages 217-223) CBS displayed the maximum electronic remote for a *one day* event; a staff and crew of 150 people at the remote, 31 cameras; 20 at the Rose Bowl and 11 more at satellite remotes including one with the U.S. 7th Army Corps in Germany. It took 20 vehicles and 20 miles of cable, 9 tape machines and six slo-mo machines, 75 microphones, 100 television monitors and talent in the truck to know all of the talent on the field.

The World Series can often be the most tedious and expensive electronic remote in sports because of the two city schedule, travel days for teams, double installations, crews that travel and the risk of rain delays on the preempted prime time regular programming. The classic remote that NBC did for the 1975 World Series between Cincinnati and Boston with the rain delays was a milestone in television sports. It was played to a record television audience.

ABC Sports in this Olympic year 1980, created unparalleled coverage in Lake Placid for the XIII Winter Olympics, both for national television as well as complete world coverage of all events. The engineering crews buried 33 miles of cable on four separate ski slopes to their cameras and microphones in the winter of 1979 for a World Cup meet only to have to remove it all because of the resident bears, raccoons and porcupines eating through the bright yellow covering of the coax and multicircuit mic cables. All cable was re-laid for the games.

Helicopters deployed 18 Philips LDK-5 triax cameras to 60 set platforms on the mountains as the events changed slope to slope. With a wind-chill factor of 60 degrees below zero, there were tough days for the crews, 14 portable generators were used to warm special heating blankets to cover *the cameras!*

The alpine needs were no more difficult than the 14 cameras 20 miles away at the bobsled run. Five separate mobile units were part of the huge remote to do hockey and ice skating. The enjoyment here in the United States and around the world was so complete and the impact of the U.S. hockey victory so wonderful that no one ever thought of what it took to see it *live* as it happened.

The nerve center for ABC was control A and B with $15 million worth of new equipment including 30 video tape machines, the Dubner Computer graphics generator and the amazing Ampex ESS Electronic Slide Store and the Quantel DUE-5000 that can do everything with a normal coverage image once it is received in control. All of this costly electronic hardware was used during the 13 days and 51 hours of broadcasting in this super remote.

I produced and directed for seven years almost entirely in film. I loved film with a passion—and I think the results showed this caring. I did the last black-and-white film remote, the first color-film remote, the first show on the electronic edit tech machines. I worked on the first live-tape show from Le Mans by satellite and was the first to take an ABC Sports film crew into the Soviet Union in 1967. It was all heady stuff. But I believe 1979 should be the last year of edited film coverage in sports for direct television programming. In the future, on special needs, film will be used and the negative sent directly to tape for computerized one inch electronic editing. In the electronic world you accept more than you do in film. You are not dealing in creative degrees but in absolute phenomena.

THE WORLD WATCHES

In 1964 I began editing videotape at the Innsbruck Olympics. On that remote and during the four years that followed, editing tape was like editing film; you would physically cut it with a razor blade. I can still remember the bin of razors and the editors gingerly handling the taffy-colored two-inch tape, miles of it on the floor winding, curling in and around and behind the hot, huge old tape machines. The editor then would carefully remove the tape from the machine head after marking it, place it on a metal block that had a microscope finder, peer through the finder to cut between pulse marks, make his cut, apply a silver tape to join the retained scenes and carefully trim it at the edges so that it would pass smoothly through the head, and then we would all hold our breath on the playback to see that it went through without the edit causing an electronic breakup. The fastest editor, when he was alert, could make a few splices during a six-hour session in five minutes each, but the average edit took fifteen minutes and some took a full hour.

In Lake Placid, we would fly the machines to the two scenes *watching* the picture as the tape advanced to the desired video, match the imprinted *time code* on the original and the dub of the original, and then in less than a minute set a dissolve, preview it, adjust it and *do it*, recording it on our master on a third machine. All this without ever touching the machine, let alone the tape itself.

The only delay was occasionally when the machines would not lock up in the correct position governed by the time code. The editor would send VTR 7 to a frame, VTR 9 would go to a matching frame, the computer would say it was there but one machine would really be a few frames off. When there was a hitch like this, the good doctor, the engineer would come by and lean in and look and say, "Well, let's see." Seconds later, Charlie Pantuso would have the set of the buttons untangled, make the computer wise up, and we would mash again.

The last night of the Games I wanted to summarize and synthesize ABC's electronic installation with all the computerized advances and the awesome technological achievement at Lake Placid. Charlie talked about the performance of the new equipment and the impending new wave of the electronic image. He appraised the conversion of two-

inch videotape, the standard that had been used for more than twenty years, to the new one-inch system that required smaller, lighter reels, smaller VTR machines, higher quality and complete computerized editing controlled through a sophisticated switcher.

"I think the main problem we've had since we've been here was time code," Charlie said. Like all good doctors, Charlie had a lovely machineside manner; he made you understand the engineering dimension without losing sight of the creative perspective he knew I cared about. "Many of our people have never worked with time code before so we had a crash training course. The people that had edited with time code picked it up pretty well, and the others are learning. Everyone realizes the power of it and knows that it is the wave of the future.

"Let's walk," Charlie said, "and I'll show you the ESS they have in the graphics room. It is the digital still store that stores nine hundred of these video frames—still pictures with no deterioration in storing it. Every alpine racer's portrait is here, every figure skater. The maximum time it takes to call up a portrait of Hans Enn, who is number 888, is twenty milliseconds. If you wanted to assemble a sequence of portraits of the entire Austrian ski team you could have instantaneous recall just by telling it in advance what you're

going to do so it could get ready to do it. You can store thirty seconds of film also, so that you can call up instantly the U.S. hockey team's winning goal against the Russians."

"I think the best thing that happened electronically here in Lake Placid was the fact that it happened at all. We're dealing with a situation where almost every piece of equipment in this facility had never been used before and a tremendous volume of equipment and of training had to go on in order to get anything to happen.

"Directors had to learn new switchers that they had never seen before. The 300 switcher in A master control is a vastly different concept in switching. (Executive producer Roone Arledge into final Olympic telecast on air, below, with GV 440 routing switcher.) It thinks for you in such a way that you have to know what it's going to do before you tell it to do something. That is really the true danger of automation—that by requiring so much technical competence on the one hand it ever more isolates you from what you're doing, and I think the challenge for people like myself who are trying to put this together is to make the human interface such that you as the creative director can completely forget about the machine; you can ignore it. You don't want to know anything about it, you just want to think about what you want to do." Just make it happen.

PRIME TIME

When a sporting event was seen as it happened, when the televising of an event was transmitted as a live experience, sports in America changed. In reality the sport should not have changed—only the audience, the sports fan as viewer—but the athlete changed. Within the ten years since the advent in 1967 of color television and the electronic devices for recording and replaying action, the athlete became part of an enormous live theater.

The traditional idea of sports in the afternoon played as a lesser event gave way to nighttime programming. Sports was played and televised live in prime time, and this changed the athlete and his influence on the American audience. He and the games he played became an enormously lucrative commodity. There was a preposterous financial escalation in the cost of the commercial minute as sports became entertainment and theater, and the athlete became aware of the viewership and the effect of his live performance, and he now plays to this audience. The young player sees it as a means for instant success without paying the price of years of grind and anonymity.

The athlete is now aware of a national audience of 30 to 60 million people. The athlete is an actor in prime time, more recognizable, more famous, and more highly paid than actors are. He is now athlete, actor, star. The athlete in prime time is hero and idol. He has replaced the movie star for the adulation of the young. The Olympic Games, the World Series, but especially *Monday Night Football* are the showcases to display the prime-time glamour of television sports. The drama of the lights has changed the look of sport, given it a polished, plastic, unreal slickness, and the athlete for the first time leaves the concentration of his game and waves to the TV audience. No athlete ever dared do this before.

PERFORMANCE PRESSURE

It is like some religion. It spreads by some evangelism, a profound faith, to new lands. Anaheim, Seattle, Kansas City, and the people who never saw the disciples in their town go to see them in an endless pilgrimage. Family. Inside the stadium it is quite another world. There is no sight like the green of a major-league field—the American diamond. Good God, what a beautiful, durable game baseball is.

High and far away to the last row of bleachers the players are only specks. But you are in the *presence* of the specks. You have seen the razor cut on the chin of the catcher on the home set closeup. You have memorized every mannerism from television's rhythmic repetition. Go out. Be there. The Yankees are in town. If Nolan Ryan is going for a no-hitter you have to be there. What are you going to say if you're not there? How can you *believe* in the home team if you're not there or you do not *see* the performance?

Only if you are there can you decide if the center fielder could have made the catch. Was it a hit or an error? You've got to see the relay from right center to cut the run down at the plate—your eye has to see the *distance*—the trajectory of the ball, the speed of the throw, the runners on the bases, the *space,* the energy, the collision at the plate, believe in the umpire's position and his call. No television camera can make you *believe* all of that.

This day you watch Nolan Ryan. You have to see the third out each inning and watch him walk to the dugout. You watch where he sits, you see him towel himself, put his jacket on, and you watch his every gesture or you imagine it if he is hidden from your view. Inning after inning the tension grows. Shadows change in the California golden twilight. His fast ball goes a hundred miles an hour. They can't see it. You wonder if he knows he has a *no-hitter* going. He's pitched four. This would be five.

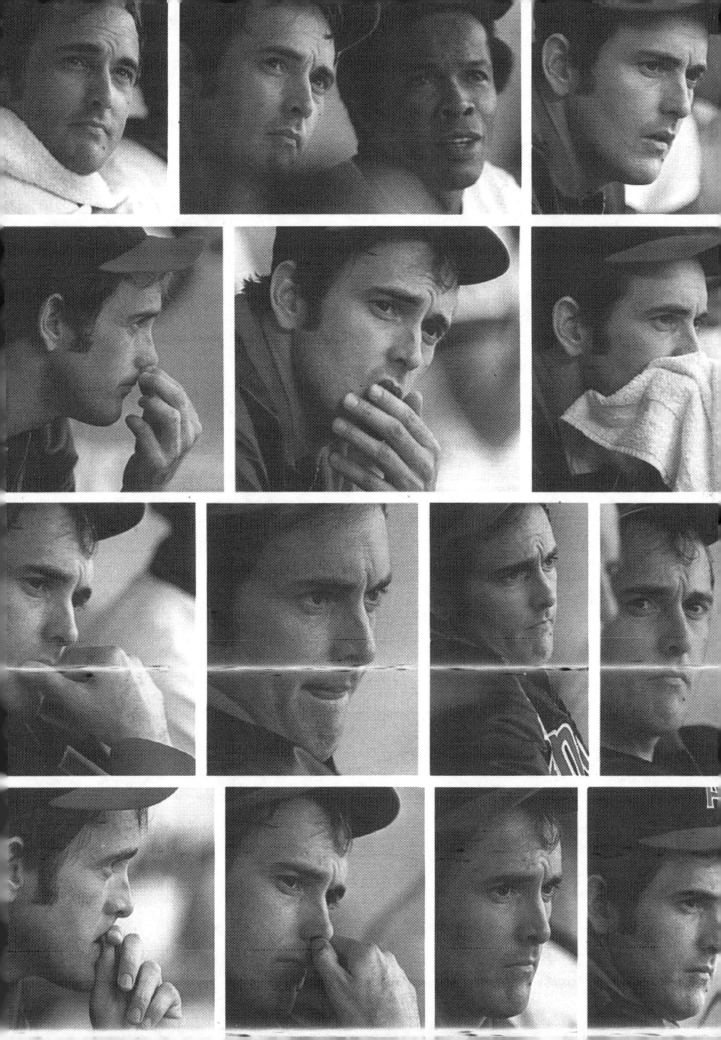

No one in the history of baseball has pitched five no-hitters. Holy smokes, and I'm here!

The fifth inning, the sixth, the seventh. Ryan bears down now. He walks to the dugout the same. He's going to make it. You feel it. The sounds in the stands are half crazy, half eerie. The whispers are deafening.

Then Spencer, the New York designated hitter, arcs a sinking drive to short center. Miller, the California center fielder, dives and it's off his glove. The official scorer rules an error. There is a long uneasiness. Ryan gets the other two outs in the eighth. Three outs to go. The Yankee bench was burning.

It seems a long time in the dugout. Nolan's eyes focus the tension that runs down the bench—a nervous row of anxious Angels hardly breathing. I study Ryan's face, the touch of his fingers on his lip.

In the ninth Thurman Munson is safe on an error by the shortstop.

Nettles pops up. Suddenly Reggie Jackson is at the plate. He rips the first pitch inches off of Ryan's glove into center. Hit. Damn! Ryah turns to the outfield and imperceptibly collapses inside as the entire stadium stands to salute him with a loving applause that flows across the field like a healing breeze. The pitcher raises his cap. Raises it again. *Almost* a no-hitter

I watched Jackson look up at the official scorer in the press box and smile. I played it all back. I talked about it that night and all the next day. All that weekend. I can still feel it a year later. I can remember Nolan Ryan's eyes in the dugout inning after inning as the suspense mounted. You knew it would have to be Jackson. Hell of a game. I was *there*.

DIRECTORS' CHOICE

Our enjoyment of sports changed on television in 1967 with the advent of slow-motion and videotape machines. Football became a whole new game. The great in-depth advances in electronic coverage have been appreciated most on defense. The slow-motion machine is the greatest exponent in showing a defensive play. Before slow-motion and the technology of the fast back-and-forth videotape machine to give an instant replay of action recorded seconds before, you never saw the defensive plays. In the first ten years of television coverage of football, it was all offense. The quarterbacks and the running backs were on camera most of the time. You were actually watching only half a football game.

Videotape allowed for a second eye to cover the defense and record that picture in the truck; saving it on videotape so it could be shown after the offensive play was run, while the quarterback was in the huddle. This was a revelation on simple defensive plays, but you could not see it all because defense was too subtle and too fast. The magnificent achievement of instant replay made possible by the slo-mo disc recorder enabled millions of viewers to enjoy the game of football more. The slo-mo disc machine is a $100,000 piece of TV magic that has revolutionized the world of sports coverage. A result of Ampex electronic engineering, this marvelous monster can record the moment and play it back at normal speed or in degrees of slow motion or stop any split second of action, within five seconds.

"For the first Superbowl in 1966, CBS won a coin toss and they ran the pickup from the Los Angeles Coliseum, where the Green Bay Packers beat the Kansas City Chiefs 35–10, but NBC shared the coverage. There were two networks and two sets of announcers. After that it was agreed we would alternate each year. My first year as director was the third Superbowl in Baltimore." NBC veteran sports director Teddy Nathanson seemed to enjoy instant recall as he remembered his role in television's biggest one-day remote—as the electronic quarterback.

"What made it memorable was that the AFC, the American Football Conference, won. It was the coming of age of the AFC when Joe Namath led the New York Jets to victory over the Colts. We had a camera in both dressing rooms, and the plan was to go into the losing dressing room. Pat Summerall was working the game for us, and the thing I remember was that Pat never went to the losers' dressing room. I saw him on the monitor standing alone on a platform with tears in his eyes. He had been a great NFL player and announcer for their league and he could not believe it. No one could. I was very nervous in the truck for that game. I can still remember being nervous in a much different sense when the Jets beat Baltimore—that I've since gotten over in directing sporting events. That game was a very personal thing. It was like your own college winning.

"No one laughed at the AFC after that, and they went on to win nine out of the thirteen Superbowls played. I directed numbers three, five, seven, nine, eleven and thirteen—that's '69, '71, '73, '75, '77 and '79—and Superbowl XIII, between Pittsburgh and Dallas, was unquestionably the best game yet played. It had everything in it. There was exceptional fan reaction in the Orange Bowl, which you don't usually get at a Superbowl because it is a once-a-year crowd.

"I think in any sporting event, I treat it just like an actor would treat a script. If he's given a great script he can do something with it. If you're given a good game you can do a lot more with it than a bad game. You can do the greatest job in the world on a bad game and no one will notice it. The event dominates.

"There is considerable planning at NBC as we come down to the game. Superbowl XIII was the first year that we used the so-called second unit to do the replays. It definitely took a considerable amount of the burden of concentration on certain areas away from me. The other unit did many of the defensive replay situations. We had six slow-motion machines and the B unit had two of them.

"We had a defensive isolate at all times in some form. This is a camera following a defensive player in close-up and recording on a tape machine—or disc-isolated from the full play action that is being aired. There may be four isolates on one play. They could always hear what we were doing.

"The second unit could not replay action because their end-zone camera was not a ball camera, it always worked in isolation. I was the only one that had an alternate angle on the play action.

"My meeting with the cameramen lasts about three hours, but I'm working with the best hand-picked twelve men and I've worked football with them for years and they know exactly what I want. They are my actors. They know what I'm looking for. They know when a quarterback throws an interception, I want to see him going off the field as much as I want to see the guy who intercepted the pass.

"The basic coverage remains the same for a Superbowl. All the time is spent briefing on how I will isolate certain players in certain situations and all based on the abilities and tendencies of *that* player and *that* team in *that* situation. In that way I'm thinking the way Terry Bradshaw is on the field.

"I give each cameraman a card so they know in what areas of the field they're going to be isolated. I break down all the kicking situations so that these six different isolated pieces of equipment—each cameraman knows exactly what he will be doing on a field goal. Once the game starts I *never* tell a cam-

eraman what to do. He knows what to do, and I know exactly what shot is coming up on the monitor. All I have to do is concentrate on the ballgame and pick my cherries—the best shots.

"My fourteen-camera placement for the Superbowl coverage is diagrammed below. Play coverage was the responsibility of our four high cameras. Camera 1 was on the left twenty-yard line, camera 2 was on the fifty, camera 3 was also on the fifty and camera 4 on the right twenty-yard line. Cameras 5 and 6 were field cameras mounted on high carts, camera 7 was the left end zone, and camera 8

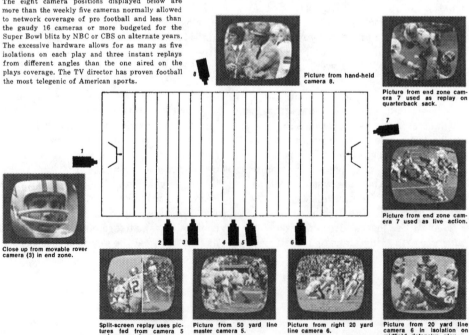

IDEAL COVERAGE
The eight camera positions displayed below are more than the weekly five cameras normally allowed to network coverage of pro football and less than the gaudy 16 cameras or more budgeted for the Super Bowl blitz by NBC or CBS on alternate years. The excessive hardware allows for as many as five isolations on each play and three instant replays from different angles than the one aired on the plays coverage. The TV director has proven football the most telegenic of American sports.

Picture from hand-held camera 8.

Picture from end zone camera 7 used as replay on quarterback sack.

Picture from end zone camera 7 used as live action.

Close up from movable rover camera (3) in end zone.

Split-screen replay uses pictures fed from camera 5 and camera 6.

Picture from 50 yard line master camera 5.

Picture from right 20 yard line camera 6.

Picture from 20 yard line camera 6 in isolation on midfield defensive play.

was the right end zone. Camera 9 was hand-held action, cameras 10 and 11 were on the team benches and camera 12 was the panorama roof camera. Camera 13 was the fifty-yard-line camera of the second unit, on a strange.Orange Bowl platform under my two midfield cameras, and camera 14 was in the blimp.

"The slow-motion discs for the first unit were lettered A, B, C, D, and X, Y for the second unit. Nothing went on the air unless I put it on the air. Everything came through us, and I think it worked very well.

"My briefing to cameramen in all areas is detailed and complete and it allows for all possible game situations. If the ball is deep in Dallas territory and there is a chance that the punt will be blocked, the following is our coverage: I isolate each of the wide defensive men who are up close and who will be slanting in from the outside. I have a camera on the middle of the line in case somebody blocks it from the middle, and I have a camera isolated on the punter. If the pressure is not on, if the defense does not rush the kicker, then the outside cameramen follow the offensive linemen downfield. All patterns and plays are covered in the briefing, and the way a cameraman handles a play depends more times on the score and the time of the game. You alert the cameraman to the Dallas flea flickers and reverses and to Pittsburgh's three possible wide receivers. On this punt situation each of the three isolated cameras is feeding three slow-motion discs. I'll take one end-zone camera and isolate the punt with the full line and I'll pick a rush angle and isolate a hand-held.

"We then cover the play with our right twenty, camera 4, the pass is blocked, and I can replay it five different ways. The producers will call out that it's best from number 8 in the end zone and we'll air it and then the bench camera will do a closeup of the defensive player that blocked it and then I'll go with camera 9, which was another angle at ground level. If the action continues quickly and I want to save the contents of one of the other slo-mo machines I will feed it to a tape machine and the associate director will log it and if it becomes a critical play we can air that third version later in the game.

"You feed the bench cameras directly to the tape machine on a high camera shot of a coach, because you do not need these reaction portraits in slow motion.

"In the pressure and shorthand of the game I never call players by name, always jersey—black 68, white 12—and each cameraman has a flip chart on his camera of all the position matchups, but this information is memorized. They know black 68 is the Steelers' left guard and that white 12 is the Cowboy

quarterback.

"As soon as I see a punt I call, 'Punting from left to right: one, three, four, six, seven, eight.'

"I don't see any monitors on slo-mo A, B, C, D. The isolated camera bank is set up in the same order as I am. As soon as the play is run I know which camera should have it best. They punch it up.

"With the added equipment at the Superbowl I could afford at all times to have a camera stay on the quarterback. In the regular season you have five cameras for a game and so you have to play hunches when you think a quarterback will get blitzed or sacked. You direct a camera to stay with the passer. No cameramen can play hunches. They can't free-lance on the action. They *can* free-lance on the color shots, the crowd, sideline bench, coaches, and they will give me good shots and I'll air them. I encourage that.

"There was a very significant thing in the game which I discovered on the monitor of camera 10 in the truck and that was there was never a moment when I asked for a shot of the Steelers' quarterback Terry Bradshaw on the sideline that he wasn't laughing and relaxed. When he was behind, when he was ahead by seven—he'd come off the field and there would be a smile on his face. He displayed absolute total confidence in what was going on with his team and this game.

"In a Superbowl I have to discipline myself to balance the coverage fairly. This is the final game for the championship, and although NBC covers one league during the year and CBS the other, when it is our year to do the big game it can't subtly feature one quarterback more or one coach more. This is all feel, a certain balance.

"With this balance you then build the game. Slowly at first. You don't rush your technological skills, you set the scene, present the offense and defense, and then well into the first quarter begin the display. If you have a long touchdown run on the opening kickoff you present it big because it may establish the momentum for the entire game, but usually you let a game shape your telecast.

"I never really know what a total sports telecast I direct is like. I never really know what a Superbowl looked like as a complete contest or drama because of the frenzied atmosphere we work in. As we were preparing for Superbowl XIII, a few of the staff sat down to screen the tapes on the Denver-Oakland championship game the previous season. It was almost spine-chilling looking at it a year later. The whole drama of what was going on in Denver was there. It was incredible.

"I hope this game between Pittsburgh and Dallas will hold up. If a 35–31 Superbowl doesn't cut it, nothing will!"

SUPERBOWL SUNDAY

"I learned something from this game. There is one thing you have to overcome as a player, and that's *fear*. I never play well against Dallas. I knew that. They knew that. They always screw me up with their defenses. They really are a well-coached football team. They force me to overthink. When I play them I try to outthink myself. I think too much.

"I went into Superbowl XIII with a different outlook. I programmed myself with a new attitude. I'm going out there today and I'm going to relax, I'm going to have some fun, I'm not going to let anything bother me. I'm certainly not going to let the Superbowl dictate to me. I'll get the Steelers doing what we've done all year. If things don't go well don't worry about it. It's a game, go out and enjoy it! *Against the Dallas Cowboys!*

"What do I do? I go out there and on the first series I beat a blitz and hit Len Stallworth over the middle for a first down, passed to Randy Grossman on the right sideline for another and to Stallworth again in the left end zone for the first touchdown.

"Then what do I do? On the second series I throw two more first downs, then a big interception. On the next series I'm sacked by Harvey Martin and I fumble. Dallas comes right back. Staubach passes to Hill for a touchdown and the score is 7-7.

"In the second quarter on the first series of downs, I'm sacked again and as I'm going down Hollywood Henderson steals the ball away and Mike Hegman picks it up and runs it in from about forty yards out. Cowboys lead 14-7. Didn't bother me a bit. It didn't upset me. It didn't frustrate me.

"Charlie Waters and Cliff Harris, the Dallas veterans, remarked about it later. They saw me smiling and they admitted, 'What ticked us off was Bradshaw was having so much fun.' And I was. I was having a good time."

Terry Bradshaw laughs and gulps his fourth cup of morning coffee and stuffs a huge portion of eggs benedict into a big, hungry, healthy, happy, intelligent face. He is one of the remarkable American athletes whose career has had full dimension.

Terry continued his reflections of the game, "I've got three downs to make ten yards—unless it's late in the game and I use that fourth down on short yardage. My philosophy as a pro quarterback is that on first down we execute so that I put myself in position to make decisions easier on second down. If we can get as close to *half* of that ten yards on first down—four yards—then I'm second and six. If I can get four yards on second down, I'm third and two, and my options for running or throwing are great because I can throw under a zone, behind zones, they can't play us tight, I've got options that I certainly do not have if we're third and long yardage. The key to my philosophy is to get as much yardage as I can on *first down*. First down is the most important down—and I'm a good first-down quarterback because I'm on a good team.

"First down is a very interesting down. In the early part of a game there is the feeling-out process. What are their tendencies, what are they going to try to do. I play three downs—they show the beginnings of a tendency. I play three more downs and you get another tendency from their defense. I move the team downfield in four sets and I have a good idea—but then I'm inside their ten and I play three downs and yet another of their tendencies is revealed. Then I've got the idea. I know what I can do. They will make adjustments, I will continue to feel their defenses out, but by the fourth quarter we will break some big plays.

"I may come out and run on two first downs. I may come out and throw on the next three first downs. I have as much confidence on running as I do on passing. In my first few years in the league I wouldn't dare throw the ball on first down. They would put too much pressure on me on second down and ten if the pass failed.

"In the Superbowl people and teams play their game. There is no experimenting. We may try a new formation to see how they react, but this is a test. There is no time to experiment. I have to outguess and confuse them. That's my whole approach to the game. Catch 'em at their weakness. Deceit is a dishonor in life but for the quarterback it's *valor*. Sometimes I get lucky and my cagy tactics work. I'm always trying to pull something on that defense. I enjoy the challenge of trying to outguess them. I thrive on it.

"Experience is facing thousands of situations over and over many times and handling them different ways most of the time and coming to a conclusion on how they should be handled properly. That's why coaches in professional football agree it takes five years for a quarterback to make it because he has to experience all the ups and downs. Everything from injuries to the critical moments of third and three on the five.

"I'm going into my tenth year and I'm very confident. I go out there and I know there are just so many things that defense can do to me and I have enough defensive keys now so that I can figure out their coverage *before* I take the snap. I've learned not to overread a coverage. I've learned not to worry, not to press, not to get frustrated. You learn all of this through experience."

Terry paused a long time and smiled a deep smile of satisfaction. "You also learn it through success. It doesn't come through failure. I would never be where I am today if our team had not been successful. That's what I mean by success and failure as a quarterback. Being successful affords you the opportunity to play. Only when you play can you gain the experience, and only when you win do you continue to play. If you don't win the coaches will look for someone else.

"Preparation of a game like this enables you to *anticipate a coverage,* walk up to the line, take that step and *know.* You don't react because a receiver is covered. You know with that coverage where the hole is and whose route is coming into that hole. I know the play. I know which receiver will be open. I go to that man. There is no indecision. I don't care who you have at quarterback, some defensive units will mask their coverage better than others, and the Cowboys, I find, do an excellent job of it. I studied them for hundreds of hours, and it all became clear. I could see from the films everything they were doing. They are very confusing to an offense. They give you one look that tells you one defense and they do the opposite.

"A quarterback coming to the line, looking at the defense, taking the snap and taking his first step should know exactly what the coverage is. I'm coached so that on certain plays if the defense blitzes, then X is the person I want to get the ball to. Every time a defense calls a blitz their coverage is going to be loose. On critical third situations, distinguishing between a blitz, faking a blitz, position of feet, hands, head, angles on the field, the corners, whether the safety sets head up or outside or inside; there are so many variables on each play and all these have to register right away as I call signals.

"You never have a game plan that sets up one receiver as big man for that game. Never. I'm a right-handed quarterback. I drop back to the right and I key to the right. When I'm going back I'm picking up people and the holes open to the right. If Lynn Swann was my only receiver he would be the big man—but in this league a quarterback can't have a favorite receiver because if you do they can shut him down and you're dead. I'm fortunate to have great backup people in Stallworth, and Cunningham and Grossman. Stallworth could have very easily finished with two hundred yards in receptions had he not been hurt in the second half. His presence has helped Swann more than anybody. He caught ten passes against Denver because my so-called favorite receiver had three people covering him.

"My receivers in the Superbowl made great catches, great adjustments on my passes. The pass to Stallworth on the first touchdown was laid up too easily; he was open but he was forced to make a great catch.

"The looper to Rocky Bleier in the second quarter, to put us ahead 21–14, was a great catch. It was an option run-pass, and the run was shut off. I had two receivers to one side. The primary receiver was covered; Rocky slipped in behind them. I threw to a safe spot where the pass just was catchable, but I knew it would take a great catch. I did not realize Rocky could jump that high. He did a tremendous -job of stopping and coming back on the ball.

"The fourth-quarter pass to Swann deep in the end zone was a case of getting it over the head of the safety. Lynn, with that great leaping ability, went up and caught the ball and dragged his feet in for the touchdown. I wasn't aware of the back line but only of getting it over the defender's head. The one thing I've learned about that end zone: the open areas don't stay there long. I gun the ball inside the ten because your lanes are horizontal not vertical.

"Some people say the only thing you can't defense in football is the perfect pass. I don't know what a perfect pass is. Is it pass or catch or both or the play call? I think it comes down to your ability to know the coverage and to call the right plays—anticipating a coverage—knowing the pass you have called will hit their weakness in that coverage on that part of the field. It is the secret of the game. *Every coverage has a weakness.* You can't let the play unfold and then find it, you have to anticipate it and have the play called to expose it.

"The constant pressure in a quarterback's life, the sacks, the hit as you release, is all normal. Against a team like the Cowboys, with their great defense ends, Martin and Jones, with their ability to blitz and disguise it so well, you're going to get sacked. No one feels worse about it than your offensive lineman or your offensive backs that may have missed a pickup. As a quarterback, you have to learn to build a mental toughness about all that you do on a football field. If you're hurt, not to show your hurt, because that will only give confidence to the other team. I try to let it appear it hasn't bothered me, accept it as a challenge to achieve a greater success on the next play. *You must overcome every single negative incident with a positive attitude.* Sacks, interceptions, fumbles, missed blocks, dropped balls, crucial offsides, all of it.

"Remembering this memorable game, I can't take anything away from Dallas. You can't take points off the board. The game was as close as the final score of 35–31 indicates. People say, 'Oh, the score was deceptive. It wasn't as close as the score indicates.' Baloney! The Cowboys could have won that game, and I was a nervous wreck on the sidelines at the end. I know how dangerous and explosive they are offensively and how tough they are defensively. They will always be there in a game. *Always*. They scored thirty-one points, which is enough to win almost every game you play.

"Dallas in this game was trying to catch us and score early. Teams automatically set up reserves. Your defense tends to overreact in one direction. They sent Tony Dorsett wide left and gained nine, Dorsett up the middle for sixteen, then a pitchout to him wide right for thirteen and a first down. Then Dorsett starts wide again but hands off to Pearson, on an attempted double reverse, and they fumble and Banaszak recovers for us. All gadgets are set up off of successful runs.

"When I was stripped of the ball in the second quarter and they ran it in I was mad at myself. I just said to myself, 'Cheap touchdown.' But it didn't bother me. If it had been four or five years earlier it would have bothered me. I don't ever get that angry on the field. I don't get involved in any one-on-one confrontations. I will never challenge any verbal slander.

"On the touchdown run to our fullback, Franco Harris, in the fourth quarter, I anticipated the blitz and called the play which is a good call. If they don't blitz it's not such a good play. I called the tackle trap with Franco, got the blitz and he scored. It is true Franco was mad and pumped up over words he had on the previous play when I was sacked by Henderson of Dallas. But he did not ask for the ball. Although if you're going to give him the ball that's the time to do it.

"My opinion of the key pass play for the Dallas Cowboys in the third quarter of Superbowl XIII, as I watched it from the sidelines, was that the pass was catchable. I think Jackie Smith and Roger Staubach were both surprised that Jackie was so wide open. There was no one there. Had Roger taken less time on his throw he would have scored. Jackie admitted he should have caught it, it was a good pass. I talked to Roger and told him I thought if he had drilled it they would have scored.

"Television can make you and it can destroy you. I hope that television does not scar the great career of Jackie Smith because of one pass. For eighteen years he played better than any man at his position of tight end. I'm glad his hometown fans welcomed him after the game and expressed their love.

"I'm successful because my team's successful. I don't care who you are, Unitas, Griese, Staubach, Tarkenton, Stabler, it makes no difference how good you are if you don't have a good football team. I'm as good as my football team. I'm not as important, or more important, but I am *a part of* it and it functions that way and it functions successfully. It's what works. Teamwork. I have been raised and schooled on the concept of teamwork and have never been a selfish player. I've always thought of what was going to work. The most important thing for me in football is to play as many years as I can, with all the championships possible, and when I retire if there was anything good to be said about what we had achieved together as a team then let it be said then but don't say it while I'm playing.

"I don't believe that I am as good as I can be—that I am a maximum quarterback. Even though we won three Superbowls, even though 1978–1979 was my most accredited season, I'm still not satisfied and believe there is great need for improvement. I feel I learn more because I'm enjoying the game so much. I feel there are many successful seasons remaining and hopefully another championship for Pittsburgh.

"The athlete as hero, as idol, is something you come to understand. The limelight is bright. If a certain athlete is in the World Series or plays on center court at Wimbledon or in the Superbowl—everyone, seventy-five million or more, sees his or her performance. Probably the Superbowl over everything else is the main event. Wimbledon is one week that builds to two key tennis matches, one on one; the World Series is seven games—after 160 games in the season. In pro football we play sixteen games, have two playoffs—then the Superbowl. People have come to regard football as America's number-one sport. It certainly has made us all celebrities in the eyes of the public all across the country because of the consistent years of winning.

"I sense through the Superbowl great self-satisfaction. A great thrill. Part of history! I've always wanted to be a part of history. It's a great feeling to know that we are. We're the first team ever to win *four* Superbowls. Fifty years from now they'll ask, 'Who was the first team ever to win three Superbowls?' *Pittsburgh Steelers!* I am so proud of that.

"I haven't been able to accept praise. A lot of people can't handle success. They just can't handle it. We've been successful before but this is the first year that I've been singled out. I have had the experience now everywhere I go of having people recognize me. People bombard me. It is totally new to me. It has been a very rewarding season, a very rewarding off season. Now I'm ready to go back. I'm ready to play. Hopefully to win another championship."

A GOLDEN COLOSSUS

The American speed skater stood on the exact ground where the skaters had entered forty-eight years before. The day was about the same, the crowd about the same, the little town of Lake Placid about the same. Eric Heiden was a bigger man than Jack Shea was in 1932 or Irwin Jaffe when they won their speed-skating gold medals on ice set on the cinder track in front of the high school. On this day in 1980 the competition was held on the new three-million-dollar refrigerated rink, only the second such oval in North America, but the high school looked the same and the spirit of the local crowd was just as gentle and warm. They had come out to see Eric win his fifth gold medal in the XIII Winter Olympic Games. No athlete in history had achieved this feat in winter sports. The United States won six gold medals in Lake Placid. Eric Heiden won five of them.

Two years before, the week the new four-hundred-meter Olympic speed-skating oval was opened, I had worked with Eric and Beth Heiden for the first time. It was so cold that day they couldn't stay on the ice for more than twenty minutes. Now we talked about the technical aspects of speed skating; in the twenty-four months between Eric had established himself as the best in the world. In Lake Placid he proved to the world he is the best of all time! His tough but compassionate coach, Dianne Holum, paid him tribute. "Eric is a jewel. His superb physical assets are just part of his success. He is a thinker. And I've never seen anyone so good at producing that one dynamic effort when it is needed, as he did today" (right).

I knelt in the snow behind the· angled yellow barricade that circled the turn at the north end of the oval. Eric had told me after his first victory that his success in speed skating was his acceleration out of the turns onto the straight. Those three strides out of the turn were critical—every lap—whatever the distance. I wanted to do super-slow-motion studies of that for my television report.

I looked across to the far corner and remembered filming his sprint start in the first race.

The big, twenty-one-year-old skater from Madison, Wisconsin, was completing a remarkable Olympic achievement. His first victory came in the five-hundred-meter race. His time was 38.03, a new Olympic record. Eugeni Kulikov of the Soviet Union was second in 38.37; Lieuwe De Boer of the Netherlands was third in 38.48. Each skater had a false start. Kulikov was ahead after a hundred meters. Heiden caught him on the back straight, Kulikov slipped on the fourth turn, and lost his concentration, and Eric won nicely in sparkling sunlight.

The second victory was at five thousand meters. Heiden won in 7:02:29, a new Olympic record. Kai Arne Stenshjemmet of Norway was second in 7:03:28, and Tom-Erik Oxholm of Norway was third in 7:05:59. At twelve degrees it was a mean, gray day. Eric had won his first two medals in two days in the two races he thought he was weakest in.

Heiden's third goal was his easiest, it seemed. In the thousand meters he won in 1:15:18, beating Gaetan Boucher of Canada, who skated 1:16:68, and Frode Roenning of Norway, whose time was 1.16.91. It was thirty degrees with a light wind. In victory Eric matched his idol Ard Schenk's Sapporo Olympic record of three golds, set by the great Dutchman in 1972.

At the finish of each race his ritual was always the same. He would glide upright through the first turn, and as he entered the second turn Heiden would pull back the cowl of his gold skin-tight racing suit and then lean over with hands on knees to rest and run out. Standing again, he would coast down the backstretch in front of the grandstand along the facade of the high school. He would raise his hand to acknowledge the cheers of the little crowd, but he scarcely looked up at them.

Eric Heiden's fourth gold medal in the fifteen hundred meters was again a new Olympic record of 1:55:44. This race held the only dramatic moment as Heiden came dangerously close to falling when his inner skate caught a rut in the ice at the exact spot where he had started the five hundred meters. The fingers of his left hand touched the ice as he held his balance.

Kai Arne Stenshjemmet of Norway was second with 1:56:81, and Terje Andersen of Norway was third in 1:56:92. I had photographed Lydia Skoblikova in Innsbruck in 1964 when the Soviet woman won her four medals in speed skating. Heiden had matched that.

In his final effort, Eric Heiden was supreme. The ten thousand meters is the longest test—more than six miles—and in winning in 14 minutes 28.13 seconds he set a new world and Olympic record and lowered the previous world mark by an

amazing 6.2 seconds. Piet Kleine of the Netherlands won the silver in 14:36:03, and Tom-Erik Oxholm of Norway won the bronze in 14:36:60.

It was a cloudy-bright morning, not too cold, and Heiden skated in the second pair with Viktor Leskin of the Soviet Union. The PA announcer continued his chant lap after lap as Eric Heiden skated against the time of the first pair winner, Oxholm of Norway, who is the European champion at ten thousand meters. Finally in the backstretch, Heiden went ahead of Oxholm's pace and the crowd exploded. The townspeople waved their flags and hand-painted banners. More than a thousand watched from store roofs, balconies, windows, trees, on top of trailers that lined Main Street and squeezed along the fence above the oval. They chanted as one, *"Errric! Errric! Errric!"*

Thirty minutes later he chewed his gum and smiled. He had done it all.

"When I went out after my fifth gold medal today I did not think the ice was going to be that fast, but after seeing the first pair and watching Tim Wood skate a 34:39 I knew I would have to go out and really do my best. As it turned out the ice was really fast; I got a lot out of each stroke. You didn't lose anything when you were pushing, and the turns were smooth and quick. I was able to almost slingshot out of each turn.

"Early in the race I thought I was in trouble. Leskin, my pair from the Soviet Union, took off, and I started going after him, but Dianne Holum, my coach, called out to relax and skate my own race, and I did and it turned out well. I was a little concerned when Leskin came out of the outer curve at the crossover and was ahead of me and he was still going hard. I figured he was going to end up winning the race, but I came back, finally ended up passing him, and then I didn't see him again.

"I think this was my best effort as a skater. I don't think I could have done any better than I did today. This is the most tired I have ever been for a ten-thousand-meter race. If there had been a couple of more laps I'd have been in trouble. The crowd's cheering really helped.

"Five gold medals? They'll probably just sit where all the rest of my medals are, in my mom's dresser, gathering dust. They don't really mean that much to me. It's the effort that went into each race that matters. Now that it's over I sure hope they don't try to stick me up on a pedestal. That would really bum me out. I'd just like to be Eric Heiden."

He smiled and headed for his television interview. He walked along the edge of the ice in his track shoes, gingerly so that he wouldn't slip.

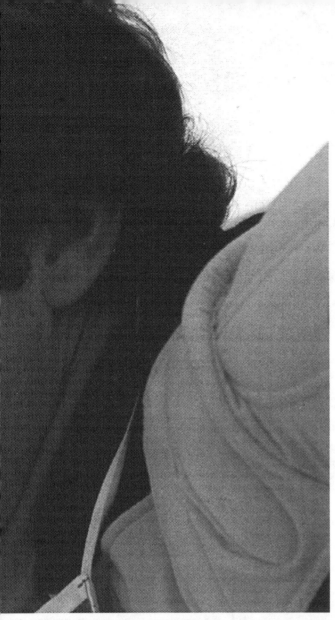

SLALOM RACER

There is no other athletic competition in which a single mistake is as costly or as dramatic as an error in alpine skiing, especially in the giant-slalom and slalom events in Olympic competition. There is also no other sport in which the best of the best who are destined to win, do win—except for the dramatic mistake, *the fall*. When Ken Read of Canada took the perfect line through the top section of the men's downhill, he was on his way to a possible medal, but his left binding broke loose, and he lost a ski and crashed. This is part of the mystique of alpine racing. With television coverage of fifteen or more cameras, every gate on the alpine courses is revealed, and a racer's ability is there for all to study—in the most amazing detail. The only way to watch a ski race is on television; you can't see everything on the mountain.

Lake Placid had few surprises in the alpine events. Annemarie Moser-Proell won her coveted gold medal in the women's downhill, and after Read's fall the gate was open for Austria's Loenhard Stock to capture the men's race with his unique style. The key to the women's race was that Hanni Wenzel of Liechtenstein lost the gold by only .7 second. The blonde athlete then duplicated Rosi Mittermaier's feat in the 1976 Games by winning two alpine golds in the giant slalom and slalom.

The twenty-three-year-old took the lead after the first fifty-two-gate run in the slalom and then blew away the competition with a blistering time of 42.59 through the fifty-two gates over a 465-meter course in the second run.

Psychologically the pressure on a slalom racer in the second run of a race is enormous—especially for the men. Ingemar Stenmark of Sweden is the world's best and has won twenty-five World Cup races by coming from behind to win on the second run. Stenmark came to Lake Placid with an unprecedented string of fourteen consecutive World Cup Giant Slalom victories, and in ten of them he came from behind. Ingemar has won races where he stood twenty-third after the first run. Preposterous. His secret? His legs and his slalom skis.

Ingemar Stenmark has super strength in his legs. He can correct a turn or an error with a body-position angle so low to the snow that it appears an impossible feat not only to keep going but to turn to the next gate with speed. At the team's training base in Val Senales in the Italian Alps, I watched him ski eight Olympic-style courses a

day, giant slalom and slalom. I photographed him skiing at speed and making position changes with the same all-out effort as he displayed in his Olympic runs. The near-fall in the first screen above, shows Ingemar during isolated practice in October.

The next two TV screens show the ace slalom racer in almost the identical trouble at the end of the first run of the giant slalom. If he had fallen he would never have won his gold. His skill, his skis, his leg strength, his mental toughness that hard work has fashioned—those are his secrets.

Stenmark was second to Andreas Wenzel after the first run of the giant slalom and beat the exceptional young racer from Liechtenstein for his first gold medal. In the slalom event he trailed Phil Mahre of the United States after the sixty-six gates of the 549-meter first slalom course. In the second run Mahre needed to stay only within .58 second to beat Stenmark, but Ingemar ripped three and a half seconds off his first-run clocking of 53.89 to win with a combined time of 1:44:26. The American won the silver in 1:44:76. "My run was frantic," Phil Mahre said after the race. "I never got my rhythm going." Ingemar Stenmark's feat of two alpine gold medals has been surpassed only by Toni Sailer of Austria at Cortina in 1956 and Jean-Claude Killy of France at Grenoble in 1968, when each won all three alpine events.

Phil Mahre's triumph was not only his silver medal and his position in victory alongside Ingemar Stenmark but his year of courage. Phil had made

his four Olympic slalom runs and his downhill race with three screws and a metal plate in his left ankle, the doctor's design to hold the broken bones together from a severe break suffered on the same mountain in a World Cup race a year before.

"Slalom" is a Norwegian word that means "turning." In World Cup and Olympic slalom racing there are two runs over two different gate settings on the same hill, and the racer who establishes the quickest and most consistent turning rhythm between the slalom poles that mark the gates will win. The efficiency of *each* turn dictates how fast a skier is able to go through a series of sixty or seventy gates on a special slalom run. If you carve too much and arc too long on an edge, you perform a decelerating turn, and if you don't hold an edge and the ski sideslips through the turn, you are also slowed and in danger of missing the next gate. If a racer does not turn enough to let the ski run free as he accelerates, he will gain too much speed, lose control, have no time to turn and so miss the gates and disqualify himself.

The technique of the slalom turn is subtle and simple unlike the turning speed of downhill racers, where impact demands heavier skis and critical bindings. The three lower screens are my slow-motion coverage of the instant the Canadian favorite, Ken Read, explodes out of his left binding and his medal hopes crash with him as he loses his uphill ski.

The ski racer's ability is really an extension of his equipment. The ski is designed with a slight camber in it as viewed on a flat surface. The tip and tail of the skis touch, but the center of the ski under the boot is off the surface. In a turn a racer takes advantage of this construction and with leg pressure *reverses* the camber, actually bends the ski the wrong way so the tip and tail are above the center. The ski becomes a bow, and this torquing action is *force* which the expert slalom racer has learned to harness and release to create turning action.

In the days of Killy they did not have this boot advantage, and they didn't have it in the 1950s in the Toni Sailer era of low leather boots.

Because of the changes in equipment the elite slalom racers today will run at the gates differently than most other competitors will. They'll come in on a higher line, not waiting until they get to the pole to turn, but beginning their turn three or four feet above the pole. With their ankles and knees angulated, and their body weight centered over the boot, they snap with a violent pressure of ankle and knee action to put the reverse camber into the ski, and combined with the centrifugal force this pressure forces the flexible fiberglass ski to bend. This reverse camber causes a deceleration of very short duration to effect a direction change, and then as the racers go by the gate pole, they let their ankles and knees release the ski torque and the ski flattens out and springs out from under them. This gives the impression, as you watch the racer, that he is sitting back on his skis, but actually the skis are running ahead, since the upper body mass cannot move that fast. The racer actually chases his skis by pulling his upper body weight forward with his arms extended and his strong stomach muscles and inordinately well-developed thigh muscles.

The arc that the racer dictates through his body action to his skis becomes the arc of the turn, especially in short-radius turns. If a racer puts too much arc into it, the ski will snap right around and stop. If he puts too little arc in it, the ski will run too straight to turn.

The exceptional slalom racers of the world—Ingemar Stenmark of Sweden, Phil Mahre of the United States, Andreas Wenzel of Liechtenstein and his sister Hanni Wenzel—have great athletic ability and tremendous balance, which enables them, with their ankles and knees, to violently put reverse camber into the skis and get them to turn in a very sharp and short arc without sliding. The racers today are skiing modifications, improvements, and refinements of the basic technique that started in the French era of the mid-1960s when Jean-Claude Killy led the way.

The one equipment change that has drastically changed the efficiency of turning is the boots. The newest racing boots are very low to the ski, with a thin sole; the racer can almost feel the ski through the sole of the boot—specifically, the racing boot used by Ingemar Stenmark. What the new, high plastic boot does is lock the ankle so that when the racer leans forward with the knee, less ankle force is used, as the force comes from the entire leg. The boot is a solid, rigid block, and this enables the racer to put tremendous torque into the ski to make it turn on a sharp radius and release with such power.

The racer then plants his inside pole to initiate the next turn. The pole action is little more than a discipline to bring the upper body back into balance over the ski again and again and again. The violent ankle and knee angulation is the secret of the turn, and only the exceptional athletes can perform it expertly over the 120 or so gates of the two special slalom runs. The key is that they are in their turning position—a decelerating position—over an entire slalom course less than the other racers are, and so they go down the course faster, especially when they have the added insight to ski the fastest line down the hill.

The deliberate racers, who make many decelerating turns, lose momentum as they go down the course. *The fastest skiers are those who are constant in their speed over the entire course.* They may not be superfast through some sections, but they have a high terminal velocity or momentum and they consistently carry that momentum through all the gates. They don't speed up or slow down or change rhythm.

The one thing that Stenmark and Mahre have in common that no other slalom racer currently has is that ability to pick the best possible line down through the gates. What the Swedish ace and the American do superbly is to look down through a pattern of fifteen gates and visualize the ideal line through. This may not always be the shortest line, but they sense where they want to be and have the athletic and skiing ability to be there under the pressures of the race at top speed—which is that speed at which each racer can maintain the balance between momentum and control.

Young racers try to memorize too much of a course before the race. Top racers, especially Stenmark, try only to remember difficult segments—a drop over a road to three sharp turns over an icy section—demand mental preparedness so that the racer can set up in time. The hallmark to the slalom expert today is that ability to react spontaneously to the gates coming up. They thrive on it as they fly down the hill in a race, and *that* is what separates them from other competitors.

OLYMPIC GAMES 1980

The American coach, Herb Brooks, glided around the rink with his head down, his players in grubby practice shirts slipping past him in warm-up drills. He tweaked his whistle and called out something, "All right, just go two and oh up to the red and back in a weave pattern." I had told him my impression of his team—I had seen the U.S. players win in Squaw Valley in 1960, seen all the teams since then, and there was no question in my mind that this was the best team since 1960, the best team of skaters and stickhandlers I had ever seen outside the NHL. I thought they could win the gold medal. I wanted to know about tactics, about strategy, about his plot for the ice war against the Russians.

"The system that we're trying to perfect here with this Olympic team is one that's been based upon my belief in the European style of play with the puck. *Possession is the name of the game.* Possession is the name of the game in baseball, football, basketball, and we're trying to incorporate the same discipline in this game of hockey. But I also want to put in the best of the North American style—the best of the play without the puck, which is something the North American athlete has always taken a lot of pride in. We feel we have to get the best of both worlds to be successful with this club. By doing this there is no question in my mind that the players' abilities on this hockey team will be accelerated and it will be a style of play that I feel we'll be very successful with.

"This possession is based on skating ability, on speed, on deception and puck control. To achieve this system you need players that are creative, that are innovative, that have the necessary hockey sense and the skating skills. This is the change from the old way, the wrong style of play where a team played negatively, a style where you would give the other team the puck and then force them into mistakes.

"I am convinced it is not the number of shots in a period but rather the high quality of shots that will make the difference. Our lines on the ice understand this and they have the necessary teamwork to make this work. They have the necessary chemistry with each other on the ice, they have the necessary chemistry to get along with each other off the ice, they have the necessary chemistry to understand the problems you have in a very emotional, difficult sport.

"Defensively we have special people. Jim Craig, our goaltender, Mike Ramsey, our defenseman. Ramsey is the youngest player on our hockey club, and he's also the youngest American player ever to be drafted by the National Hockey League. He is Buffalo's number-one choice. He gets better each day. He has that great instinctive feeling of when to mesh with the forwards that is so difficult to find with a young defenseman.

"The team and I both work with Jim Craig in the same way. We both have enormous confidence in Craig as a goaltender. The players know that he will not give up the fluke goal, the cheap goal. They will use him. Use him to control the rebounds, to direct action. They know he knows his way around the net. They know he will stay on his feet. All too often goalkeepers are not used properly by the defenseman and by the forwards.

"As the coach of this Olympic team I'm very aware of the opposition. The Russians are probably the greatest hockey team in the world. Look at who they have beaten. Historically speaking, you have to respect the Czechs and the Swedes. The United States is one of four teams that have a chance for an upset. We have to maximize the resources we have, and our resource right now is our skating ability, and that is why I've installed this style, this system—*to use our players effectively* against the immense opposition we're up against.

"We don't want to beat ourselves when we have the puck, and we don't want to beat ourselves without the puck. I really feel this team has the mental toughness to withstand all the pressures playing here in Lake Placid. We will not become unglued when we're faced with the great hockey powers of the world. We have a great deal of pride in ourselves and have the necessary practice and belief in ourselves to withstand this kind of world team pressure—even though this is the *youngest* Olympic team in United States hockey history."

Coach Herb Brooks seemed quietly confident as he talked in the locker room six weeks before the games, and his intensity and serious demeanor continued as we glanced at each other and nodded in the passageway during the games as the U.S. team began to put its string of victories together.

Twenty young men. Jim Craig with Steve Janaszak behind him in goal. The defensemen: Ken Morrow, Mike Ramsey, Bill Baker, John O'Callahan, Bob Sutter. The forwards: Rob McClanahan, Dave

Silk, Neal Broten, Mark Johnson, Steve Christoff, Mark Wells, Mark Pavelich, Eric Strobel, Captain Mike Eruzione, Dave Christian, Buzz Schneider, Phil Verchota and John Harrington. They played seven games *together!* They won six and tied one. No one beat them. They retired undefeated. Their moment of destiny came twice. The first time there were twenty-seven seconds left in a game with Sweden; U.S. goalie Jim Craig was pulled out of the net, and Bill Baker sent home a forty-foot slapshot. A beautiful hockey goal.

The second was not Captain Mike Eruzione's winning goal against the invincible Soviet team but Mark Johnson's rebound with one second left in the first period to tie the score with the Russians at 2-2. That score gave the Russians the message. You could see it on their faces. Johnson had faked the pads off of Vladislav Tretiak, the world's greatest goaltender. He was flat on his belly. Implausibly, in panic, the Russians yanked him for the rest of the game. There was now a balance of power on the ice.

But Eruzione's goal belongs to sport history, and as you watch the replay on television over the years you'll see how deft, how artful, it was. The quality shot. Masterful. Just the right speed, the right angle, an ideal screen and under the right arm of the Soviet backup goalie Vladimir Myshkin.

Never in the world of sport will celebration mean more, will euphoria be better expressed, will youthful enthusiasm run higher, than it did that moment on the ice, in the seats with the marvelous crowd of joyous people, and in the nation.

After the significant victory against the Soviets, Coach Brooks, on camera for ABC national and world television, talked to President Jimmy Carter by telephone and accepted congratulations from the chief executive. The coach told the President that he would support the boycott that had been leveled against the Summer Olympics.

"I just think that too many athletes in North America are rather selfish," he said to newsmen later. "We must be careful we do not lose our sense of values. I don't think that we have to prove to anyone that our democratic way of life is better than the iron-curtain countries. When we have to do that we're in trouble. This means to me that our institutions don't really have the depth and the strength to stand the test. We've impeached our President. We know our system works. To say that the democratic way of life will work because we have the best hockey team and we beat the Russians to prove it makes no sense.

"The significant idea here in Lake Placid in our victory over the Russians was I felt it was *not* political. It was sport. It was a game. It was a young fighting team against the unbeatable veteran team. I think the fine thing was that the players treated it as a game and the crowd treated it as a game. I think the arena was void of any 'Russia, go home' curse as we beat them 4-3."

The memorable joy of victory is achieved in this set of hockey pictures taken by my daughters. The united strength of the entire U.S. team on the winners' podium (overleaf), and the fans, flags and action on the two historic days of the American team against Russia and Finland. Soviet veteran Boris Mikhailov (top left) clasps the hand of Sweden's Mat Waltin as U.S. Captain Mike Eruzione proudly watches. U.S. goalie Jim Craig in net stopped 36 of the USSR team's 39 shots. A crush hug by the U.S. team follows a goal past Soviet Tretiak in the first victory over Russia since 1960.

The world came to the United States for the 1980 Olympic Games, and all the world was with it. It had been a bittersweet meeting of the nations. Many believed the Olympic movement would have to change because the grand ideal had been worn thin by excessive nationalism and world politics. Others saw the Olympic ideal strengthened, the creed of striving, of amateurs competing in an atmosphere of fair sportsmanship, of all nations great or small with an equal chance—all personified in the microcosm that was Lake Placid.

The United States hockey team, Eric Heiden, Hanni Wenzel of Liechtenstein. Sweden's Ingemar Stenmark embraced by his king. The small town in upstate New York couldn't get a busload of tourists into town on time, but the town became a television studio and 300 million people throughout the world watched every detail. Beyond the gift of gold for the athlete there was indeed a greater gift. The intelligent, introspective, exceptional Herb Brooks expressed it in those final minutes in a hidden corner of the ice arena as he spoke of his hockey team.

"Winning 4-2 at the Olympic Games in this final game against Finland was not for the medal. What I'm competing for and what I think the players will understand very shortly in their lives is that they are not competing for a gold medal but for *peace of mind.* That idea of peace of mind is something that seems to escape the youth of today—but that is what this hockey club is going to live with. They are not going to walk down the street for the next five years with a gold medal hanging around their neck. What's in their minds and how they look at themselves is what matters. That peace and certitude of how they played their games. How they conducted themselves—their faith and pride in each other—the execution of their God-given talent. This is their victory, their honor."

Epilogue

Most men agree that life is short. I sometimes think it is just a few days long. Perhaps that is why I am obsessed with the jewel-like particles of time and why I keep dissecting seconds in this wide world of sports. When the fractions of seconds are stretched out side by side, drawn forever in a few hundred pictures, when the lines of movement never cease to describe a thousand details and the intensity of a single thought, then the seconds have an eternity, and when we study them and enjoy them, we are all young and strong and we know we will live forever, and the victory will never fade.

I would sacrifice anything to draw a face. I would give half my kingdom to photograph a face that is alive somewhere in a corner of some stadium or racetrack or arena, a face that I will never see again, a look, a laugh, a gesture that is quick and gone. I want to take it and the lovely rare spirit in which it exists and keep it in a book forever. I want to walk through every race, every game, every event with a fanatical hunger, and look into the faces of every crowd and save them forever.

But most of all I want to explore one second of an athlete's skill and save all of its million facets and enjoy it forever.

Perfection is the flawless second of time that no one sees. I've tried in this book to split open this magic molecule of an athlete's art and see why youth prevails.

Like some obsessed miser I try to hoard every breath and pulse beat, every stride and leap and step, every shout and cheer, until we are buried in this wide world of caring, striving and achieving.

The strength and beauty of our television show is the "constant variety" of sports. On this wide stage we see the clear portrait of an athlete. I think the spirit of this book might paraphrase Thomas Wolfe when he wrote: "Play us a tune on an unbroken spinet. Play lively music when the instrument was new. Let us see Mozart playing in the parlor, and let us hear the sound of the ladies' voices; let us move backward through our memories, and through the memory of the race; let us relive the million forgotten moments of our lives. Unwind the fabric of lost time. Repair the million little threads of actual circumstance until the seconds grow gray, bright and dusty with the living light. . . ."

Play us a tune on an unbroken spinet and let us hear the skiers as they whisper to each other in the stillness atop the mountain waiting to make their run; let us see the faces of the people crowded on the lifeline along the course in the forest and watch their eyes as they see the racers go by; let us see just one graceful, elegant figure of perfection on the ice by the Russian pairs and let us hear their skate blades cut the ice as they glide past and the sound of *Swan Lake* playing; let us see the great jockeys talking and see them laugh together and watch a horse take a terrible fall at a wicked hedge and see the glamour of victory and the beautiful women sip champagne. Let us see the tactics of two boxers in the ring and the cunning of a helmsman on a majestic sloop; let us see the great veteran begin the last track meet of his career and let us see a young schoolboy winning a long race and let us study his face. Let us see the mighty swimmers and the most agile tennis player in the world and remember the sound on the court; let us remember the ferocious roar of the engines of the grand prix cars and the eyes of the drivers. Let us see everyone and hear everything and go every place to prove that art and style and the one thoughtful look last forever.

This spirit sustains you long into the night.

If I look upon these years of work as a string of ballgames, tickets and travel, of men and women at play, of reporting a game, a race, a match, then I would believe the effort is not important or a very significant way to spend one's time and energy compared to work in government or law, science or architecture, or in medicine, certainly not a valid contribution to the nation or to peace, survival or any part of history.

But if one looks upon it as theater and sees each of the athletes as an artist and each of their performances synthesized into one performance, if one sees and understands all the action as a tribute to the perfection and fulfillment of the human body and in this perfection knows an athlete attains the maximum skill and expresses the highest beauty and grace—if one sees sport as the purest expression of man's freedom—then I believe I've been about a noble business.

We wander there, we wander here,
We eye the rose upon the brier,
Unmindful that the thorn is near
    Among the leaves;
And tho' the puny wound appear,
    Short while it grieves.

With steady aim, some Fortune chase;
Keen hope does ev'ry sinew brace;
Thro' fair, thro' foul, they urge the race,
    And seize the prey
Then cannie, in some cozie place,
    They close the day.

— Robert Burns

CATALOGUE OF PICTURES

First sports photograph: Richie Ashburn steals second. Polo Grounds, 1950.

★*Original in color. All other picture references appear in text.*

First pro football photograph: Les Bingaman in his old hat.
Detroit Lions, Polo Grounds, 1950.

First car racing photograph: Sterling Moss winning
the Grand Prix of Monaco, 1960.

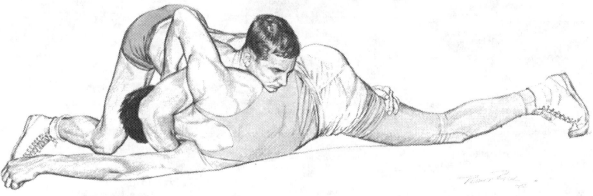

First Sports Illustrated Series drawing: West Point wrestlers. Lithograph and water color.

★*Original in color. All other picture references appear in text.*

First night photograph: half-time marching band. Los Angeles Coliseum, 1960.

ABOUT THE AUTHOR

ROBERT RIGER *is currently writing his
second screenplay and first novel
and has just completed the
second unit direction on a major
motion picture with John Huston directing.*

ACKNOWLEDGMENT

*My career with pictures over the years
has been successful with more than a little
help from my friends. I am grateful to the
following: Al and Bill Corvelle, Peter Sansone,
Ray Walsh, Jack Mara, Jim Wright, Jerry
Snyder, Sid James, Peter Schwed, Hugh
Edwards, Fred Roe, Marty Forscher, Robert
Northshield, John Szarkowski, Harold Hayes,
Clay Felker, Roone Arledge, David and Michael
Samuelson, George Flynn, Ken Lieberman,
Ralph Baum, Al Striano, John Petersen, Abe
Milrad, Tom Moore, Dave Burke, David Travis,
Igor Breght, Marty and Morris Rosenthal,
John Kay, the Kodak people and my family:
Christopher, Victoria, Robert, BZ and Eleanor,
who are all photographers now.*

Editorial assistance:
Margaret Uihlein, Dawn Aberg, Dorothy Gordineer

ALSO BY ROBERT RIGER

*The Art of Raceriding (Arcaro/Tower), 1958
How to Teach Yourself and your
Family To Swim better (Champlin), 1959
The Fun of Figure Skating (Owen), 1960
The Pros (Maule), 1960
Best Plays of the Year, 1962
Best Plays of the Year, 1963
Run to Daylight (Lombardi/Heinz), 1963
The Last Loud Roar (Cousy/Lynn), 1964
Wide World of Sports, 1964
Wide World of Sports, 1965
The American Diamond (Rickey), 1965
Man in Sport, 1967*

Printed in the United States
By Bookmasters